ARSENAL

The Agony & The Ecstasy

Ian Castle

For Steph, Gerry, Dickie, Prinders and Andy.
They share the agony and the ecstasy with me.

Published in 2012 by FeedARead.com Publishing – Arts Council
funded

A CIP catalogue record for this title is available from the British
Library.

CONTENTS

Introduction

On 27 February 2011, as I walked down Wembley Way on my first visit to the 'new' Wembley, the skies were leaden; it was cold and raining. Forty years earlier, in 1971, I had walked the same route in glorious sunshine on my way to an FA Cup Final that created a dramatic milestone in the history of Arsenal Football Club. That had been my first visit to the 'old' stadium.

Some hours later, on this grey and gloomy day, I shuffled away amidst a throng of subdued, downcast faces. I edged back down Wembley Way, trying unsuccessfully to avoid the puddles, to the Underground station and deliverance from this place of misery. In the 88th minute a piece of slapstick defending had handed a 2-1 victory – and the Carling Cup – to Birmingham City. Their fans were delirious. I was not. When I got home I sat on the sofa and stared blankly at the television, not really aware of what was on. My mind grappled with mental arithmetic; the answer to these calculations was stark and depressing – that afternoon I had personally witnessed my team – Arsenal - losing a tenth final. Ten! One after the other those bleak occasions flickered through my memory like clips from an old movie, an image here, an emotion there. I thought I had exorcised those depressing memories of past years, but they were all there still: 1972…1978…1980 (twice!)…and still they kept coming as the years rolled by…and now 2011 too. And then I remembered there were others that I hadn't attended and could add 1968, 1969 and 2007 to this roll of pain, when I had listened in anguish to the radio or watched TV as other teams took the glory. That just didn't seem fair to me that evening, and the fact that I'd seen Arsenal lift eleven Cups in that same period, from Copenhagen to Cardiff, and, of course, at Wembley too, did not lift my mood at that moment. And I shouldn't forget six winning League campaigns. But none of that mattered right then, it was what seemed to be the injustice of so many losses that occupied my thoughts. And if anyone says, "At least you got to the final", well, they just don't understand. It's not a "great day out for the fans" if you lose. Your team means everything to you; they give you rushes of emotion that very little else in life can match and only other genuine football fans understand, but they can also take you to depths, so dark and deep, from which it can take an eternity to emerge back into the daylight.

My journey as an Arsenal fan has had many such highs and lows – agony and ecstasy - and over the next few days I began thinking more and more about them, and how it had all begun. Like so many other football fans, in the beginning it was all Dad's fault.

1

In The Beginning

It all started for me in January 1966. I was an eight-year-old from north-west London and an avid reader of comics as befitted someone of that age. That January I bought one called The Hornet. Free inside were four postcard-sized photos of football teams. I bought the next issue the following week too and got four more. They were an eclectic mix: Wales, Northern Ireland, Brazil, Celtic, Rangers, Liverpool, Tottenham and West Ham. They were part of a series called 'Top Cup Teams', a title defined loosely with the inclusion of Wales and Northern Ireland who earned their place in the collection on the back of their performances at the 1958 World Cup when they'd punched above their weight. I did not collect the final four cards in the set because the fickle mind of this schoolboy responded to the temptation of a football booklet given away by another comic. Which one it was I don't recall but I do remember on the inside back cover I was required to fill in the details of 'my' football team. Now that was a problem for me to wrestle with; I didn't have one. It was only these cards that awakened an interest in football. I had no grounding in my new subject. I had no knowledge of traditions, history, local affiliations, and there was no such thing as a 'glory hunter' back then, which I wouldn't have understood anyway. So, my football world was pocket-sized in the form of those eight cards and I would have to select 'My Team' from amongst them.

Despite this narrow field and my limited knowledge it was clear that I would have to dismiss international teams, so I quickly discarded Wales, Northern Ireland and Brazil. Next I eliminated Celtic and Rangers, what did Scotland have to do with me? That narrowed my choice to three teams: Liverpool, Tottenham and West Ham. I studied the pictures closely and rejected Tottenham; their kit looked boring. After a little more deliberation I plumped for West Ham, I thought they had the prettiest kit of the three; they would be 'my' team. Decision made, I sharpened a pencil before filling in the page of my new booklet in my very best handwriting, gleaning information from the back of the card and that was that – I was a West Ham supporter, well for a few hours anyway.

When my Dad came home from work that evening I approached him as he sat in the armchair and, showing him the booklet, said, "Dad, this is my football team." He looked at the details I had filled in and without looking up he simply said, "You don't want to support them, Arsenal's the best team." Unquestioningly and without more ado I rubbed out the details I had pondered over for so long and, with my Dad's guidance, boldly wrote Arsenal in the section that required me to fill in the name of 'My Team'. He told me the name of their ground and the colours of their kit, but we had to leave the 'Honours Won' section blank. He said there were too many for the space the publishers had allowed. It seemed odd that I hadn't had that problem with West Ham. And that was that. I had seamlessly transferred my allegiance from West Ham to Arsenal – I now know what a lucky escape that was. Task completed I returned to my comics. Although I couldn't know it at the time, that brief conversation was about to embark me on a life-shaping journey, one of incredible highs and lows, not only a mixture of unbridled joy, celebration, camaraderie and lasting friendships, but also frustration, anger, pain and deep, deep despair. As a naïve and innocent eight-year-old, I had no comprehension of what I had just committed myself to.

It was in fact not until August 1967, 19 months later, that my life as an Arsenal fan really began. In the meantime I had watched England win the World Cup on TV – in black and white of course - and foolishly missed the chance to see the team return to their hotel with the trophy. I'd watched the final at my grandparents' house in Hendon. After the toothless Nobby Stiles had skipped deliriously around the pitch, my grandfather suggested we drive over to the hotel nearby where the team was staying, to see them return. I thought we'd have no chance of seeing anything so I stayed behind watching events unfold on TV while my grandfather and sister headed off. It was a spectacular own goal. They were indeed present when the team alighted from their coach with trophy in hand. Forty-six years and eleven World Cups later there has never been another opportunity and maybe there never will. As an aside, a few months later a feature film documentary of the World Cup opened at the cinema, called Goal! I went to see it with a school friend and was mesmerised. Here was football in glorious colour and literally larger than life – it was the first football I had ever seen in colour and I've never forgotten the impact it made on me.

The moment when I really became an Arsenal fan happened on Bank Holiday Monday, 28 August 1967. My Dad worked on Saturdays so taking me to football had never really been an option, but on the Bank Holiday he was free and decided to take me to Highbury for the very first time – the match was Arsenal v Liverpool in a Division One match (for anyone born post the launch of the Premiership that was the top division). To be honest I don't remember the details very clearly, other than my first view of the pitch and the final score. We sat in the East Stand Lower Tier; my Dad just paid at the turnstile – no advance ticket required - and I pushed hard against a heavy revolving turnstile that clanked loudly as it reluctantly turned before depositing me inside the stadium. I felt I had entered another world. My Dad may have bought me a drink or something to eat, I don't remember, but I do remember my first incredible sighting of that lovingly tended luminous green sward. My only previous experience of football pitches were the muddy battlefields in my local park, dotted with the odd spot of dog mess. This was something completely different; it was an unforgettable moment.

I always found sitting in the lower tier at Highbury a rather strange experience. Because of the upper tier seating above, the ceiling – if you can call it that – was low and I would come away at the end of a game with the feeling I'd watched the match peering through a letter box. If anyone hoofed the ball up in the air, and I can assure you they did –

often - it would disappear from view for a few moments, leaving you to watch the players jostling for position as though they were part of a life-sized spot-the-ball competition. To be honest I don't remember any details of that first game other than the fact that Arsenal won 2–0. My lack of any memories of the game bothered me and I wondered why that was. I decided to investigate and I think I found the answer; one newspaper report unenthusiastically described it as "a generally poor game." But I had no comprehension of good football or poor football back then, just football – and Arsenal had won. I was hooked.

Reading that report also made me realise I had seen two future Arsenal managers in action: Terry Neill and George Graham played that day. I also discovered that if I hadn't been there the crowd would have been 33,419 instead of 33,420! I'd made a difference. These things are important when you're ten. For the record Tony Hateley scored an own goal, managing to rise, "high above everybody to head the ball at tremendous speed" past the unfortunate Liverpool goalkeeper, and the much-maligned Jon Sammels lashed home the second goal from 25 yards. I now remember neither, but at the time I knew I wanted to go again.

Before I got the chance to repeat the experience Arsenal went to Wembley for the League Cup Final of 1968, on my birthday. Only the FA Cup Final received live television coverage back then, so, preoccupied with my eleventh birthday, it did not feature too highly in my day. But here we were at the beginning of my testing relationship with Cup Finals. Arsenal played Don Revie's Leeds United that day, a team that was to become our bête noire in the early Seventies. Leeds won a poor game 1-0 to give them their first significant trophy and started them on their assault on, or some would say against, English football. Writing in *The Observer* Hugh McIlvanney, one of sport's great journalists, summed up the game succinctly. Lamenting the lack of quality on display, his honest appraisal said it all. "Examples of creativity and individual brilliance were so rare as to appear positively out of place...Rarely can so many gifted players have provided so little entertainment." The result upset me, but the whole

Arsenal thing was still new, and I had only been to one game. I didn't yet feel the pain of Cup Final defeat – that was still to come. But anyway, at least I had my birthday.

My second opportunity to go to Highbury did not come for some time. With Dad working Saturdays, the chances remained limited. Football back then was straightforward and easy to understand. You played on Saturdays at 3.00pm and if you had a midweek game it kicked off at 7.30pm on a Tuesday or Wednesday – end of story. My return to Highbury finally came eight long months after the Liverpool game, on the Easter weekend, April 1968. It was Leicester in the League, and I loved it. Inexplicably a newspaper reporter considered it "a match of stunning mediocrity", he clearly he didn't get it. Then again, it appeared quite a lot of others didn't either as only 19,108 bothered to turn up. Maybe they'd lost the faith because Arsenal were without a home league win since the turn of the year. But what did they know, Arsenal won 2–1, and in my young, impressionable mind something became very clear. When Arsenal played a team whose name began with L we'd (I'd already started using 'we') win and score twice. Simple. I guess I can consider it my first 'sign'.

I've seen many signs over the years, football fans do, we like the comfort of thinking there's something out there helping guide our team's success. They're not the same as superstitions - those 'lucky' things. The lucky tag adheres when your team wins an important game and you realise, "Oh, I had those new pants on today" or you walked a different route to the stadium or had/didn't have a beer before the game. Currently for me 'lucky' Murray Mints are the order at half-time. All those early goals we score in the second half – those are down to the Murray Mints, honest! And when you realise you did something different and your team gets a great result, well, it's all down to you and you have to make sure you do exactly the same for the next game. This can become quite a burden at times, particularly if your name is David and you realise one Saturday when you get home from a game that you had the lawnmower in the car boot. Inevitably, that lawnmower went on quite a few more football outings after that until the winning sequence broke down. Sadly, David is no longer with us – he emigrated to Australia! I wonder if the team realises the sacrifices fans make to spur them on to victory.

For me, the 1967/68 season ended with that Leicester game. There were still five more home games but I didn't get to any of them. However, I now considered myself a fully-fledged Arsenal fan – firmly initiated into the Brotherhood.

Around this time I first encountered another team that was to haunt me in future years. That May I watched on TV as Manchester United beat Benfica at Wembley to win the European Cup. I remember wanting United to win, and being amazed and delighted when they did; 31 years later I was at the Final when they won it again – which is a story in itself – and I can't say I experienced the same sentiments. But that first victory, combined with public sympathy following the 1958 Munich air crash, spawned widespread support for Manchester United, taking it beyond traditional local allegiance, a trend that has continued and grown in football, fuelled by the late 20th and early 21st century global coverage of football by satellite television. But Manchester United's victory that night didn't sway me, I had two Arsenal games under my belt and I was in for the long haul.

2

The Magic of the Cup

As the next season approached it was clear to my family that I was smitten with football, or rather with Arsenal. Dad's work meant I was only likely to get to the very occasional game, which was not good news, but then my grandfather stepped forward. He'd take me to Highbury. For the next eight years he became my constant Arsenal companion. Thank you grandad.

We were at the first home game of the 1968/69 season, against Leicester – again; brilliant, another L game, I knew we'd score twice. And what made it really special was that it was my first evening game. It was school holidays so Mum didn't mind. Confusingly we won comfortably – 3-0 – and I learnt an important lesson; signs can't always be relied on. My theory that we'd always score twice against teams beginning with L destroyed at a stroke. However, there are still times when I seek out signs to help allay doubts before matches. It's now a running joke amongst the friends I go to games with.

I went to quite a few games that season. My Dad also seemed to get the bug because he started going to evening games. I'd be in bed before he got home from matches, but I'd lie awake waiting for him to get back. When he got in he'd come up to my bedroom, tell me the score and hand me the programme. Only then could I allow myself to go to sleep.

Grandad and I usually sat in the Lower Tier of the East Stand but occasionally we stood on the North Bank. I don't think he really enjoyed that, and I must admit I couldn't see much when we did – but it was exciting. Casting my mind back, I think the last time I stood on the North Bank was at an FA Cup Fourth Round tie against Charlton Athletic in January

13

1969. Arriving at the ground I was dismayed to find that all the Lower Tier seats sold out in advance, something the club only did for cup ties, but we didn't know that. Instead, we headed to the North Bank, and took up a position near the front, just to the left of the goal. As more and more people arrived, however, it got pretty tight and the pressure gradually edged me further back. A woman standing nearby spoke to a policeman and pointed to me saying that I'd been so quiet and patient he should let me go to the front. I was a nice boy! Clearly he was unmoved – like me – because my view of the game consisted of occasional glimpses of scurrying players or a whizzing ball. We won 2–0 and everyone around me was in a great mood.

The FA Cup had real standing then, it really was exciting and every supporter dreamt of seeing their team lift the Cup at Wembley. Boy's comics were full of stories of unlikely heroes scoring the winning goal in the final, and I read a lot of comics! After a Saturday victory in the early rounds of the Cup, excitement built through the weekend as you studied the other results and considered who you might meet in the next round. Finally, on Monday lunchtime you learnt the answer. All over the country supporters gathered around transistor radios and waited in awed silence as the numbered balls dropped into a velvet bag. A satisfying click confirmed the balls were receiving a good shake then a stern disembodied voice informed you that "No.1…Arsenal …will play…No.16…" This collective experience was part of what we considered 'The Magic of the Cup'. Much of that magic has now evaporated as expensively purchased TV rights demand maximum game coverage, leading to challenging kick off times, resulting in poor attendances at many games. In 2011 the draw for the FA Cup quarter-finals took place on a Sunday afternoon just before we kicked off our 5th Round tie at Leyton Orient and over a day before West Ham played Burnley. And likewise, in 2012 the draw for the 4th Round took place more than 24-hours before we'd played our 3rd Round tie against Leeds United. Where's the magic in that?

Any dreams I may have had of the FA Cup Final in 1969 after that victory over Charlton quickly evaporated. The revered numbered balls sent us to West Bromwich Albion in the next round where we lost 1–0. But that wasn't the end of the Wembley dream for that year – there was more to come – but dream is not the right word, nightmare would be more appropriate.

In 1968 we had lost the League Cup Final to Leeds United. In 1969 we got another chance. Progress to the final had been smooth and efficient. Sunderland and Liverpool were beaten by single goal margins while Scunthorpe and Blackpool were swatted aside easily, leaving a two-legged semi-final against North London rivals Tottenham between us and a return to Wembley. My Dad went to the first leg at Highbury when we gained a narrow 1-0 victory thanks to a last minute strike by John Radford. But after 68 minutes of the return leg at White Hart Lane, Tottenham scored to bring the tie level again, in a game described as "90 minutes of brutally hard, recklessly fast, intemperate football." Sounds like a typical North London derby to me. But Arsenal didn't crumble and right at the end John Radford leapt high to meet a corner and crash a header past Pat Jennings in the Tottenham goal - and Arsenal were back at Wembley. This time the opponents were lowly Swindon Town of Division 3 – what could possibly go wrong?

I didn't go to the Final. Back then, if you weren't a season ticket holder you qualified for a ticket by collecting coupons printed in the match day programme. You cut them out, stuck them on a form and sent them off – the more coupons you had, the better your chance of getting a ticket. I probably had enough to get lucky, but my grandfather didn't buy a programme and clearly, having just reached my 12th birthday, I couldn't go on my own. This meant that when the fateful day arrived I was condemned to listening to live commentary on the radio. I have a copy of the programme in front of me as I write this. Stapled within its pages is a copy of the Football League Review, a magazine that ran for about 10 years from the mid 60s to mid 70s. It was heavily supported by tobacco advertisers because within its pages I find that I could buy twenty Senior Service for 3/9 (about 19p) – not that I was old enough, or interested. I also learnt that "a pipe does something

15

for a man, St. Bruno does something more, man!", and if I smoked Old Holborn I could "Join the men". I was still a boy so they wasted their budget on me.

The pitch that day looked more like a farmyard than the Mecca of English football. The week before, the Horse of the Year show took place on the pitch, followed by a deluge of rain that hit London during the days leading up to the final. Wembley claimed they had pumped 25,000 gallons of water from the pitch, I think there was probably another 25,000 gallons still in it, leaving it "glutinous mixture of ankle deep sludge and sand" for the final. But even so Arsenal's thoroughbreds should certainly dispose of the carthorses of Swindon. At that stage in my football knowledge I had no awareness of the terms 'plucky underdog' or 'cup upset'. Swindon scored in the first half, resulting from a mix up in our defence between the centre half Ian Ure and Bob Wilson in goal. It was horribly similar to the goal scored by Birmingham right at the end of the 2011 final. Arsenal threw everything at the Swindon goal in the second half and, just when it looked like all efforts would come to naught, a mud smeared Bobby Gould popped up with three or four minutes remaining to force home a header into an empty net. I watched the game highlights on TV the following day and will never forget the smile on his face, he was so happy he cried.

Sitting at home, hanging on every word of the radio commentary, I was convinced that during extra time the dominance we'd shown in the second half would continue and ensure another goal, and victory. But as the game wore on the Arsenal players sank ever deeper into the mud while Swindon, and in particular Don Rogers, seemed to skate across the surface. In a role reversal it was now Arsenal looking more and more like the carthorses. Swindon got a second and then, with time running out, Rogers broke clear and slotted home a third. Listening at home, after Swindon's second, I crawled under the dining room table, after the third, my schoolboy dreams shattered, I cried and I cried. The despair I felt that day has never left me.

It was my first really painful experience of defeat in my brief time as an Arsenal fan; a pain that increased tangibly

16

when I returned to school on the Monday. There were just as many Spurs and Chelsea fans as there were Arsenal amongst my classmates. That game taught me two important lessons that are as valid today as they were then: firstly, take nothing for granted in football, and secondly, previously un-noted goalkeepers will invariably play a blinder against us.

3

One Giant Leap

During the summer of '69 something remarkable happened, something besides the crew of Apollo 11 landing on the Moon and taking "one giant leap for mankind." Something far more important; my grandfather suggested we get season tickets at Highbury. I was ecstatic, and amazed when my Dad agreed − because he'd have to pay for mine − pocket money didn't stretch that far. Later that summer we heard the tickets were ours. For the princely sum of £19.10s (£19.50) I gained access to 21 league games, up to six cup ties and all reserve games at Highbury. I was in heaven. These days I pay about £50 per game! A quick calculation tells me that while I got a whole season's football for £19.50 in 1969, today that buys me just 36 minutes of one game.

As you can imagine, waiting for the new season (1969-70) to begin was agony. My grandmother bought me a red and white scarf − which I still have - and I was ready and raring to go. At the end of the previous season we had battled to finish fourth in the league, the highest position we'd attained since 1959, and by virtue of that we had qualified for the European Fairs Cup (the forerunner of the UEFA Cup which later morphed into the Europa League). That was sure to add an extra exotic twist to the season ahead.

While I'd been looking forward to my return to Highbury as a season ticket holder, the club were busily preparing the stadium for the new season by installing seats in what had been terracing underneath the West Upper tier. My grandfather and I sat on those new seats in the curtain raiser to the new season. Like most of our fans, it seems that the club needed to exorcise the demons of Swindon Town, as they had invited them to a pre-season 'challenge match' at Highbury. A young, gangly – short-haired – forward played and scored; his name was Charlie George. We won 3–0, mission accomplished. But then I thought back to Wembley – the pain was still there. And a dull ache remains to this day - I still get a little flutter of pleasure when browsing the latest scores if I see that Swindon have lost!

My appetite for football that season was insatiable. I saw all 21 home league games, all six European games, the three domestic Cup games, only missed one home reserve game, and even went to Tottenham for the away leg of the reserves Combination Cup semi-final. As it happened the season started badly, with a 1–0 defeat at home by Everton, but I liked my new seat: West Stand, Upper Tier, Block U, Row S, Seat 20. It was a big cushioned seat covered with slightly grubby looking heavy duty canvas – and it had arm rests! The position was level with the 18-yard line at the North Bank end. It was a marvellous position, with no one, no matter how tall, able to block my view. And that seat was to be mine for the next 37 years, until Highbury was no more. I think they changed the canvas cover once, and later they put in new seats, but number 20 was mine until the end – no one in the history of Highbury ever sat in it longer than me.

We put up poor showings in the League Cup and FA Cup that season: knocked out of the former by Everton in the 3rd Round and lost away at second division Blackpool 3-2 in a 3rd Round replay of the latter, after being 2–0 up at half-time. Cup competitions and pain were beginning to form an uncomfortable alliance. But glorious deliverance lay over the horizon.

That season our European campaign got off to a comfortable start with a 3–0 home win over Glentoran of Northern Ireland (away leg 0–1). It was a game marked by a strange crowd dynamic. We were 3–0 up by half time, all goals scored at the Clock End. At half-time the majority of the crowd standing at that end of the ground, anticipating a further glut of goals in the second half, emigrated to the North Bank, which was possible then by walking through the standing enclosure that ran along the front of the new West Stand lower tier seats. The club clearly were uncomfortable about that and quickly erected gates to prevent it happening again. In the next round we won 3–0 at home again, against Sporting Lisbon (0–0 away) and then scraped through 1–0 against Rouen of France on aggregate with a goal right at the end of the second leg at Highbury. This game fell in the middle of an extraordinary series of fixtures. These days, when we hear regular complaints concerning fixture congestion, I wonder how Arsène Wenger would react when told he must play four games in eight days across three competitions. On Saturday 10 January 1970 we were away to Manchester United in the League, followed on the Tuesday by the home game against Rouen in the European Fairs Cup, then on Thursday the team travelled to Blackpool for the FA Cup replay and finally faced Chelsea at home in the League on Saturday 17 January. And in December there had been a full League programme on both 26 and 27 December – on Boxing Day we drew at Nottingham Forest and then drew at home to Newcastle the following day. Squeezing the games in was necessary due to the World Cup taking place in Mexico that summer. The football authorities wanted the season to finish on 15 April but in fact this proved impossible, and while we played our penultimate League game on 4 April we then had to wait until 2 May to complete our fixtures.

For the quarter-finals of the Fairs Cup we were drawn against the Romanian unknowns of Dinamo Bacau and emerged from behind the Iron Curtain with a 2–0 victory, which led on to an amazing 7–1 win in the return. It was more goals in a game than I thought possible and I was giddy with excitement. I felt like I had spent more time leaping out of my seat than sitting in it. I still remember the headlines in *The Sun* the next morning, "Seventh Heaven.".

By the time the first leg of semi-final against Ajax came around we had only one league game left to play. In summary, my first season in the League as a season ticket holder can best be described as average: at home we'd won 7, drawn 10 and lost 4. We were definitely average, but in Europe everything was different. We'd played eight games so far, won all our home games and only lost once away. The first leg of the semi-final was at Highbury and Ajax had an exciting young player called Johan Cruyff. Following on from the recent British record transfer of World Cup winner Martin Peters from West Ham to Tottenham for a breath-taking £200,000, the programme notes suggested that a similarly inflated fee for Cruyff would in fact be a bargain for any club.

It proved another night of huge excitement. An early goal had me out of my seat and already dreaming of the final, but the quality of Ajax was ominous and as the game wore on they seemed content to keep the score at 1–0. But we kept pressing and with two late goals the game ended 3–0; the dream was very much alive. A week later a solid defensive performance frustrated Ajax, limiting them to one goal and, incredibly, we were in a European final. It was an outstanding result when one realises that this Ajax team was on the brink of greatness and about to blossom into one of the outstanding football teams of all time, going on to win the European Cup for the next three seasons in a row.

The final saw us face the Belgian club Anderlecht, with the first leg in Brussels. I spent a tense night with the radio, a night punctuated with increasing points of pain as Anderlecht scored three times, suggesting this latest final was leading me again on a familiar path to misery. Surely no one deserved to lose three finals in three years? But just as despair began to settle on me there shone a ray of hope, Ray Kennedy to be precise. With five minutes left on the clock he popped up to head home a George Armstrong cross. With the final score now 3–1 instead of 3–0 there was hope. With away goals counting double in the case of a draw we now just needed to win 2–0 at Highbury…just 2–0!

The second leg of the final followed six days later, on Tuesday 28 April. I had been a teenager now for a few weeks and I guess I should have been concentrating on school work, but the only subject for discussion in the playground was the game. On the Monday the *Evening Standard* published a souvenir issue of the newspaper; it had a full colour cover with pictures of Frank McLintock and Bob McNab under the bold headline "Come on Gunners, Shoot to Kill!" I remember how it inspired me; I have just unearthed my copy, kept safely tucked away for the last 42 years, and reading that headline again has just sent a shiver through me, reminding me of the excitement I felt at the time. But the less said about me hoarding old Arsenal newspapers the better!

I rushed home from school, had a bite to eat and waited for grandad to collect me. Then off we went, parked near Finsbury Park and joined the expectant throng heading towards the ground. There were 51,000 there that night and inside Highbury the atmosphere crackled with excitement. But as I took up my seat I was taken aback to find we had four Anderlecht supporters sitting right in front of us. There were familiar faces around too though. On my right sat a large velvet collared, camel-coated business man. Mum called him 'the cigar man'; she'd never met him but always knew when he'd been to a game - he smoked cigars of Churchillian proportions and I used to reek when I got home.

Right from the start the crowd urged the team to attack but they looked a little nervous at first. Then, half way through the first half, Eddie Kelly scored at the Clock End and everyone went wild. One more goal would do it. Half time came and the feeling in the crowd was electric. In the second half we attacked the North Bank end, my end, whatever fate had in store would play out right in front of me – and those four increasingly isolated Anderlecht fans. They were subdued.

The second half continued with us attacking but not getting the breakthrough we needed, then Anderlecht came back and hit the post; oh no, could it still go wrong? But, with 15 minutes to go, right below me Bob McNab swung a cross in from the left to find John Radford rising to make a 'giant leap' – but not for mankind - and connect with his forehead to arrow the ball downwards and into the net. The North Bank exploded and I flew into the air and continued jumping up and down uncontrollably; the Anderlecht fans remained quietly seated. As was the way of the late 60s and early 70s, toilet, till and bus ticket rolls cascaded down from the North Bank to drape untidily over the goal. The crowd was still celebrating when we struck again; Jon Sammels strode onto a pass from midfield and lashed the ball home past the bewildered Belgian goalkeeper. 3–0!! Dreamland.

When the final whistle blew we had won the European Fairs Cup, glorious victory after successive defeats and the first trophy since the League title back in 1953 – ancient history to me. The pent up frustrations of Arsenal fans exploded on that blast of the whistle and a surge, a tide of ecstatic delirious fans, flooded on to the pitch. I stared wide-eyed and disbelieving from my lofty perch in the West Stand, a mad, happy grin fixed and unmoving across my face as fans danced, cavorted and congaed across the pitch. The Anderlecht fans were magnanimous in defeat and left to face a long melancholy journey back to Belgium. I know how they felt as I was to experience a similarly bitter journey in reverse 10 years later. The players disappeared for a while until the captain, Frank McLintock, reappeared in the Director's Box in the East Stand and received the trophy, which shone magnificently in the lights of a bank of cameras. With the players back on the pitch the fans sought out McLintock and carried him and the trophy shoulder-high through a sea of joyous faces. It was a night I'll never forget. I pondered on this reward for having a season ticket – was it a sign – did it mean if I had a season ticket we would always win a trophy – could it be true? I couldn't wait for the start of the next season, 1970-71, and the good fortune a new season ticket must surely bring.

4

On The Road To Glory

In fact the new season was to be a truly remarkable one — one of the genuine milestones in the club's history. And a milestone in my own life too as, now aged 13, I joined the workforce — Ian Castle, newspaper delivery boy! However, I was rubbish at getting up in the mornings, still am, so it was the evening round for me, after school and Saturday's too. I think I earned £1 a week. Fortunately, Dad continued to fund my Arsenal addiction.

Unexpectedly, that newspaper round gained me entry into a new 'man's' world. Every Saturday evening at about 6.00pm a group of middle-aged men would gather at the newsagent and earnestly discuss football news. I stood on the periphery and listened intently to their views until the door flew open and a bundle of newspapers landed heavily on the counter. A brief flurry of activity, an exchange of coins and the group would disperse again leaving just the newsagent and me. The focus of their attention were the Classified editions of the London evening papers, containing results from the day's games and match reports on those involving London clubs. It was then my job to deliver the rest.

And if I wasn't at school, delivering papers or playing football in the park I'd be playing football games. Waddington's Table Football was a favourite where you passed the tiddly-wink-like 'ball' between your plastic players before flicking it — hopefully — into the net. Another was a card based game called "Penalty" where you played directional cards from your hand to guide the ball around the pitch, and then of course came Subbuteo. What football fan has never played Subbuteo? Actually I got quite good at it. As late as 1990 I played in a lunchtime tournament at work inspired by the World Cup. I won playing for Cameroon. I was a collector too: cards, stickers, anything football orientated. It probably started getting serious with the Esso World Cup coins marketed in 1970. The following year I collected Soccerstamps issued by *The Sun*. I cut vouchers from the newspaper and sent them off and sometime later a little pack of specially created football stamps arrived. The following year *The Sun* issued 3D cards and ActionPix – cards that showed players moving when you tilted them back and forth. In the 3D set I had Bob McNab, Charlie George, Frank McLintock, Bob Wilson and Alan Ball – or rather that should read, still have. In 1972 Esso issued another set of coins – FA Cup winners to mark the 100th anniversary of the competition. They were white metal but Esso also announced a special 'gold' one for the winners after the Final. I hoped so much that it would be Arsenal – my own FA Cup winner's medal. I was disappointed.

When the 1970/71 League season finally began it started reasonably well, and by the time we commenced our European Fairs Cup run in September we were lying in 4th place. The first game was the away leg against Lazio of Rome with the match ending 2–2. It was a little bad-tempered at times – as games between English and Italian clubs always used to be. But there was no hint of the 'Battle of Rome' that followed. When the news leaked out it was the only topic of conversation at school.

After the match the players and officials of both sides attended a dinner. The Arsenal players reported punches, kicks and spitting aimed at them during the game but Bertie Mee, the manager, was delighted that his players had not responded to the provocation. Intriguingly, the manager of Lazio was the same man who led Argentina at the 1966 World Cup, a team labelled 'animals' by England manager Alf Ramsey. A reporter present at the dinner, however, noted "a distinct feeling of an edgy undercurrent." At the end of the evening, as the Arsenal players assembled outside the restaurant prior to boarding their coach, two Lazio players attacked Ray Kennedy, kicking him in the groin. Bob McNab, our left back, tried to intervene, then, according to Peter Blackman, a reporter from the *Evening*

Standard, "All hell broke loose; the side street was in bedlam with more than 30 men exchanging blows... George Graham and George Armstrong were quickly drawn into the fiercest exchanges and several other of their Arsenal team-mates were forced to fight dockyard style: back to back with as many right-handers as possible." Another reporter present was Bob Driscoll of *The Sun*. He added that, "Arsenal skipper Frank McLintock and fellow Scot George Graham rushed to assist 19-year-old Kennedy and then the whole Lazio team descended on them in a crazy, screaming, kicking and punching mob." John Woodward, a fringe player, was grabbed by four men and hurled over the top of a parked car as "Young Italian women who had been dining in the restaurant were screaming in terror." The police arrived quickly and hurried the bruised and battered Arsenal players onto their coach while one officer brandished his revolver in the air. As the coach pulled away the Lazio players bid the team a final farewell with an aimed volley of bottles and stones.

It was of course all rather shocking, but everyone at school loved it. To us the players were real heroes, fighting for the team; we were really proud of them. Initially there was talk of cancelling the return leg in the post match media furore, but it went ahead, with an appeal for fair play from the FIFA president Sir Stanley Rous before kick off. Lazio ran onto the Highbury pitch to a cacophony of boos from a crowd eager for revenge but the match passed off without further significant incident, which I think everyone there that night found rather disappointing. The Roman gladiators were in the arena but they spilt no blood. We comfortably won 2-0 and progressed to the next round.

Back in domestic football we were also going well in the League Cup. By October we were in the 4th Round and faced an away tie at Crystal Palace. I only mention this really because my grandfather suggested we go and it must have been school half-term as my Mum agreed. I was going to see my team play an away fixture for the first time. We headed to deepest south London that evening on the train, squeezed in with all the homebound commuters. They must have really enjoyed the experience, because 40,000 made their way to Selhurst Park that night. Sadly, after an exciting build up, the game was an anti-climax — a 0–0 draw. But I had enjoyed the buzz of the away trip, of entering enemy territory. Any hopes, however, that I harboured of the team returning to Wembley for a third consecutive year in the competition quickly evaporated when we lost the replay at Highbury two weeks later. But I made a mental note to consider the possibility of further away matches later that season when the FA Cup began.

When the draw for the 3rd Round of the FA Cup eventually took place it gave us an away tie against Southern League Yeovil Town, a team with a much-heralded giant-killing history. Fortunately I didn't apply for tickets, because a frozen pitch caused the game's cancellation, the match re-scheduled for the following Wednesday afternoon — kick off 2.00pm. Yes, 2 o'clock on a Wednesday afternoon. It was still school holiday's and I was at a friend's house as Yeovil's chances melted with the ice and a comfortable 3–0 win followed, taking us into the 4th Round, and an away tie at Portsmouth. Now was the time. I had a good friend at school, Colin, a fellow Arsenal fan — I don't remember the term Gooner being in common usage then — and we decided we'd go. Times were different then and, although we were only 13, our Mums raised no objection, so on 23 January 1971 Colin and I headed by train to Portsmouth — it was very exciting, and incredibly wet. It rained all day long and we got soaked. And in another demonstration of how times have changed, we stood on a terrace filled with supporters of both clubs, although significantly more Pompey than Arsenal. We got right down the front and were at the end where Peter Storey scored from the penalty spot in the first half on a mud-bath of a pitch. It is a strange experience celebrating a goal while those around you stand sullen and silent.

In the second half second division Portsmouth threw everything at us and for a long time it looked as though they would equalise, but we entered the final rain-soaked minute still leading. Then, with just 20 seconds left on the clock, a bad defensive error close to goal — a recurring theme - and Mike Trebilcock, hero of the 1966 FA Cup Final for Everton, lashed the ball home for Portsmouth and the match ended 1–1. The delirious Portsmouth fans went mad. The final whistle following shortly afterwards left us feeling dejected as we became caught up in their celebrations, and we had nothing left to look forward to but a cold and wet journey back to London. Following the team away from home was not quite developing in the way I had hoped.

The first attempt at a replay fell foul of the weather, but when it finally took place on 1 February, we won a close-fought match. In fact the match did boil over at the end after Peter Storey had again scored from the penalty spot to put us into a match-winning 3-2 lead. One of the Portsmouth full backs took a kick at Pat Rice. Unimpressed, Rice kicked him back and another Portsmouth player took a swing. "Whereupon", The Times reported, "some half-a-dozen unidentified shadowy figures were at it, hammer and tongs, as the crowd roared – a good, old fashioned rough house in Hollywood style, red-blooded and ugly." The team certainly appeared to have fighting spirit.

The weather continued to exert an influence on the competition and delayed our 5th round tie away at Manchester City until Wednesday 17 February, but it still took place on a paddy-field of a pitch. Television pictures of the game shout '1970s' at you. An evening midweek away game was a non-starter for me. That night the team put in a really strong performance, the hero, Charlie George, now resplendent in his trade mark flowing locks. He scored both goals in the 2-1 win – celebrating his second by lying flat on his back in the mud – to earn us yet another away tie, at Leicester City. It would not be the last time we were to see that celebration in the Cup run, but the next time was an even more memorable occasion, and there was certainly no mud that day.

In that same round of the Cup, Leeds United, our big rivals in the League, suffered one of the greatest cup shocks in the history of the tournament when they lost 3–2 at Fourth Division Colchester United. I was so excited I cut out and kept the newspaper reports of the game. Now journalists were beginning to mention the Double when discussing Arsenal's progress. Caught up in the excitement Colin and I made plans for our second away FA Cup tie.

We caught a packed train up to Leicester on the Saturday morning, feeling part of Arsenal; the team, the fans – we were all in it together. The game turned out to be another disappointment – ending 0–0 - but it was still an exciting day out and we were able to boast about it back at school on Monday. With the draw already made before the replay, which we won 1–0, we knew our semi-final opponents were Stoke City – the venue, Hillsborough. There was no question – Colin and I were off to Sheffield. The only concern was that six months earlier we'd lost 5-0 to Stoke in the league. Results like that breed doubt.

Because we were only 14 we could get really cheap children's train fares so went up from St.Pancras on a normal train – avoiding the delights of the infamous football specials. However, we were not the only ones travelling that way. The station was awash with red and white, as was our train; we quickly realised we'd be standing all the way to Sheffield. And every time we pulled into another station it got ever more crowded. I remember a man – a professional Yorkshireman - getting on at Chesterfield and deciding the pair of us needed educating on the hardships of Yorkshire mill workers during the industrial revolution. Fortunately, Chesterfield was the last stop before Sheffield.

We didn't go straight to the ground. A former classmate had recently moved to the city so we met up with him first and by the time we got to Hillsborough it was heaving. Our tickets to stand on the East Enclosure, a huge banked terrace known as 'The Kop', cost 60p and we ended up right at the very back, and I really mean the back, there was no one behind us. We made a dreadful start to the game and by half-time were 2–0 down, the second resulting from an awful mistake by Charlie George – the theme continues to develop - and memories of the 5–0 drubbing were pulsing uncomfortably through my mind. But right at the start of the second half Peter Storey lashed one in from the edge of the Stoke penalty area past Gordon Banks and we were back in it. But the second goal didn't come as the clock ticked down.

Arsenal fans began drifting away in a steady stream and from my position I could see them making their way out down the stairway. That sick feeling in my stomach that comes with impending defeat had taken hold as we entered injury time. But in the dying seconds we won a corner at the far end of the ground and I realised this was our final chance. The ball swung over and Frank McLintock rose above the Stoke defenders to send a bullet-like header downwards towards the goal. A Stoke player shot out a hand and deflected away a certain goal. Penalty! I remember screaming incoherently at the fans that were leaving as we celebrated like the penalty was already nestling in the back of the net. The tension was unbearable on the terraces; I can't begin to imagine what it felt like for Peter Storey who stepped forward to take it. Storey v Banks, one shot, a semi-final replay or elimination. In fact I remember it was not a great penalty. From my lofty perch I looked on helplessly and held my breath as Storey hit it low and almost down the middle, but Banks shifted his weight to his right and could not readjust in time. The final whistle blew – 2–2 – we'd survived. Now my mate Colin had ears that stuck out a little, a bit like the FA Cup really. He was on the terrace step below me and as that great bank of Arsenal fans exploded in celebration, I grabbed those ears as if I was lifting the FA Cup itself! He howled in pain but I didn't care. The dream was back on.

I was absolutely convinced we would not make the same mistakes again. I was right. Four days later we won the replay comfortably at Villa Park. I was going to the FA Cup Final! And there was one extra twist. On the day of the Hillsborough semi-final we were due to play away at Tottenham in the League. A busy fixture list meant that we could not re-scheduled the game until the Monday before the FA Cup Final, becoming the last League game of the season and in the process claiming a glorious place in the annals of Arsenal's history.

There were now five weeks left of the season and we still had ten League games to play after the victory over Stoke. We trailed the leaders Leeds United by six points but had three games in hand (two points for a win). We went on a fantastic run and won the next six games which saw us overhaul Leeds and take a two-point lead, still with a game in hand. And then the wheels appeared to fall off the wagon. On Saturday 24

April we drew 2–2 away at West Bromwich Albion and then two days later we played at Leeds who we were racing neck and neck with for the title. Leeds scored in the 88th minute to record a 1–0 victory, our two point lead reduced to a one point deficit in the space of three days. Leeds had one game left to play, we had two. Both teams won their next game, ours a tense narrow victory at home to Stoke, which left it in our hands. We remained a point behind Leeds whose season was now complete, so we needed to go to White Hart Lane and beat Tottenham, or hold out for a 0–0 draw. The complexities of the old 'goal average' system meant that any other draw or a defeat would condemn us to second place. It meant the game at Tottenham became a Cup Final in its own right – one game, winner takes all. For Tottenham fans, the thought of their hated local rivals winning the title at White Hart Lane, giving us the key to the elusive League and Cup Double – a feat only achieved once previously in the century - by Tottenham – was too appalling for them to contemplate.

Monday 3 May was the day set for the Tottenham match, just two days after the League victory over Stoke. It was a very tense day at school and I probably didn't learn very much. I remember a cartoon in *The Sun* that morning. It showed a battery of guns arranged on the half way line facing a bemused referee and Tottenham players, while an Arsenal player enquires "How much time to go for our scoreless draw?" I thought about that all day – more fighting spirit. Once school was over I rushed home, grabbed a bite to eat then set off for White Hart Lane with Kevin, a Tottenham supporting friend.

Arriving at the ground it was clear this was going to be a special night. We must have arrived some time after 5 o'clock but already the streets around the ground were full of people milling around. Kevin and I went our separate ways, he to the Park Lane end and I to the Paxton Road entrances. As I turned into the road I was amazed to see a massive queue snaking away from the turnstiles which were not open yet. Games were rarely all-ticket then so huge numbers were turning up early to ensure they got in. I walked along the queue and came to the conclusion that it was not too bad, but as I got to the corner of the next road the true size of it became apparent. It turned down this road, curled back on itself and down the next road. I followed it all the way to the end and took my place, for the first time it occurred to me that I might not see the game. Always patient though, I prepared to take my chance. Eventually the queue began to move as the turnstiles opened but I was genuinely shocked to see how much it had grown since I first arrived. I must admit that the closer I got to the entrance the scarier it became as the crowd pressed together on nearing the turnstiles. For the only time in my life I found myself physically lifted off the ground in a crowd, my body held up by the crush until the pressure spat me into the stadium. It wasn't a pleasant experience, but I quickly put that behind me; I was in. Newspapers later reported that 50,000 unhappy supporters found the gates closed on a full house when they arrived. Incredibly, after all that, I found myself sitting directly behind a father and son, Arsenal season ticket holders, who had sat in front of me at Highbury all season.

The game has of course passed into legend. Ray Kennedy soared above the Tottenham defence to head home a George Armstrong cross two minutes from time into the Paxton Road end goal – right before my eyes. I jumped up and hugged the boy in front – he'd sat in front of me for the whole season but I never knew his name. The tension as the clock ticked down was unbearable – we were about to become League Champions - but if Tottenham equalised we'd end as runners-up. Tottenham had one more chance but Bob Wilson smothered it and then the referee's whistle blew. The lateness of our goal meant Tottenham fans had not had a chance to leave and so could not avoid witnessing the mass invasion of joyous Arsenal fans on to the White Hart Lane pitch to celebrate this incredible moment – we were indeed Football League Champions! I watched the celebrations from the seats for a while but eventually decided I needed to join in. I clambered down the front wall, onto the terrace below, over the pitch boundary fence and there I was on the pitch just where Kennedy had been when he scored. I grabbed a few blades of grass and placed them carefully in my pocket before becoming part of the mass of fans in the middle. I am sure I can spot myself in a photo published in the commemorative book, *Arsenal! Arsenal!*, in the bottom left hand corner, the boy with long hair and wearing glasses. One down, one to go – this was heady stuff, was the Double really on?

Five days later bright sunshine heralded the FA Cup Final. During the build up over the previous weeks ITV's football highlight show, *The Big Match*, had decided Arsenal needed a song for the occasion to rival Liverpool's "You'll Never Walk Alone" so launched a competition. A few schoolmates and I decided to write one, to the tune of Simon and Garfunkel's "Are You Going to Scarborough Fair." It started, "Are you going to Wembley to see, Arsenal beat old Liverpool…" Fortunately I can't remember more. Embarrassingly, one of our teachers made us sing it in front of the class, but we didn't enter the competition – our contribution was obviously rubbish. But it seems most of the others were too because ITV dumped the competition and Jimmy Hill, one of the show's hosts, decided to write a song himself, which is how we ended up with "Good Old Arsenal", sung to the tune of Rule Britannia. I never really thought that much of it but it still pops up every now and then.

I went to the Final with my grandfather; our seats cost £2.00 each. Football entertainment then still belonged to an earlier era. That day we listened to a selection of marches and waltzes played by the combined bands of the Grenadier and Scots Guards. All very familiar because at every game at Highbury we were regaled by the Metropolitan Police Band who played a selection of dated tunes accompanied by Constable Alex Morgan who would sing a song or two. The only real element of entertainment on those occasions for a 14 year old boy – and most of the North Bank - came at half time when the band marched around the pitch with a drum major at their head. In front of the North Bank he would toss his mace up into the air as the roar of crowd anticipation built up to a crescendo, to end in a groan as he always caught it again. Except once! That day the crowd celebrated as though we'd just scored the winning goal, but, undaunted he tossed it up in the air again, caught it and, unruffled, marched on as though nothing had happened. But we knew.

Football fashion in 1971 dictated that the 'must have' item for supporters was a silk scarf, which for a brief blip in history replaced the woollen version in popularity. I had two, a red one and a yellow one and wore them both to Wembley – but not in a traditional way. It had become lucky for me to wear them around my neck as normal, but also tucked into the waistband of my jeans and under a jumper. And despite the fact it was a hot day I had to wear my 'lucky' jumper to Wembley. In addition, this method of wearing my scarves also prevented any awkward confrontations. Back then a lone football fan was an easy target for rival fans' 'aggro'. In fact, having grown up during a period of skinhead 'boot boy' violence, even now I am never completely comfortable openly displaying my 'colours'.

Brilliant sunshine illuminated the Final, but the game was tight with few clear chances in the opening 90 minutes and ended 0–0. After an exhausting season the team made ready for one final extraordinary 30 minutes, but almost immediately disaster struck. Just over a minute into the first period of extra time Liverpool's Steve Heighway, attacking down the left, unexpectedly beat Bob Wilson at the near post. He scored at the Arsenal end and there was a split second of silence before the Scousers realised the ball was in the net and their roar thundered across the stadium. I sat silent; I don't remember saying anything to my grandfather. The goal was hugely deflating and I really thought that was it. But this Arsenal team were real fighters – we'd seen that in Rome. Ten minutes later, at the Liverpool end, the ball emerged from a confused penalty area scramble and rolled into the net. At the time we thought George Graham had scored it, but later TV replays credited the goal to Eddie Kelly. I didn't care who scored; I shot out of my seat, jumping up and down, screaming like a madman. Fortunately the end of the first period of extra time followed and gave me the chance to calm down a little. Then, about half way through the second period Charlie George took a pass from John Radford and unleashed a thunderbolt that rocketed past Ray Clemence in the Liverpool goal. The sad thing now is that I can only 'see' the TV images of the goal in my mind, not my own real view that I had on the day which was on the opposite side to the cameras. The goal has become one of the iconic images of Cup Finals at 'old' Wembley, the ball hitting the back of the net and George lying on his back on the Wembley turf, just as he'd done in the Manchester City mud back in the 5th Round. Liverpool could not come back and at the final whistle the world turned yellow and blue.

It was an amazing feeling, almost of disembodiment. It was hard to see Frank McLintock lift the trophy through a wall of supporters, but I caught glimpses of the players' bright yellow shirts and a flash of silver. This was what all football supporters dreamt of back then, to win the FA Cup – and we'd won the League too. It was an unbelievable experience for me. Until the Fairs Cup win the previous year the club had gone 17 years without winning any major honours, now, in only my second year as a season ticket holder I'd seen three trophies lifted. It was all quite clear to me, buy a season ticket and Arsenal will win. I've now had one for 43 years and sadly know that isn't actually true. But on a sunny Saturday afternoon in May 1971 anything seemed possible, and I wanted to be a part of it.

5

Reality Check

In fact there was a slight complication at the start of the 1971-72 season – I was on a family holiday in Norfolk on the opening day of the season. A game against Chelsea on the first day of the season was enough of a draw for me anyway, but when the club announced that they planned to parade the League Championship trophy and FA Cup around the pitch before kick off, well, how could I not be there? I made a very strong representation to my Mum that, as a true Arsenal supporter, it was an occasion I could not miss. I don't think I appreciated at the time how much my Mum did for me when it came to football. She eventually agreed that I could go and on Saturday 14 August I caught a packed train from Norwich back to London. Tediously, with so many returning holiday-makers on board, I had to stand in the corridor the whole way. One incident broke up the monotony of the journey though.

As a child I suffered from car sickness, but on this journey I discovered I also was a victim of train sickness. I started feeling really ill and pushed down the corridor to the toilet, only to find it occupied. I knew I was going to be sick any second and desperately sought an alternative. The windows in corridor trains were high up and with no alternative I climbed up on a suitcase left in the corridor, stuck my head out of the small sliding window and threw up. The effect of being sick from a train moving at great speed had never been something to occupy my thoughts before, but I learnt an impressive lesson. My eruption of vomit instantly smeared itself, with great violence, across the windows the length of the carriage. I felt a bit sorry for anyone who might have been enjoying the view at that moment, but with my deposit sliding across the windows I decided it was an appropriate time for me to find another carriage. And after all that I arrived at the ground just too late to see the parade which was extremely disappointing, well it's not everyday you get the chance to see the Dagenham Girl Pipers marching around Highbury! I consoled myself with the fact that it was the just club's junior players, not the first team as I'd imagined, that paraded the trophies. But the trip definitely proved worthwhile. We beat Chelsea 3–0. And after that I enjoyed an incident-free return journey to Norwich, relaxed in the knowledge that the team appeared to be in the mood to carry on where they'd left off.

In fact it was a false dawn. By the end of December we had just crept up to eighth in the table after being very mid-table for most of the first half of the season. Our attempt to claim the League Cup for the first time had ended in November when we lost to Sheffield United in a 4th Round Replay, but in Europe we were competing in the European Cup for the first time and looking good. We brushed aside Stroemsgodset Drammen of Norway 7–1 on aggregate, and then followed that with a convincing 5–0 aggregate victory over Grasshoppers of Zurich. All that meant that come March we'd be playing the mighty Ajax again, who'd won the trophy at Wembley a few weeks after we'd completed the Double there. But while I waited for Europe to come around again, it was time for the FA Cup once more.

I'd enjoyed my trips to away Cup ties the previous season, even though all had resulted in draws, and had every intention of continuing the trend. But then the 3rd Round draw gave us an away game at Swindon Town, bringing back those terrible memories of Wembley 1969. I decided not to go. Fortunately the team did not share my qualms and won 2–0. The draw for the next round offered up the exotic delights of a trip to Fourth Division Reading. It was a temptation I could not resist. I went to the game with Colin and, as only schoolboys can, we sniggered when we saw in the programme that the Reading goalkeeper's name was Death! It was not a great game and despite the difference in League positions, the typical 1970s muddied pitch levelled the playing field and created a pretty even game. Our winning goal in a 2–1 victory coming from an unlikely source, a 30-yard screamer from Pat Rice's left foot. I guess you could say Death didn't see it coming.

Our victory – the first I'd seen away from home - didn't make many headlines; they were all reserved for one of the great FA Cup upsets of all time. While we'd been toiling against Reading, elsewhere Newcastle United suffered humiliation at the hands of non-league Hereford United in an oft-postponed 3rd Round replay. And a strange parallel did not go unnoticed by Arsenal fans: the Hereford goal scorers bore the names Radford and George. The scenes of the Hereford fans invading the pitch in celebration after the winning goal are as familiar to football fans today as they were back then. And who can forget that overwhelming fashion statement – just about everyone of that invading horde wore a fur-trimmed, hooded, olive-coloured parka. I had one too, I wore it to Reading that day; no self-respecting teenage football fan could be without one in 1972.

Our reward for beating Reading was another away tie, this time against the upstarts of Derby Country who, under the inspired management of Brian Clough, went on to win the League title that year. This time my grandad wanted to go, and again there was no segregation so we found ourselves sitting amongst 'home' fans. This was particularly unfortunate as it developed into a rather feisty game, but nothing too unusual I thought, although I seem to have been in the minority. "Unremitting and frequently violent action was the currency of an occasion that was constantly in danger of being ruined by the wild malpractices of certain players" was how Hugh McIlvanney, summed up the game in *The Observer*. The game featured a mass brawl of the 'handbags' variety, some overly aggressive tackling and Charlie George flicking the 'V' sign at the home fans after he'd put us 2–1 up, which for some reason seemed to wind them up! They eventually, however, forgave him because three years later he became a Derby player. Derby equalised with two or three minutes to go and a snarling, aggressive crowd greeted this goal as some kind of divine retribution. An over-excited middle-aged Derby fan nearby seemed to blame me personally for all that had gone on and, with misplaced teenage bravado, I advised him "We'll murder you in the replay!" With some vehemence he spat back "What, literally?" It was not the time or place to engage in post-match banter. Things were beginning to look ugly; it was time to go.

The replay at Highbury was a most unusual one-off experience. The 1970s was a time of strained industrial relations and in January 1972 the coal miners went on strike, leading the government to introduce electricity rationing in February. This meant no games under floodlights and led to the replay kicking off at 2.45pm on a weekday! That looked like a problem – it was a school day. I don't remember how I convinced Mum but she wrote a note to school saying I had an afternoon dentist's appointment and off I went with my grandad again. I'd imagined we'd be almost alone in the stadium, but how wrong can you be? That afternoon it appears a pandemic of toothache struck North London. Highbury strained at the seams as a crowd of 63,000, the largest of the season, squeezed into the ground. Despite considerable hype after the excesses of the first game, the replay was a dull affair and after extra time the score remained 0–0. There was however a certain smugness the next day when I told schoolmates where I'd really been.

Back then there were no penalty shoot-outs to resolve drawn cup ties, you just kept replaying the game until one team came out on top. The stalemate was finally resolved on a Monday night two weeks later at Leicester City's ground when a Ray Kennedy goal gave us a narrow 1–0 victory; our reward, a 6th round tie away at second division Orient. I could sense Wembley again.

I went to Orient, but I can't remember who I went with now. Orient went for it and smacked the ball against the woodwork more than once, but we scored early in the second half and hung on for a 1–0 victory. It was another example of the battling, fighting spirit and a foretaste of the future when "one nil to the Arsenal" rung out proudly wherever the team played. Mike Langley, in *The People*, admiring the quality of the team wrote, "Even when tired and strained, when outplayed overwhelmingly in the first half, and with their rhythm disrupted by instant tackling…Arsenal are a hell of a team."

And now we were in the semi-final of the Cup, and, as fate would have it, our opponents were Stoke City again.

But before then we had the minor issue of resolving our European Cup quarter-final against Ajax. We'd played the first leg in Amsterdam already and although outplayed had only lost 2-1, with Ray Kennedy again stepping up to slot home the crucial away goal. All we needed in the return leg at Highbury was a 1–0 victory and we'd knock out the holders, Cruyff, Haan, Krol, et al. And the memory of our 3–0 victory over them in 1970 still burnt brightly in my memory. All the anticipation evaporated though when a mix up in defence saw George Graham head an own goal tamely past Bob Wilson in front of the North Bank. It was a sickening moment and I think everyone realised that our dream of European Cup glory was over. With a 3-1 aggregate lead Ajax were not to be beaten and subsequently went on to win the trophy again. It was a sad end to what proved to be our only participation in the original format of the competition. Despite the disappointment of our European exit there was little time to dwell on it, for it was time to face Stoke City once again.

This time the game took place at Villa Park and I went with my grandfather. The previous year's semi-final had been a tense, desperate affair, as semi-finals usually are. This one was no exception. We had taken the lead and were in command until our goalkeeper Bob Wilson injured his knee. He played on but was hobbling badly and completely caught out when Peter Simpson's back pass eluded him for Stoke's equaliser. It was a terrible blow; Wilson was a great 'keeper. Teams could only name one substitute then and it was never a goalkeeper. With about 20 minutes left Wilson, who missed the rest of the season, left the field, with his place between the posts taken by striker John Radford. I feared the worst. Yet Radford astounded me by doing really well. He made a couple of good saves while the defence concentrated on keeping Stoke at arm's length as much as possible, although the extended period of injury time meant that when the referee finally blew for full time it felt like we'd just won the cup itself rather than just hanging on for a replay.

I couldn't go to the replay because it took place four days later on a Wednesday evening at Goodison Park. We were trailing 1–0 at half-time but a couple of controversial refereeing decisions allowed us to fight back and claim the tie 2–1. I stayed up to watch the highlights on TV that night and went to bed excited about a return to Wembley and the chance of another FA Cup win. I had total belief in the team then, and I felt nothing, not even our Cup Final opponents and hated rivals, Leeds United, could stop us.

But before I could get back to Wembley there was an administrative hiccup. My grandfather thought I was applying for our Final tickets, I thought he was doing it. It was rather late in the day when we realised neither had done the deed. We contacted the club as soon as we discovered the error but by then all the seats were gone. We did, however, secure two standing tickets, but grandad didn't fancy that, so I offered his ticket to Colin who gratefully accepted.

The game was the 'Centenary Final', the 100th FA Cup Final, and so the FA made the day a celebration of Finals past. I brought a book, '100 years of the FA Cup' – I was always into history – and, as mentioned earlier, collected the commemorative set of FA Cup Winners' coins issued by Esso. Dad got one every time he filled up the car with petrol. By the day of the game my earlier confidence in victory had begun to wane; like us the previous year, Leeds were challenging for the Double. I remember I had been looking forward to the pre-match 'Parade of FA Cup Winners' but was hugely disappointed when I realised it was just a number of people walking around the pitch holding up large badges of the FA Cup Winners through history. I'm not sure now what I expected, but I was definitely disappointed. Still, according to the programme there was always Tommy Steele singing "Abide With Me" to look forward too. For some reason I don't remember that.

The game followed the pattern of previous games between two such close and fierce rivals. The tackles flew in from all angles. Our left back Bob McNab was booked in the first minute, which set the tone for the first half. Leeds scored about ten minutes into the second half through an Allan Clarke header which Geoff Barnett, Bob Wilson's replacement, at full stretch could not reach. From then Leeds took control and we struggled to get back into the game. There was just one moment when I thought for a split second that things might change. A shot from Charlie George, at the same end where he'd scored the winner against Liverpool, seemed to be heading towards the Leeds goal right in front of us, but it smacked against the bar and bounced away. There was little to cheer after that. Numbed, we stayed to watch the team collect their medals then headed homewards. As we queued in silence for the station, a police horse nonchalantly swung its head to the side, plucked a rosette from the lapel of the person in front of me, chewed it then spat it out. The victim raised no protest; it was just another bad moment on a bad day.

Two days later Leeds required just a draw at Wolverhampton Wanderers to secure the Double. I must admit I took great pleasure from their 2–1 defeat, which handed the League title to Derby Country. And such was the fixture backlog that we played on the Monday and Thursday after Wembley, the season fizzling out with a draw at home to Liverpool and defeat at Tottenham. How things had changed in a year. And my theory that Arsenal would always win trophies when I had a season ticket had inevitably been destroyed. I remained a season ticket holder but the quest for more trophies entered a depressingly barren period.

6

Seven Seasons Without A Trophy
Part 1

After the astounding start to the 70s, much of the rest of the decade was a massive disappointment. However, 1972-73 did, at one point, promise much – even a repeat of the Double was on the cards for a while, but the promise faded away weakly. The league title was a real target and we were in genuine contention until the final run in (that sounds familiar) when we won only one of our last six games and finished three points behind Liverpool. Our last four games were all away from home and I know Colin and I finally accepted it was all over on Easter Monday. The team was away at Southampton and drew 2-2 while we had gone ten-pin bowling at Edgware with some girls from school. We had a radio with us; it just about killed the afternoon.

Our League Cup run that season had come to an abrupt and shocking end. In November Norwich City came to Highbury in the 5th Round and ran away with the tie 3-0, all the goals scored by Graham Paddon, the first opposition hat-trick at Highbury since 1964. I felt sick. Maybe we'd fare better in the FA Cup.

We overcame Leicester City and Bradford City before the 5th Round draw gave us an away tie at Carlisle United. Carlisle in February, that sounded exotic, Carlisle was almost Scotland! Colin and I decided to go. Our analysis appeared to receive confirmation as we progressed further into north-west England; there was snow on the hills. Then, as our train reached its destination and the Arsenal horde flooded from Carlisle station, I was amazed at the large crowd of locals gathered around the forecourt, silently watching the spectacle.

It struck me at the time that this was a pretty odd thing to do and considered it a reflection on how dull life must be in the North. However, with the benefit of hindsight I realise just how alien we must have looked.

Football fashion in the early seventies was, err, unusual; replica shirts were for a far off distant future. One of the stranger items of clothing was the white butcher's coat decorated with the names of players, cannons, AFC, etc, all added in red felt-tipped pen. Then of course there was the classic skinhead attire of tight jeans coming only half way down the calf to show off the Dr. Martens 'bovver' boots. Denim or Harrington jackets or Crombie overcoats covered Ben Sherman or Brutus shirts and braces. Scarves generally did not hang around necks, more frequently you could see them tied to wrists or threaded through the belt loops of jeans. This London invasion was a sight to see; personally I was never one for fashion. As for the game, it was a tough one and we had to work hard, but held on for a 2–1 win, goals courtesy of Frank McLintock and Alan Ball.

In the next round the draw took us to Chelsea, to the building site known as Stamford Bridge. My ticket on the North Terrace cost me 40p and I saw us draw 2-2, earning a replay at Highbury three days later which we won 2–1 after some controversial refereeing decisions. We'd reached our third FA Cup semi-final in three years, and all that stood in the way of a third Final was second division Sunderland. Easy. Oh dear.

The semi-final was at Hillsborough again; this time I went with grandad. Our seats in the North Stand cost £3.00 each. That was as good as it got. The triple-final dream ended there. Sunderland outplayed and outfought us; they wanted it more and duly won 2–1. Our solitary goal five minutes from time made it look as though it had been a close run thing, but we were well-beaten. My cup of gloom runneth over. The only pleasure left that season was Sunderland continuing their remarkable run and actually winning the FA Cup. They beat our rivals Leeds United in the final and in the process gave the history of the FA Cup one of its most enduring images: Sunderland manager Bob Stokoe galloping across the Wembley pitch at the final whistle in his tracksuit and raincoat, clutching his trilby, to embrace his goalkeeper Jim Montgomery. Personally though I'd have preferred it if we'd dumped Sunderland out in the semi and to hell with FA Cup history.

The summer of 1973 brought a great change in my life. Now aged 16 I chose to leave school. I could have stayed on to do 'A' levels but I didn't see the point. I reasoned that two years in the workplace would put me ahead of anyone coming in later with extra qualifications. I had five 'O' levels and two CSE grade ones to my name – and they counted as 'O' levels – and so with that I looked to my future. I've never regretted that decision. In fact a year or two earlier, so infatuated with Arsenal had I become that I wrote to the club enquiring about jobs there. I received a very pleasant letter back from Ken Friar, then assistant secretary, now a director of the club. Sadly the letter is no more but I remember him saying how delighted he was to hear that I was considering employment at a football club and that I should write again nearer my time of leaving school; I don't know why, but I never did. Instead I got myself a job at an advertising agency, my thought process being, "I like television, I'll try advertising, that's to do with television." It was nothing glamorous though, I started working in the despatch department of a London advertising agency, earning £686 a year, but had seamlessly exchanged school for the workplace.

And while I entered an exciting new era of my life, my football team took a path in the opposite direction. For the next three seasons, as the Double team broke up, a poor inconsistent Arsenal finished 10th, 16th and 17th in the league, leading to the departure of Bertie Mee as manager at the end of the 1975-76 season and the appointment of former player Terry Neill as his replacement. The only slight glimmer of hope for the future during this period lay in the emergence of a young and extremely gifted Irish midfielder, Liam Brady.

Little football action, however, was available to the great television audience. Live football on TV was a rare occurrence at the time. It was one of the reasons why the FA Cup Final was so popular as, other than the occasional England game, it was just about the only Live football available to the population at large. There were highlights of selected matches at the weekend with *Match of the Day* on BBC Saturday nights and ITV's *The Big Match* on Sunday afternoons and there were also highlights of midweek cup replays on *Sportsnight With Coleman* on BBC or *Midweek Sport Special* on ITV, but that was it. Without the blanket media coverage of football we now enjoy it was perfectly feasible to avoid the score of these midweek games and tune in expectantly to the highlights – although I never did that with Arsenal games, they were far too important. These days I am regularly amused by the BBC news bulletins before match highlight programmes which genuinely seem to believe there are vast numbers of people who still do this, but then they get it completely wrong anyway when the newsreader helpfully says, "And if you don't want to know the score, look away now", then proceeds to read out the results. However, my efforts to enjoy these late night football shows often ended in disappointment as my Dad unknowingly ruined them for me. If he'd been out and came home just before the highlights started I would implore him not to tell me the score. He'd agree and we'd sit down to watch, but when he knew that the last goal had been scored he'd pick up the newspaper and begin to read. It didn't take many games before I worked out what was happening – evenings of anticipation ruined with the flick of a newspaper.

The mid seventies also brought a whole raft of mediocre or poor players to the team. Just browsing through squad lists while writing this a number of names slip apologetically off the page that never made it into the pantheon of Arsenal greats: players such as, Richie Powling, John Matthews, Trevor Ross, Pat Howard, Jimmy Harvey, Mark Heeley and John Kosmina, to name but a few. Then of course there were players like Terry Mancini, definitely not a great player but a cult hero all the same. He seemed permanently out of his depth but never gave up – fans appreciate that.

On a personal level, by 1975 my career had begun to progress and I had moved from the despatch department and found a place in the media department of the advertising agency I worked for, learning about TV, radio and press campaigns; I'd also met the girl I was later to marry, left home and moved into a rented flat in Paddington – all by the time I was 18. My life was rapidly changing, but for Arsenal things were moving at a slightly slower pace.

Under Terry Neill there was a gradual improvement in the league but sadly my grandfather was not there to see it. We'd been to every home game together for seven years but he passed away in April 1976 and my trips to Highbury became solitary affairs for a number of years. In 1976-77 we were back up to eighth and the following season climbed to fifth, but that season, 1977-78, finally promised a return to cup glory. In the League Cup we fought past Manchester's United and City on the way to the semi-final where we narrowly lost out to Liverpool over two legs. But by then we were already in the 5th round of the FA Cup having disposed of Sheffield United and Wolverhampton Wanderers. Then, after a comfortable 4–1 victory over Walsall, we travelled to Wrexham where we won a breathless game 3–2. And so it was semi-final time again – our opponents Orient, struggling in the lower reaches of the old Second Division. This time it couldn't go wrong – could it? I made my way nervously to Stamford Bridge for the game; my years as a committed Arsenal fan had taught me never to take anything for granted and of the law of the underdog in the FA Cup. As it happens I needn't have worried; an untroubled Arsenal confirmed the gulf between the two sides and strolled out 3–0 winners, securing a return to Wembley. This time, surely, the Cup would be ours again – our opponents, unfashionable and unfancied Ipswich Town.

Well no, it wasn't. I remember nothing of that day, my brain seems to have erased all memories, for which I'm grateful. Although we started as firm favourites to win, Ipswich outplayed us that day. They hit the woodwork three times before they scored the winner 13 minutes from the end. The ever-entertaining Hugh McIlvanney writing in *The Observer* the following day noted that Ipswich "had already inflicted enough punishment on the woodwork…to suggest that the referee might have to send for a joiner before the hour and a half was up." The goal followed a half-hearted attempt at a clearance by Willie Young that trickled across the goal area to a grateful Roger Osborne who lashed it back into the net. Game over. I had now experienced League Cup final defeats to Leeds and Swindon and FA Cup final defeats to Leeds and Ipswich. To balance those there was of course the Fairs Cup win and the Double, but those defeats really hurt – and now it was seven achingly long years since I'd last seen Arsenal lift a trophy.

7

One Glorious Day In May

By the time I handed over the £56 to renew my season ticket for 1978-79 my salary was slowly on the up, which was useful because Dad was no longer funding me. I had changed jobs twice in the last couple of years, but remained in the advertising industry, working first in the London offices of ITV station Border Television and then at Associated Television (ATV), the forerunner of Central Television. I also had to face up to the soul-destroying concept of a long commute to work. My wife-to-be and I had been looking to buy a flat in the Harrow area when that curse of the late 70s and early 80s, gazumping, was rife in the housing market. By the time we'd lost out twice on properties we could no longer afford to buy in the area and had to cast our net wider. In the end we found somewhere in Berkhamsted in Hertfordshire. I did not take well to commuting.

The money I invested in my season ticket that year was well-spent. The season provided one of those truly unique experiences, one of those massive and sudden adrenaline surges and highs of emotion that I believe only football fans can ever experience.

We were solid again in the League, finishing 7th, but our 5th place the previous season had earned us a return to European competition, in the UEFA Cup. But thoughts of cup glory seemed a million miles away after a humiliating defeat at third division Rotherham in August abruptly ended any ideas I may have had of a good run in the League Cup. However, there was a promising start in Europe with an aggregate 7–1 win over Lokomotive Leipzig of East Germany. But before the next round, against Hajduk Split of Yugoslavia, was complete, another significant moment in my life took place; in October I became a married man. For the record, we played away at Bristol City on my wedding day, and I admit, I had taken that into account when planning the wedding. We won 3–1 with two goals from Liam Brady and one from Frank Stapleton. Thanks for the wedding present guys. We went on to overcome the Yugoslavs on the away goals rule, but sadly our European adventure came to an abrupt end as we exited the competition in early December to another team from Yugoslavia, Red Star Belgrade. So, any chance of cup glory rested with the FA Cup. We opened that competition with a nerve-wracking and traumatic start, against Sheffield Wednesday - of the third division.

The first game at Hillsborough, played in wintry conditions at the beginning of January, ended 1-1, but I felt sure we'd finish the job at Highbury three days later. Surprising this replay also ended with the same score after extra time. A second replay was required, the venue, Leicester's Filbert Street. We went ahead twice but were pegged back each time, Wednesday's goals scored by a former Gunner, Brian Hornsby. And so it went on; a third replay two days later produced a pulsating 3–3 draw before this extraordinary tie was finally settled in a fourth replay with us finally emerging 2–0 winners, but not without the odd scare along the way. When the final reckoning was made it had taken us nine hours of football to dispose of a third division side, playing the five games within a period of seventeen days and managing to squeeze a league game against Nottingham Forest in between them. These days, when the police require at least a week's notice of games, if we had retained the replay system we'd still have been playing the third round of the Cup in the middle of February, six weeks after the initial tie. The much-debated and unsatisfactory solution of settling matches by penalty shoot-outs has removed this problem which would never fit within the structure of the modern game.

After the third round marathon we sprinted through the next two rounds, doing a Nottingham double as we first by-passed County at home then disposed of Forest away. The 6th round draw threw up a very tough away tie at Southampton;

we were fourth in the league at the time with Southampton in ninth. However, the game took place on a Monday instead of the traditional Saturday – because Southampton played in the League Cup Final that day. They lost to Nottingham Forest in the Final – and two days later faced us in the FA Cup! Southampton rallied from their disappointment and an evenly balanced game ended 1–1 leading to a replay two days later. For Southampton, their third cup-tie in five days proved too much as we dominated and emerged fairly comfortable 2–0 winners. It was semi-final time again; standing between us and Wembley, Wolverhampton Wanderers. I went up to Villa Park for the game on my own and for my £3.50 ticket I witnessed a very competent, no nonsense performance with goals from Frank Stapleton and Alan Sunderland securing a 2–0 victory. It is possible to get to the FA Cup Final playing just five games, we had managed to take ten, but, however long the path, I was going back to Wembley.

Our opponents in the 1979 FA Cup Final were Manchester United. Having been relegated in 1974 - allowing most football fans to revel in a sense of schadenfreude - they returned to the top flight for season 1975-76, reaching the FA Cup Final that season but losing out to Southampton before returning and winning it a year later. Now, in 1979, they were back again. It was set up to be a real Cup Final.

I went with Walli, a mate from work. We met at Preston Road station and walked to the stadium to take in the Cup Final atmosphere, but then went our separate ways as he was standing and I had a seat. It was perhaps a rather unfair system, but as a season ticket holder I could get two tickets for the Final, one through my own ticket and another if I collected the programme vouchers. Walli was the lucky recipient of my second ticket. It was a sultry hot day, the sun seeming to make our yellow and blue colours positively glow with expectation. I bought a programme (50p) and took up my seat (£8.00) while enduring the most excruciating headache I can ever remember.

The game was so completely different from the previous year's disaster against Ipswich. We looked confident and assured, with Liam Brady pulling the strings. The game opened with some cagey, scrappy play without any real chances until the twelfth minute. Liam Brady picked up the ball in midfield, brushed off the challenges of three United players before pushing it out to Stapleton on the right. He took a few steps forward and played a low pass into the penalty area. David Price ran onto the ball, jigged past a defender and took it to the goal line before playing it back towards the penalty spot where the onrushing Alan Sunderland and Brian Talbot crashed into two United defenders, but an Arsenal toe got to the ball first – it was Talbot's – and we were one up. Talbot had signed for us in January from Ipswich, having been one of our chief tormentors in the previous Cup Final.

Much to my surprise Manchester United offered little in the way of real threat for the rest of the first half, other than a disallowed Maradona-style 'hand of God' goal by Gordon McQueen. Then, just as I was preparing for the relief of half-time, Brady worked his magic again. Picking up a pass half way inside the United half he strode forward down the right, shrugged off two challenges before ghosting into the penalty area and arching a perfect cross onto the head of the unmarked Frank Stapleton whose downward header put us 2–0 up. Joyous celebrations and a thumping headache do not sit well together.

As the second half kicked off, the sun beat down on what had developed into a red hot scorching day. I thought my head would explode and considered that I'd be happy for the game to play out with no further excitement. Both sides created chances in the second half but with United failing to get a goal back the game edged closer to the final whistle and memories of the pain of the Ipswich game, unlike that in my head, were fading. And then everything changed.

With five minutes to go Steve Walford came on to replace David Price and play out the remaining minutes. No doubt he envisaged a gentle jog up and down the pitch before climbing up to the Royal Box and claiming his medal. It didn't quite work out like that. Seconds later Manchester United scored, a cross from the right poked back into a melee of players in the penalty area where McQueen stuck out a boot and saw the ball roll into the net. OK, only a few minutes to go, I was happy with 2–1, just concentrate. Moments later United came forward again and in spite of having a couple of chances to clear we failed to hoof the ball into touch. Coppell fired a pass into our penalty area to McIlroy who bamboozled O'Leary and Walford for the unthinkable to happen; after cruising comfortably for 85 minutes Manchester United equalised with just a couple of minutes left. It was impossible, inconceivable. I sat with my throbbing head in my helpless hands. Everyone about me was stunned. We'd thrown it away, mentally now the momentum was with Manchester United as the torture of extra time lay just seconds away.

When the game restarted I was hurting inside. But out on the pitch Brady picked up a chested pass from Stapleton on the half way line and surged forward; he skipped past one challenge and flicked the ball out to Graham Rix on the left. Surely not… Rix floated a cross into the box over Bailey in the United goal…no, it's not possible…and there, rushing in at the far post, was Alan Sunderland to slot the ball home. I shot up in the air like a rocket, my head feeling as though it was about to detonate with a mixture of uncontrollable joy and incredible pain! I looked around me and just stood there repeatedly mouthing "I don't believe it, I don't believe it" – predating Victor Meldrew by at least ten years! We'd won the cup in one of the most extraordinary Finals ever and in the process brought an end to the unwelcome run of seven long seasons without a trophy. I was so happy. My only disappointment came when Brady, Stapleton and Rix swapped shirts at the end of the game and went up to collect the Cup and their medals wearing Manchester United shirts. I thought it rather spoilt the post-match photos.

I met up with Walli after the game and we went back to his parents' house for some food before heading into London for a few beers. Pubs didn't have televisions then but, undeterred, we blagged or way into a university bar somewhere in Bloomsbury and caught the *Match of the Day* highlights to revisit the moment of extraordinary victory. The following morning, still floating on a wave of euphoria, I was up early and headed to the nearest newsagent emerging minutes later clutching a bundle of Sunday papers: the *Sunday Express*, *Mirror*, *People* and *News of the World* – the 'proper' papers didn't have enough photos! I intended spending Sunday reliving that unforgettable day. It's probably wrong to admit it, but I've still got those newspapers.

In 1979 video recorders remained outside the mass market, so for those who wanted to enjoy special Cup Final moments again and again the BBC produced LP records of highlights of their radio commentary – no, they did, honest. And I for one eagerly awaited its release. When I finally listened to it the turmoil in the commentary box caused by Alan Sunderland's sensational late winner particularly amused me. Stunned by what we'd all just seen, someone in the commentary box just exclaims one word - "Jesus!" It was that sort of a day.

With the pulsating memory of the Cup Final win sustaining me through the summer I couldn't wait for the new season to start, convinced that win would be a springboard to more successes in the coming months, and the Cup win also added the excitement of Europe again, this time in the Cup Winners' Cup. But being a Gooner can be a cruel love at times.

8

Double Despair

My summer of promise and anticipation soon withered. We only won three of our opening ten games in the League, but the Cup competitions seemed to offer a lifeline to my rapidly sinking season. In the League Cup progress was smooth – including a 7–0 replay victory over Leeds – until we encountered third division Swindon Town, my childhood nightmare-inducing nemesis, in the 5th Round. A poor performance at Highbury resulted in a 1-1 draw and in the replay we lost 4–3 with all but one of the Swindon goals finding the net off various Arsenal players' body parts. The result induced much embarrassment and pain at work the next day. One cup down, but at least there were still two to go.

Steady but unspectacular progress was the order in Europe in the first half of the season. Before the competition went into cold storage in preparation for the onslaught of the European winter we had disposed of Fenerbahce of Turkey and Magdeburg of East Germany. While mainland Europe shivered we made compelling progress in the FA Cup for the third year running, pushing our way passed Cardiff City (after a replay), Brighton and Bolton (again, after a replay). In March, when Europe reopened for business, we squeezed in an exhausting eight games, of which only three were at Highbury: we played five in the League, beat Watford in the 6th Round of the FA Cup and easily disposed of Sweden's Gothenburg in the Cup Winners' Cup. Our reward, semi-finals against current League champions, Liverpool and Juventus, one of the giants of the European game. However, if the players – and fans – thought March was tough, April would test them even more; that month we played ten games. But such was the mental strength of the team at that time that they overcame every obstacle put in their path. It was a remarkable month.

I went up to Hillsborough for the Liverpool semi-final on 12 April; it was not a memorable match. The game ended 0–0 prompting *The Observer* to report "that this was a match from which no one was due a victory. Rarely can so many gifted players have combined to produce so much scuffling mundanity." The replay at Villa Park followed four days later and provided a far more competitive game, but again it ended with the scores level. And so it went on. Three days after the replay, one of those oddities of the League calendar meant we played Liverpool in the League at Anfield – another 1-1 draw – then the Cup marathon continued at Villa Park with yet another 1–1 stalemate. Finally, in the third replay, at Coventry, when I'm sure the players must have hated the sight of each other, we won. A Brian Talbot goal early in the game secured a 1–0 victory. The four games, lasting seven hours, entered the record books as the longest ever FA Cup semi-final in history. With tied games now decided by penalty shoot-outs, it will remain there for all time. I must therefore take my hat off to my long-standing friend Steph and her father Gerry who went to every game. But as the tie had taken so long to resolve we now had only nine days to wait for the Final – this time our opponents were West Ham of Division Two. Another FA Cup appeared within reach.

However, remarkable as it may seem, during the Liverpool marathon we also played a two-legged European Cup Winners' Cup semi-final against Juventus, the favourites to win the competition. I feel exhausted just thinking about it all.

The first leg at Highbury developed into one of those games that typified the British view of Italian football at the time; niggling fouls, outrageous challenges - "dirty tricks" as one newspaper called it - and in-depth defending. In the end the game revolved around the Italian forward Roberto Bettega. Only eleven minutes into the game he latched on to a poor back pass and broke into the penalty area; a desperate attempt by Talbot to save the situation saw Bettega tumble and the referee point to the spot. 1–0 to Juventus. About ten minutes later Bettega's over the top challenge on David O'Leary saw our Irish defender carried off on a stretcher, then, a few minutes later Marco Tardelli, booked in the melee that surrounded the challenge on O'Leary, hacked down Liam Brady and got his marching orders. The crowd was baying for blood. One man down but a goal ahead, the Italians withdrew into their shell. There seemed no way through the solid 10-man defence, until, with just five minutes left on the clock, Brady took a free kick out on the right. In a crowded anxious penalty area the ball flicked off the shoulder of Bettega, past Dino Zoff and into the net. Final score 1–1. But Juventus, with an away goal, had the advantage, and having just witnessed their defensive qualities – well for 85 minutes anyway - I could see our European dream coming to an end in two weeks' time.

By the time the game came around I had convinced myself we'd lose. On top of everything else, no British club had ever won there before, nor, for that matter, had any other European team for ten years. I listened to the first half on the radio (no such thing as TV coverage of anything as unimportant as a European semi-final) with increasing fatalism. Juventus demonstrated little enthusiasm in pressing for another goal, preferring to rely on their solid defence to see them through on the away goals rule. At half time the score remained 0–0 and stayed like that into the second half. Depressed by the whole thing I retired to the bathroom with the radio and wallowed disconsolately in the bath as the clock ticked down.

Unexpected gifts remain long in the memory and so it was that night. With just two minutes to play, and with the sound of the already boisterously celebrating Juventus fans in Turin penetrating all the way to my bathroom in Hertfordshire, Graham Rix got the ball out on the left, just like he had done at Wembley a year earlier. He moved forward, noticed Dino Zoff at the near-post, and so floated a high cross into the penalty area. Advancing unmarked toward the far post, 18-year-old substitute Paul Vaesson leapt to meet it and head home. It silenced the Italian crowd in an instant – everyone knew what that goal meant. Sitting in my bath it probably took me a half second longer. Then, like Vaesson, I too leapt into the air - and screamed. And as we all learnt at school, for every action there is a reaction; in this instance my action caused a flood of tsunami magnitude to sweep unstoppably across the bathroom floor. An historic moment in the history of Arsenal Football Club but also, sadly, the highpoint of Vaesson's all too short injury-ravaged career. Forced to retire from football aged just 21, his life took a downward spiral leading to his premature death in tragic circumstances eighteen years later. But in April 1980 his face shone out from the back page of every newspaper, hailed the Hero of Turin.

Two Cup Finals! Two chances of glory – incredible. But it never really occurred to me at the time that the team was entering unknown territory. By the end of the season they had played 70 games – a total never equalled by any other team. What is perhaps even more remarkable is that Brian Talbot played in every single one. Our season ended on 19 May, in those nineteen days of May we crammed in seven games, including the two finals. When viewed in the context of those last three remarkable months of the season the outcome should not have come as a surprise – but it did, and it hurt, it really hurt.

After finally disposing of Liverpool in the semi-final of the FA Cup on 1 May we played League games on 3 and 5 May, and then had just five days to prepare for West Ham in the Final. The possible tiredness of the players never entered my mind as the big day approached. I had my ticket; £13 this time, but a better seat than the previous year. But that's about all I remember of the day – my bad memories generally erased. The always witty Hugh McIlvanney, writing in *The Observer*, recognised the problems the team faced when we wrote they were "emerging from a programme of work that would make hod-carrying on the Pyramids look like a rest cure." The difference in status between the two teams, however, ensured that despite this the smart money was on Arsenal, only for West Ham to take the lead after just 14 minutes. A West Ham attack resulted in the ball pin-balling around the penalty area, evading a number of tired-looking attempts to clear it before finally finding the net off the head of a stooping Trevor Brooking. Ever since that day the media has painfully and regularly reminded me of the rarity of a Brooking headed goal.

Only the day before the Final Brian Clough had added a twist to the words of Mohammad Ali when he wrote that Brooking "floats like a butterfly - and stings like one!" Thanks Brian. We kept pressing but the incisiveness was missing and then I could sense the players didn't believe any more. We'd made history by reaching three consecutive FA Cup Finals, but one win was a poor reward. I was beginning to hate Wembley. Still, we had the European final to come – but now the nerves were jangling – I couldn't contemplate losing again. I had only four days to discover my fate.

I went to Brussels for the final, held at the ill-feted Heysel stadium, our opponents the Spanish team, Valencia. It was my first overseas trip to support the team. I went with Walli from work again. The club offered a number of travel options; we took the cheapest, a train to Dover, ferry to Calais and coach to Brussels. Well that was the plan anyway. It was an early start and all went smoothly until we boarded the coach at Calais. The authorities in Brussels decided they didn't want thousands of fans wandering the streets of their city so re-directed us to Ostend, leaving us to amuse ourselves until such time as we received permission to continue our journey. Ostend was incredibly dull and tedious. The only memory I retain is of wandering around aimlessly and the incongruous sight of Gooners hurtling along the seafront, racing each other on four-wheel cycles.

Eventually our time came and the coaches departed for the 70 mile drive to Brussels. I think I must have heard Dexy's Midnight Runners sing "Geno" at least ten times that day on the coach radio as we travelled through France and Belgium and back again. Over 30 years later, whenever I hear that song, it instantly transports me back to that day and all the emotions I endured.

We arrived at the ground around 5.00pm with the stadium not yet open – and the game didn't kick off until 8.15. Even so there were plenty of police on duty and they made it very clear that we were to immediately form orderly queues at the locked turnstiles.n Our turnstile finally opened at about 6 o'clock and the queue began to shuffle into the stadium. Unfortunately the next turnstile along didn't open. A middle-aged man near the front of that queue got annoyed and started shouting at the police to get the gate open. In a split second he was grabbed and frog-marched away – his distraught wife remonstrating fruitlessly in his wake. I doubt he ever saw the game. It was my first experience of heavy-handed policing European style, but not my last. And for the next two hours Walli and I stood on that featureless open concrete terrace watching the ground gradually fill and the atmosphere build. Now, finally, it was getting exciting - and vocal.

The origins of terrace songs are always obscure, but why a song sung by a cheesy school choir called "I'm Only a Poor Little Sparrow" found its way into the repertoire of football fans all over the country will remain a mystery to me. A crowd favourite amongst our fans that day – bearing in mind it was the 80s - was this 'charming' regional variation with our Spanish opponents in mind:

> He's only a poor little Dago,
> His face is all tattered and torn.
> He made me feel sick,
> So I hit him with a brick
> And now he don't sing anymore.

Once the game started there was, perhaps surprisingly, little sign of the team's tiredness so apparent at Wembley, and as the game developed both sides created chances without result. And so the game continued with the defences on top. 90 minutes came and went, as did 30 minutes of extra time; all that remained was the dreaded penalty shoot-out. Valencia's star player, the Argentinian World Cup winner Mario Kempes went first – and Pat Jennings saved. Advantage Arsenal. Next up was Brady, our number one penalty taker, who, inexplicably and unbelievably, virtually passed the ball to the Spanish keeper. All square again. Both sides then scored their remaining spot kicks leaving the game balanced at 4–4 as we entered 'sudden death' spot kicks. Valencia scored, Graham Rix didn't. It was all over. It really did feel like sudden death to me. Only a week before I had been dreaming of winning two cup finals – now it was all over and we had nothing; it was the most dreadful feeling of loss, it was cruel and the pain was raw.

The journey back to Calais was long and silent – except for bloody "Geno" on the radio. We got back to the port at some ridiculous time in the early hours of the morning and waited for our ferry. We settled in a waiting room which in reality was little more than an elaborate bus shelter enclosed in glass. There were not many seats so most were slumped disconsolately on the floor. I was aware that a couple of gun-toting French policemen were watching us, wandering away and then returning. I didn't think anything of it until, all of a sudden, a handful of Gooners at the far end of waiting room started coughing and shouting. Moments later everyone dived through the door, spluttering out into the fresh air. Those two policemen had let off a canister of tear gas by the ventilation grill of the waiting room, presumably for their own amusement. As we piled out, drinking in the fresh air, they stood there laughing – guns pointing in our direction – their body language suggesting "Say something – if you dare." We finally got back to London – Charing Cross - incongruous amongst the hurrying commuters rushing to work. As we walked towards the Underground I remember staring at the blank faces and thinking "You have no idea what I've just been through." They were the lucky ones. That season, after 70 matches, we had absolutely nothing to show for it other than the pain of defeat. My first European adventure - like the season - was, thankfully, finally over.

9

Seven Seasons Without A Trophy
Part 2

Any Arsenal fan who has been around for a while will tell you the same thing, the early 80s was not a good time. The club, unsurprisingly, failed to replace the irreplaceable Liam Brady who moved on to Italy, and the high water marks of this period were a third place finish in the League in 1981 and reaching the semi-finals of both the League Cup and FA Cup in 1983 – but then losing both to Manchester United. The 4–2 home defeat in the League Cup semi still remains a particularly traumatic experience in my mind. There were other low points aplenty. Defeat on away goals by Winterslag of Belgium in the 1981-82 UEFA Cup, (miserable), a 5–2 thumping at Highbury by Spartak Moscow in the same competition the following season, (shocking), and a 2–1 defeat, again at home, by third division Walsall in the League Cup in November 1983 ("a night of shame" as manager Terry Neill called it). Two weeks later the club replaced Neill with Don Howe.

The mid-80s were also a dark time for English football in general. At the 1985 European Cup Final between Liverpool and Juventus at the Heysel Stadium in Brussels – the same stadium where we lost the 1980 Cup Winners' Cup Final – 39 supporters of the Italian club died. A group of Liverpool fans had charged towards Italian supporters inside the ground before the game and a retaining wall separating the two sides collapsed causing panic. UEFA reacted by imposing a five-year European competition ban on all English teams. Less than three weeks earlier 56 fans died when a fire broke out in a stand at Bradford City's Valley Parade ground on the day Bradford received the trophy for winning the old Third

Division title. I was at home and watched the disturbing live broadcast of this tragedy on television. The stand was an old wooden one and I remember feeling thankful that Highbury stood strong on solid bricks and mortar.

On a personal note my life had moved on. In late 1979 I'd left ATV and moved to the media department of a London advertising agency, then moved on again to another in 1981 – it was the way to increase your earnings. However, in June 1982 a significant change in my life took place when my wife and I divorced, and with that I abandoned Hertfordshire to return to London. For a brief period I had no furniture in my new flat, but I did have a TV and video-recorder. I spent the first month as a single man again watching every minute of the 1982 World Cup. I can honestly say I was not unhappy.

Although the club had changed management, it didn't bring an end to Cup embarrassments. In 1984-85 we sunk to double depths of despair when losing 3-2 at second division Oxford United in the League Cup in October (embarrassing) then in January we exited the FA Cup in the fourth round, losing 1–0 to a last minute penalty at Third Division York City (humiliating). The squad continued to include numbers of players who were just not good enough – players like Lee Chapman, Chris Whyte, Colin Hill, John Hawley, John Kay and David Cork spring to mind. It was not until 1987 that Arsenal fans could lift their heads again; by then George Graham had begun his reign. We were back, but with Arsenal there was always the chance of a setback or two on the way.

Before then I had managed one particularly interesting afternoon's football watching. In 1985 Pat Jennings retired from football, having been a great goalkeeper for Tottenham and then, somewhat surprisingly at the time, for us. Although retired from first team football, he returned to Tottenham to keep match-fit by playing for their reserves as he was in line to play for Northern Ireland at the 1986 World Cup. In 1985 Jennings was due to play his last reserve game for Spurs against us at Highbury; the game scheduled for a Wednesday afternoon in November. Now normally the game would not have even registered on my radar, but as it happened I was leaving my job and working through my notice period – I'd had a falling out with my boss at a time when I was at a bit of a low ebb anyway and wasn't happy with the direction my life was going. After one particular disagreement I resigned without a job to move on to. Married at 21, divorced at 25 and a mid-life crisis at 28 – I didn't believe in hanging around. As it happened, things worked out all right and about a year later my former boss asked me if I would go back as a freelance to help out during a busy period. I did, anticipating the arrangement would last for two or three months. Well over 20 years later it continues to work, spending six months each year there which allows me the rest of my time to follow another passion – military history – and write a number of books. But, back to Pat Jennings.

One of the people I dealt with at work, Kevin, worked at a TV company and was a Tottenham fan (I know, I know – but it's not as bad as my mate Prinders – he's Arsenal, and married Zoe, a Spurs season ticket holder). As I was leaving my job anyway I suggested to Kevin we 'disappeared' that particular afternoon and went to the game to mark the end of Jennings' career. He agreed. What could possibly go wrong?

It was a typical weekday afternoon reserve team game – the crowd, a few senior citizens and the proverbial 'two men and a dog'. We took up our seats in the East Stand Upper Tier feeling very pleased with ourselves. And then it started to go wrong. We were not the only people who had recognised the significance of the game; the BBC's *Sportsnight* programme had spotted it too – and sent a camera team to make a short film for that evening's programme. Everything was fine while the camera concentrated on Pat Jennings, but not so good when it swept over the crowd. With no safety in numbers we had to duck down every time the camera moved in our direction. I spent a nerve-wracked evening waiting to discover if the camera had exposed our crime. While I was not bothered for myself, unlike me Kevin wasn't working his notice. With some relief we got away with it – there was a shot of the crowd on the show later that evening, but we must have hidden well because there was no sign of us.

It was in May 1986 when George Graham took over the managerial reins. At the time the club had just, for the second time since I'd been a Gooner, completed seven seasons without claiming a trophy. But he immediately made his mark. In his first season we conceded the least goals since the Double season of 1970-71, although we finished 16 points – in fourth place – adrift of the Champions, Everton. In the FA Cup we suffered an embarrassing elimination in the 6th Round at home to Watford after a controversial refereeing decision, but it was in the League Cup that everything clicked into place that season. And it was in the semi-final that it exploded into unforgettable life.

Before games I'd meet up with Steph. I used to deal with Steph at work and discovered she and her father Gerry had season tickets in the next block to me in the Upper West Stand. We'd meet under the clock in the bar area. We still referred to meeting up 'under the clock' years later when all that remained of it was a metal spike emerging from the wall. Steph's father, Gerry, has been supporting Arsenal since the 1940s, and started going at a time when it was common for fans to watch Arsenal one weekend and Tottenham the next. Occasionally Gerry entertains us with stories of long forgotten players – including a former Tottenham player, the delightfully named 'Butcher' Ward - but he retains very fond memories of George Eastham, a star of the sixties, at a time when Arsenal was rather short of stars. And it is Gerry who is responsible for the 'lucky' Murray Mints. But, let's get back to the League Cup.

Steady progress through the early rounds in 1986/87 led us to a two-legged semi-final against our North London rivals Tottenham Hotspur. The draw gave us the first leg at Highbury, but unexpectedly the game went against us. Clive Allen scored the only goal, putting the ball in the net after it had been ricocheting around our penalty area for what seemed an age. It was not a great Arsenal performance that night and I left Highbury feeling that the odds were now stacked against us, as I often do. We needed to go to White Hart Lane in three weeks time and win. The chances looked even more remote as the two league games in between were both away – at Sheffield Wednesday and Oxford United – and both ended in draws. The second leg took place on a cold and wet 1 March. Steph and I got tickets together while Gerry sat with Peter, his brother-in-law, a Tottenham season ticket holder. As we all lived more or less in the same area Peter had, very considerately, offered to give us all a lift home after the game – or maybe he just felt sure Tottenham would win and he'd enjoy having three miserable Gooners in his car.

The game did not start well and after just a quarter of an hour that man Clive Allen scored again. Fortunately he just failed to touch in a second and at half-time Tottenham were leading 2-0 on aggregate and things, frankly, looked bleak. And then something extraordinary happened during the break. The stadium announcer broadcast details over the PA telling Spurs fans how to apply for tickets to the Final. Arsenal fans reacted as one to that. Rumour has it that word of this arrogance also reached the players in the dressing room. Whatever the truth, both fans and team began the second half fired up. We pulled a goal back within a few minutes of the restart, Viv Anderson squeezing the ball between 'keeper and near post after a Niall Quinn flick on. As the Arsenal fans erupted in celebration a real surge of belief and determination seemed to sweep through everyone. Tottenham had a couple more clear chances but, about 15 minutes after our first goal, David Rocastle broke on the right and sent a ball skidding across the Tottenham six-yard box which the onrushing Quinn tucked in at the far post. The red part of White Hart Lane went wild. With the score now 2–2 on aggregate it was game on again. The momentum was with us as the fans urged the team on into 30 minutes extra time. Both sides made further chances but in the end the defences held firm and the tie ended all square.

It was only after I got home that night that I heard George Graham and Tottenham manager David Pleat had tossed a coin to see who would get home advantage in the replay. Newspaper reports claim that the coin initially stuck upright in the White Hart Lane mud before falling to favour Spurs. And so we had to return and do it all again three days later. It can be draining being a football fan. But it is amazing now when you look back at how the distribution of tickets worked back then that games like these were always sell-outs. Getting your hands on those precious tickets involved juggling work responsibilities and a lot of queuing outside Highbury at unsocial times to collect tickets in person. But all the efforts proved worthwhile when the game went on to firmly establish itself as one of the great nights in Arsenal's history.

At the time, however, things did not look promising. At half-time the teams were still level at 0–0 and I felt a general air of nervousness in the stands during the break. Then, after about 15 minutes of the second half, Clive Allen scored again. Once more the odds were stacked against us - until fate took a hand. Much to the delight of the Tottenham fans, Charlie Nicholas took a bad knock just after Allen's goal and couldn't continue; in his place Ian Allinson jogged on. Signed in 1983 from Colchester, Allinson had been our leading scorer with 10 goals in 1984/85, but now was only on the fringes of the first team, most of his appearances coming from the substitutes' bench.

At that point Wembley appeared to be drifting inexorably out of our reach. Then, with just eight minutes left to play Paul Davis picked up the ball in midfield and, spotting Allinson sprinting down the left, sent a high looping pass directly into his path. Allinson ran on into the penalty area – every Arsenal fan was on their feet, every Tottenham fan held their breath – then, as he neared the corner of the six-yard box, he swivelled through 360 degrees to throw off a Tottenham challenge and poked the ball towards the near post. Ray Clemence in the Tottenham goal, wrong-footed, could do nothing as it kissed the post and trickled over the line. The Arsenal supporters around the ground erupted. After that we kept pushing forward, our fans lifting the roof while the Spurs players looked dejected as the clock ticked down and extra time loomed again. I can honestly say I didn't feel worried about that – Spurs looked broken. And I was right. In the last seconds of the 90 minutes David O'Leary took a free kick near the half-way line and pumped it towards the towering figure of Niall Quinn. The ball eluded Quinn and his marker but dropped to Allinson on the left hand corner of the penalty area. He lashed the ball towards goal where it cannoned off a Tottenham defender straight to David Rocastle by the penalty spot. I held my breath. One stride, two strides, GOAL, and an explosion of hysterical, jubilant madness. After 300 minutes of football we were in front for the first time – there was no time for Tottenham to hit back even if they could have mustered the energy; they were a shattered team. The scenes on the pitch and amongst the supporters after the referee blew the final whistle were akin to those that greet the final whistle after a Wembley win.

I don't think I've ever had a broader grin on my face as when Steph and I met Gerry and Peter after the game. Peter had generously repeated his offer of a lift home and Gerry quickly indicated that his brother-in-law was upset and we were not to gloat. And so we did not. The conversation on the homeward journey was a little stilted. We all offered the usual platitudes: it was a great game, a pity someone had to lose, it could have gone either way, etc. etc – while all the time thinking, "Yes! We stuffed 'em!" And so it continued to the end of the journey. Peter dropped Steph and me off at Swiss Cottage to complete our journeys, but as he and Gerry drove off we couldn't bottle up our joy any longer: as the car pulled away we stood in the road jumping up and down and punching the air in celebration. Gerry later said he'd seen us in the wing mirror and chuckled to himself – if Peter saw us too he kept his thoughts to himself. In an interview given twenty years later the Tottenham manager, David Pleat, said that he gave George Graham a lift home that night after the game (!). I bet Graham punched the air in celebration too as Pleat's tail lights disappeared into the night. And so, seven years after the double disappointment of 1980, I was heading back to Wembley. Incidentally, Spurs actually made it to Wembley too – they reached the FA Cup Final that year where they lost to Coventry City. I enjoyed that game immensely.

And so our date with Wembley was rapidly approaching, our opponents in the League Cup Final, or with sponsorship taking a hold in football I should say the Littlewoods Cup, were Liverpool, the dominant team of the Eighties.

I met up for beers before the game in Swiss Cottage with Roger, the guy who had the season ticket next to me at Highbury at the time, and his two sons, and then we travelled up to Wembley together on the Tube. It was another gloriously sunny Wembley day. My ticket cost £20 (a 54% increase over my previous visit for the 1980 FA Cup Final, in the same section of the stadium) and the programme – with what must be one of the worst pieces of cover artwork ever – was £1.50. The relentless price increases at Wembley have always made me shudder.

The game did not start well and after just 20 minutes disaster struck. Liverpool exploited poor defending and an unmarked Ian Rush slotted home with ease. And through the mind of every single Arsenal fan ran the all too familiar statistic: Liverpool had never lost a game in which Rush scored. Over a six year period he'd scored in 145 games, not one of them lost, and now he'd scored again. But this was the Arsenal team that had refused to surrender to Tottenham in the semi – and records are there to be broken. As the clock edged towards 30 minutes we won a free kick just outside the Liverpool box. Four players positioned themselves around the ball which was touched to Paul Davis whose shot hit a Liverpool defender and bounced out to Kenny Sansom. In the bewildering sequence that followed the ball zipped wildly around the penalty area until it fell to the irrepressible Charlie Nicholas who poked it home from six yards. It was not what you'd consider a classic goal, but it was a goal. The Liverpool defence looked ragged and shell-shocked at that moment.

In the second half we began to look more confident. With 15 minutes left to play George Graham brought on Perry Groves to replace Niall Quinn. Groves started operating wide down the left, stretching the Liverpool defence. Seven or eight minutes after entering the game he skipped past a challenge, burst into the Liverpool penalty area and cut the ball back to Nicholas whose first time strike seemed to change direction slightly as it spun into the net off a Liverpool defender. Nicholas wheeled away in triumph and once more we had clawed back a deficit and found ourselves in a winning position. All records are eventually consigned to history, and so it was that day with Ian Rush's one too. I remember thinking about that for just a moment. The Arsenal end of the stadium was now a seething, boiling mass of red and white flags and triumphant voices, belting out all the fans favourites, equalled only by the roar that greeted the final whistle. We had done it, we were winners again. And as our 1979 FA Cup victory had done before, it brought an end to a run of seven trophy-less seasons, the second that I had endured.

At the end of the season the club announced the exciting news that for the price of £3.50 you could have your photograph taken at Highbury with the Littlewoods Cup. The club had never offered anything like this before and I was even more amazed when led out onto the hallowed Highbury turf for my photo. I would have happily paid the £3.50 just to walk on the pitch! I've returned many times through the years for more trophy photographs but never again got a chance to go on the pitch. In 1989 and 1991 photos were taken on the North Bank terracing but by 1993, following the opening of the new North Bank stand, those trophy-holding photos were staged inside the new stand, the turf exchanged for specially created backdrops. But on the pitch or inside the stand, those photos have always provided a tremendous personal souvenir of the club's achievements, not to mention an amusing insight into how I've changed over the years!

Winning is like a drug, when you win once, you want more – but you don't always get what you want. I began the next season – 1987/88 - with my regular levels of optimism. Although the post-Heysel ban denied us a return to European competition as reward for the winning the League Cup, come Christmas time we were lying in second place in the League, were safely in the League Cup 5th round and our FA Cup campaign was about to begin. Sadly, that was as good as it got.

We played another 20 League games that season, winning only six, and despite beating Manchester United in the 5th Round of the FA Cup we lost in the next round to Nottingham Forest. Although our average home attendance in the League that season was just under 30,000, the final home League game – against Coventry City – attracted a crowd of just 16,963. By then my dream of claiming the League Cup again had also been shattered.

Despite our indifferent League form we made a fairly untroubled return to Wembley, without any of the dramas that had accompanied the journey the previous year. Our reward, a Final against Luton Town; we were overwhelming favourites to win the Cup again – just as we had been against Swindon in 1969, Ipswich in 1978 and West Ham in 1980. Oh…

Another brilliantly sunny Wembley day, but as with most of my bad experiences at Wembley I now have few memories of the day; they have been deleted. But my Wembley price-watch tells me I paid £25 for my ticket and £2 for the programme.

Our first half performance was hopelessly uninspiring and after 14 minutes Luton scored following a free kick when Brian Stein left the bewildered Gus Caesar standing and slotted past John Lukic. 1–0 down at half-time and little to suggest matters would change in the second half. But change they did after an hour of the Final when Martin Hayes came on as substitute and began to put pressure on the Luton defence. With about 18 minutes left, a floated free kick reached the Luton penalty area and broke to Hayes who poked it home from about six yards. Suddenly everything changed.

We came pouring forward and just three minutes later Hayes' persistence out on the left enabled Michael Thomas to push the ball out to Alan Smith who smacked it home past Luton reserve 'keeper, Andy Dibble. Now it was one-way traffic, the game turned on its head. Moments later Smith's header was on its way into the net but a despairing dive by Dibble pushed it onto the crossbar; the ball fell at the feet of Hayes who lashed it against the post. As ball rebounded back to him he fired it goalwards again from close range but Dibble saved his second attempt. Dibble then saved a goal-bound headed flick from Hayes, and then saved in a one-on-one with Alan Smith; it was breathtaking. Surely a third goal would come. With 10 minutes left a Luton leg tripped Rocastle in the penalty area – PENALTY – every Arsenal fan was up in the air – this was it. Quite why Nigel Winterburn stepped up to take it I do not know. Michael Thomas had scored three penalties already that season. Winterburn hit it low down to Dibble's left, well paced but lacking power. Dibble got a hand to it and pushed it behind.

We could have been 3–1 ahead and there would have been no way back for Luton. But they seemed to take heart from their 'keeper's performance and two minutes later, after some comedy defending – all too familiar in more recent times – Luton equalised. Gus Caesar hesitated to clear a bouncing ball before missing his kick, stumbling and falling to the ground, allowing Luton to pounce: from being home and dry it was now 2–2. Then the inevitable; with 30 seconds left Luton scored again. Game over. Crushed and finding it very hard to accept what I had just witnessed I stared blankly at the pitch for a while as angry fans all around me loudly gave voice to what I was thinking. I shuffled away devastated, feeling badly let down by the team, and wishing that we hadn't made it to the final at all, for only that would have spared me from the pain I was feeling. We had shockingly managed to snatch defeat from the jaws of victory. I am very happy to forget 1988, but 1989, now that is something entirely different.

10

The Zenith of Glory

There can't be any Arsenal fan reading this – or any football fan in general - who doesn't know what happened in 1989. Such was its impact it has even entered mainstream culture in the film adaptation of Nick Hornby's book, *Fever Pitch*. It is without question the greatest single moment in my addiction to Arsenal Football Club, the greatest moment for anyone associated in any way with the club. Surely nothing yet to come in the club's history will ever, can ever, surpass it.

After the end of season collapse the previous term I cannot say that I felt particularly confident that the 1988-89 season offered much hope for the League, but with Arsenal there was always the chance of another crack at Wembley.

As it turned out there was no early promise of a return to Wembley that season. We exited the League Cup after two replays against Liverpool in the 3rd Round, and having drawn at bottom of the table West Ham in the 3rd Round of the FA Cup, in a very menacing atmosphere (my only visit to Upton Park), we lost the replay 1–0 at Highbury. And so, by mid-January any chance of cup glory had evaporated. But in the League we had been surprisingly consistent and at the opening of the New Year we stood proudly at the top of the table.

By the end of March we were still there but Liverpool were on a great run and ended the month five points behind us with a game in hand. After 18 long years without the League trophy could this be our time again? In April we were due to go to Anfield in what could be a deciding clash – as things stood a draw would be great. But before that game came around disaster struck at the FA Cup semi-final at Hillsborough between Liverpool and Nottingham Forest.

73

Rumours began flying around Highbury that something had gone badly wrong as we played out a League game against Newcastle; the truth, when understood, was shocking. The death toll eventually claimed the lives of 96 Liverpool supporters. The tragedy led to the postponement of our game against Wimbledon scheduled for three days later, and also our crunch meeting with Liverpool scheduled for the weekend after. Before this hiatus, Liverpool had overhauled us into top spot, on goal difference, but while the Hillsborough tragedy was unfolding we'd beaten Newcastle to retake our position at the top of the table. It now remained to re-schedule the postponed games and ITV, who had the contract for live games, made sure our game with Liverpool became the last game of the season, arranging it for the night of Friday 26 May. Whether that would still be the crunch game depended on how we fared in our next four games and Liverpool in their five. It was the beginning of an unbelievably tense period of my life.

Liverpool drew the first of theirs, an emotional return to football against Everton, and then went on to win their next four games. With typical Arsenal flourish we won our first two games then imploded: first, losing, unbelievably, at home to Derby County, and then, despairingly, drawing at home in the re-arranged game with Wimbledon. It was hard to take in. Having been in pole position for most of the season, we appeared to have thrown it away at the final hurdle; it was too cruel. The desire to be crowned League Champions was a gnawing ache, an all-encompassing obsession for every Arsenal fan, but having got within touching distance the image of Tony Adams lifting the trophy was fading like a desert mirage. I was disgruntled, angry, bitter and so very, very unhappy.

And so it came to the last game, at Anfield, with Liverpool three points ahead and a goal difference four better than ours; so if Arsenal were to win by one goal, although the teams would be level on points, Liverpool would still win on goal difference. It meant we needed to win by two clear goals which would leave us level on points *and* on goal difference, meaning the deciding factor would be goals scored, and there we had the advantage. So, all we needed was to win by at least two goals, *all* we needed! The true magnitude of the problem became apparent when you looked at the records. We hadn't won a League game at Anfield for 15 years – November 1974 to be precise – and we had lost all of our last seven League games there with an aggregate score of 16–3 to Liverpool; and the final nail in the coffin was the fact that no one had beaten Liverpool at Anfield by two or more goals for over three years. Liverpool had also just won the FA Cup on the previous Saturday and now, with their confidence sky-high, they had one hand on the Double. Everything screamed "No chance", and the media made it very clear that they felt we were making a wasted journey.

Friday 26 May 1989 seemed like a very long day at work. It was the only topic for conversation, but I had a big decision to make. Like most Gooners I felt that a cruel end was in sight, what I had to decide was where I was going to watch the last rites of our challenge. The game was going out live on TV, the first time a television audience would witness the League decided as it happened. There were various offers but in the end I chose to go home on my own, I wanted to be alone with my grief. Others I know did the same.

I started watching the first half sitting on the sofa, the tension cranked up even more by a ten-minute delay at kick off. The Kop, unfazed, used this time to get in some early practice for celebrating their inevitable title win. I felt resigned to that outcome too. When the game finally kicked off George Graham had selected three centre backs: Adams, Bould and O'Leary, with O'Leary – the only non-English player in the team – playing sweeper. Clearly he wanted to make sure we didn't give away an early goal and make the task even more impossible than it already was. In fact we made a very solid and positive start, with an excellent header from Steve Bould seemingly destined for the Liverpool net until a defender headed it clear from under the crossbar. At half time the game remained goalless.

Just 45 minutes of the season to go. I started the second half sitting on the floor leaning against the sofa as the tension increased. The game continued very much in the same vein as the first half, with few if any clear-cut chances for either team, prompting the Liverpool fans into an irritating and premature

75

chant of "Champions!" and "We're gonna win the League." And then, as the clock showed 52 minutes played, Nigel Winterburn floated an indirect free-kick into the Liverpool box and Alan Smith ghosted in behind the defence to make the faintest of glancing touches with his head. GOAL! Or was it? The Liverpool players surrounded the referee demanding he consult with his linesman – they hadn't become assistant referees yet – desperately claiming that Smith had failed to make contact with the ball. But it was to no avail, the linesman agreed with the referee; the goal stood.

We began to look confident on the ball; the Liverpool fans stopped singing "Champions!" We were fighting for every ball, never resting, then, as we neared 30 minutes of the second half, there was a chance; Kevin Richardson slide the ball forward to Michael Thomas unmarked on the edge of the Liverpool penalty area – was this it – I stood up – Thomas turned with the ball and poked it towards the goal – YES? – NO! The shot lacked power and Grobbelaar in the Liverpool goal gratefully smothered it. There had been few clear chances in the match, that was one and we'd missed it. I couldn't imagine there'd be many more. To me, right then, it looked like Thomas had blown it. I sat down again – but found I had edged closer to the TV.

With just 15 minutes left the home crowd were getting their confidence – and voice - back, while we prepared for our final push. Graham replaced Steve Bould, one of the three centre backs, with Perry Groves, to increase our attacking threat. But the clock ran down far too quickly and with one less defender now Liverpool looked more threatening. With just two minutes left to play we smothered another Liverpool attack but it left Kevin Richardson in a heap in our goal area and needing treatment. The 90 minutes were up by the time the game restarted. During this break I reflected on how well we'd played, and how at least we'd won at Anfield, although only by 1-0 – no one even gave us a chance of doing that. The players had given their all. And then TV pictures showed John Barnes nodding 'job done' to John Aldridge and focused on Steve McMahon telling the players just one minute to go. That seemed arrogant and irritating, and now the Liverpool fans were celebrating too. I returned to the sofa for the last moments of the game, pondering once more on the cruelty of football. No one could have anticipated at that moment that the delay caused by Kevin Richardson's injury was about to grant us the time needed to write what surely will always remain the most incredible chapter in Arsenal's history.

Liverpool came forward once more but the limping Richardson won the ball back and gave it to Lukic in goal (at a time when passing back to the 'keeper was still legal). He swiftly threw it out to Lee Dixon who looked up and fired it on to Alan Smith. Smith trapped the ball, turned and looped it into the path of the onrushing Michael Thomas, in a similar position from where he'd missed 15 minutes earlier. In reality it was incredibly quick, but at the time everything appeared to be in slow motion. As the TV commentator, Brian Moore, uttered those immortal words, "It's up for grabs now", I thought, no, not Thomas again. Then, GOAL! I leapt from the sofa high into the air, hit the ground and wriggled like a crab turned on its back and screamed. It was like an out of body experience and I'm sure I started hyper-ventilating. As they played out the final minute I sat with my nose about a foot from the TV screen, then as that sweet final whistle blew I screamed and rolled around the floor some more. The phone rang. It was Chris, a Watford fan; he wanted to congratulate me. I seem to remember just screaming incoherently down the phone at him! Another phone call or two later, when I had regained the power of speech, and it was party night! Over 20 years later, whenever I see Thomas charging through the Liverpool defence to score, I still feel a tingle shoot up the back of my neck. That unique moment in my life, in the life of every Arsenal fan, remains indelibly etched within me and forms part of my DNA. Surely nothing else can ever happen in my relationship with Arsenal Football Club – or in life - that will again unleash such a sudden, uncontrollable explosion of raw emotion; of joy, of exhilaration, of achievement and of release.

11

Into the Nineties

In the summer of '89 I had the opportunity to visit Communist governed Czechoslovakia at a time when eastern Europe was about to embark on a dramatic political upheaval. In Poland the country had just rejected Communism and Czechoslovakia soon followed suit.

Although the days of Communism were drawing to a close in Europe, back home I had dreams of my own 'Red Revolution'. I hoped our dramatic Championship winning end of season would pave the way for back-to-back titles, but that dream, like European communism, faded and died. I should have anticipated that after the euphoria of Anfield anything that followed would be an anti-climax, but I had hope. In all my years we have never managed to secure back-to-back League titles, which has always been a source of great disappointment to me. For many it remains the yardstick by which great teams are measured. And with UEFA's post-Heysel ban on English clubs' participation in European competition still in place we missed out on the chance to test ourselves against Europe's finest. Back then just one team – the champions – from each European league qualified for the European Cup. This ensured a number of unfancied teams, with the benefit of a kind draw, could progress some way in the competition before eventual elimination. Looking at the teams involved that season I think we would have made a good showing. In the last 16 teams like Malmo, Mechelen, Tirana, Honved, Dnipro Dnipropetrovsk and Swarovski Tirol were all still involved. Compare that with the last 16 we see now and it shows clearly why UEFA embraced the money-making concept of the Champions League so enthusiastically.

Once the season got underway we were dumped out of the League Cup by Oldham in the 4th round and departed the FA Cup after a 4th round replay at QPR. In the League we'd done well up until late December and were only a few points behind Liverpool who were back at the top again. After that, though, we started dropping points on a regular basis, but in April we faced two crucial midweek home games a week apart, against Aston Villa and Liverpool. If we were to have any chance of achieving anything in the League we needed to win both games as our opponents were second and first respectively.

I was working at the advertising agency I freelanced for at the time and was invited along with a couple of colleagues to watch the Villa game from the Thames TV box at Highbury as it was being transmitted as a Live game on ITV. We had finished dinner when a production man popped his head around the door and asked our representative from Thames if it was all right if England manager Bobby Robson came in and sat with us while they made the studio ready for him. It turned out that George Best was supposed to be the studio guest that day but he had arrived at the ground having had a drink or ten. Following a desperate search for a replacement the production team had found Robson, but it struck me that they must have found Robson in the bar because he didn't seem quite on top of the situation. Sitting with us around the table he opened by saying that it was a bit of a nothing game. No one said anything so I piped up and explained that actually, if Arsenal won they'd move up to third, three points behind Villa with a game in hand, and the following week we'd be playing Liverpool who were first, and that actually the game was vital. He seemed genuinely surprised and kept repeating what I'd said as though it was all completely new to him. A few moments later someone came to collect him and next thing we knew there was Bobby Robson on the TV in the corner of the suite, quoting word for word everything I'd just told him. The studio was only a few doors away and the cheer from everyone around our table was so loud I'm surprised it didn't come out on air.

It is the only time I've ever watched a game from a hospitality suite – it bears no comparison to watching with your mates. I was disappointed, though, that I'd not had the chance to meet George Best, but I did actually get another opportunity six years later when, through work, I was invited to a 50th birthday celebration in his honour hosted by a marketing company and held at Football Football, a now-defunct sports bar in London. I managed a few words with him and apologised for not wearing a tie as most others were. He leant forward and whispered back conspiratorially, "Don't worry, *they* made me wear one."

But after all the promise offered by those two games we took only one point from them. Our challenge fizzled out once and for all after that and as the final curtain came down on the season we remained in fourth place, 17 points behind Liverpool. But as we moved into the '90s that disappointment quickly faded as George Graham's team set about adding more exciting pages to Arsenal's illustrious history.

Our Cup runs in the following season, 1990-91, are not something I need dwell on. We did make it all the way to the FA Cup semi-final where we faced Tottenham in the first ever semi played at Wembley. We didn't win. We had already faced humiliation in the League Cup (by then, the Rumbelows Cup) when Manchester United had come to Highbury for a 4th round tie in November and crushed us 6–2 with a hat-trick from Lee Sharpe. Just a month earlier, at Old Trafford, we had met them in a league match. We won 1–0 with a goal from Anders Limpar, but it was an incident off the ball that made the biggest impact. Following a crunching tackle by Nigel Winterburn a mass brawl developed after Brian McClair and Denis Irwin repeatedly kicked Winterburn on the ground. Everyone on the field piled in – except David Seaman – it was like a return to the 70s. Three weeks later an FA Tribunal decided to deduct us two points and Manchester United one point – our punishment greater due to a bit of 'previous'. Rather than derailing our season, though, it seemed to make the team even more determined to succeed.

A further set back came in December when inspirational captain Tony Adams was sentenced to four months imprisonment for drink driving. That's how football was back then. But this was a mentally tough team and we continued to rack up the points. Adams returned after serving two months of his sentence, having missed eight league games, with us on top of the League.

Liverpool pushed us all the way but they were unable to keep up the pressure and results elsewhere meant we knew before we kicked off against Manchester United on the early May Bank Holiday that we were Champions. The noise in the bar area in the Upper West was deafening and the mood jubilant – a favourite song that day, sung raucously to the tune of "She'll be Coming Round the Mountain", went along the lines of "You can stick your effing two points up your arse, etc., etc!" How it must have hurt the United players to form a guard of honour for the team as they ran out before kick off. But their time would come, again and again and again. The party mood continued as we won 3–1, and carried on to the final game, at home to Coventry. With the League title in the bag it was probably the most relaxed match I have ever attended, the team treating us to a glorious 6-1 festival of football. It was a remarkable season for which I believe the team never received the respect it deserved. After 38 games, and having had two points deducted, they went on to win the League by seven points from Liverpool; we scored 74 times, conceded just 18 goals and lost only one game. Incredible; I was so proud.

That achievement kept me buoyant all summer, although the announcement of the new away kit for the following season did come as a bit of a shock; to me it is clearly still the worst we've ever had – the yellow and blue shirt with the zig-zag 'car tyre' track all over it. And I accepted, without question, the large hike in the price of my season ticket – from £180 to £328 – but when the kick off came around, as is generally the case with Arsenal in the season after they win a trophy, it proved to be a great disappointment: we took just one point from the first three games. But moves were afoot behind the scenes and in September 1991 we signed Ian Wright who went on to become a true Arsenal legend. In that first season he scored on his debut in the League Cup (Rumbelows) and stunned everyone with a hat-trick on his League debut at Southampton three days later; in all he scored 24 goals for us in 30 league games that season. Six years later, in September 1997, Ian Wright became our record goal scorer. But despite Wright's contribution that year the trophy cabinet stood empty at the end of the season.

Our long awaited return to European Cup action was brief, going out to Benfica of Portugal in the 2nd Round, and defeat at Coventry saw us exit the League Cup in the 3rd Round. But neither of those results was as depressing and embarrassing as our defeat in January at Fourth Division Wrexham in the 3rd Round of the FA Cup. It was a particularly bleak time for me as I went into hospital just after New Year for an operation on a detached retina. I came home to open a number of 'get well' cards that focused more on gloating over this Cup catastrophe than displaying any concerns for my health. In *The Observer*, Hugh McIlvanney wrote,

> ...the League champions found themselves dumped from the last of the major competitions they had a realistic hope of winning. They will go on striving in the First Division but only a fanatic could believe that a team as traumatised as they are now will salvage consolation there.
>
> Nothing they have endured recently – their expulsion from the European Cup by a stylishly superior Benfica, their dismissal from the Rumbelows Cup or their struggles in the League – can compare with the horrors inflicted on them by Fourth Division opposition late on this chilly afternoon in North Wales.

And horrible it truly was. I needed an escape and I had one lined up – subject to swift recovery from my eye operation. The hospital was a little concerned, they did not recommend flying with an eye pumped full of gas, but in the end they gave me the nod. So off I went to Senegal, West Africa, via Banjul in Gambia, to watch the closing matches of the African Nations Cup. I had clambered aboard the Cameroon bandwagon at the 1990 World Cup very early – actually I feel I was the driver as I had predicted to anyone who would listen during the run-in to the competition that Cameroon were going to surprise a lot of teams – I even wore a Cameroon badge - although I must admit I didn't anticipate them beating Argentina in the first game and coming close to knocking out England in the quarter-final.

As a consequence I thought it would be fun to go and see them play in the Nations Cup and convinced my girlfriend of the time to come too. The trip was organised by the magazine *When Saturday Comes* and was a little chaotic at times – but always fun. I'd planned to be there for more of the tournament but my operation prevented me flying out earlier and had to organise my own travel as the group had already departed by the time I gained permission to fly – their concern being something to do with the effects on my gas-filled eye if the aircraft suddenly lost pressure! Probably best not to dwell on that. The travel went smoothly until we reached Banjul where flight tickets were supposed to be waiting to take us on to Dakar. Unsurprisingly they were not.

I must have spent an hour with desk staff at this very low-key airport trying to discover where my tickets were. At one stage they invited me to climb over the counter and look at their computer myself. There was nothing. It was then suggested I go and see the Head of Security and was led into a very sparse office with little more than a desk and a couple of filing cabinets. Behind the desk sat one very large, balding, stern-looking man. I was not really sure where this was leading and so a little nervously I explained the problem. The big man's face lit up into a broad smile. "Oh, you've come for the football!" After that we chatted for about 15 minutes about the tournament, at the end of which he asked which flight we wanted to go on, sorted out the tickets and sent us on our way – onto an aircraft with piles of luggage tied to the first few rows of seats and all the safety instructions written in Chinese! But it got us to our destination and after that the only problem we encountered was when walking along a curiously deserted beach. About half an hour into our walk I discovered why it was so empty when I heard the unmistakeable ziiip of a bullet over my head. We beat a hasty retreat and later discovered that the French Foreign Legion had a base nearby with a firing range that backed onto the beach.

We saw the semi-finals, the third-place play-off and the Final. The football, however, was not great. For the record, the final between Ivory Coast and Ghana ended 0–0 before a marathon penalty shoot-out finally ended 11–10 in Ivory Coast's favour. But all the time I was away Wrexham was there lurking in the corner of my mental luggage.

When the season finally ended we had secured fourth place, 10 points behind the Champions, Leeds United. But football was about to change. It was the last season of the First Division of the Football League, the next season would trumpet a new beginning; the much heralded arrival of the FA Premier League.

12

My Cups Runneth Over

With a season out of the limelight – except for the Wrexham horror show – I spent the summer wondering what lay ahead, while watching on TV as the England football team stumbled out of another international tournament, this time the 1992 European Championship in Denmark. England played three games, drew two and lost one, scoring just one goal. It was rubbish, but defeat for England just does not – can not - hurt as much as when Arsenal lose.

I'd already consigned that tournament to history by the time August came around again and another season kicked off. Yet it marked the end of an era at Highbury; the North Bank, the spiritual home of Arsenal fans, was no more. A new North Bank stand was under construction and in the meantime we had the much-maligned mural, painted to show how the new stand would look when finished, complete with happy smiling fans. It didn't take long, however, before someone pointed out that all the faces in the mural were white, forcing the club to quickly get out their paint box to create a more representative image of their wider fan-base.

With immaculate timing Manchester United won their first league title for 26 years in 1993, at a point when football finances leapt forward on the back of the Sky TV deal that had bankrolled the formation of the Premier League. We were average in the league in 92/93, we won 15 and lost 15 games and finished in tenth position: average. But this was not the year of the league, for Arsenal this was the momentous 'Year of the Cups'.

There was symmetry on the road to Wembley as we made it to the finals of both the League Cup (now renamed the Coca

Cola League Cup) and the FA Cup. In the 5th Round of both competitions we beat Nottingham Forest at Highbury 2–0, and Ian Wright scored all the goals. Our League Cup two-legged semi final against Crystal Palace was completely one sided; we progressed to the Final with a 5–1 aggregate score. The FA Cup semi-finals, featuring a Sheffield derby – Wednesday against United – and a London derby, prompted the FA to stage both matches at Wembley. The ease of the League Cup semi was behind us, this would be a far tenser affair – the prize the FA Cup Final, our opponents Tottenham, with all the baggage that would entail.

I've just looked at my ticket for the game (cost £20) and had a chuckle at one of the conditions of issue; how times have changed.

4: The use of cameras or recording equipment is prohibited.

Amused by this I checked the 2011 terms and conditions and extraordinarily Wembley still officially prohibit cameras, but if you do flout this regulation you are required to assign the copyright of any photographs to the stadium management! Try telling that to 90,000 photo-taking fans who want to celebrate their day at the stadium.

Our Wembley semi was not a memorable game from a football point of view, but on an emotional level it was right up there in the Hall of Fame of great victories over our nearest and dearest. Beating Tottenham is always an uplifting experience. This result brought particular pleasure as the only goal in the 1–0 victory was scored by Tony Adams, a regular butt of opposition fans abuse, but to Gooners everywhere he was simply 'Mr Arsenal'. And so we headed to both the League Cup and FA Cup Finals, where remarkably our opponents in both games were Sheffield Wednesday.

Wednesday were a good, enterprising top division team then, orchestrated on the pitch by Chris Waddle and managed by Trevor Francis, who, in his playing days had been Britain's first one million pound footballer. The League Cup Final took place on a blustery but bright April day with neither team a clear favourite to win. My Wembley 'price watch' tells me I paid £35 for my ticket and £4 for the programme, and, with an eye to the future, the players wore their names on the back of their shirts.

The game was quite open and lively at the start. Then, after nine minutes, a well-worked free-kick resulted in Wednesday scoring in front of our fans, the goal put away by an American, John Harkes. All the previous Wembley defeats flickered through my mind – surely not again. But the goal didn't seem to affect the team and with Paul Merson playing really well we came back. About ten minutes after the Wednesday goal the scores were level again when Merson popped up to send a swerving volley into the net beyond the despairing dive of Chris Woods.

We looked really solid in the second half, our midfield dominating as we won tackle after tackle all over the pitch. Then, on 68 minutes, Merson pushed forward on yet another run before sending over a cross as he neared the goal line. A weak attempt at a clearance by a Wednesday defender saw the ball roll into the path of the incoming Steve Morrow, a player who had never before scored for the first team. Undaunted, he smacked it into the net from just outside the six-yard box to instigate mad joyous celebrations amongst the red and white half of the crowd. After that Wednesday never really threatened again and for the last 20 minutes we were completely on top, it was a perfect Final as far as I was concerned – but probably not one for the neutral. Final whistle, 2–1 to Arsenal, we were back to winning ways at Wembley. Much joy and huge relief. But amidst the joy there was sorrow – sorrow for Morrow. Throughout a long and magnificent career Tony Adams often experienced ill luck, and here it was again. While the team playfully celebrated before going to collect the cup, Adams lifted the smiling Morrow up into the air, but the pair toppled over; Morrow landed awkwardly and broke his right arm. It prevented him going up to collect his medal and he had to leave the pitch on a stretcher; he didn't play again that season. Agony and ecstasy seem to be an inescapable part of any relationship with Arsenal Football Club.

Four weeks later I was back at Wembley again for the FA Cup Final. What was it to be this time – agony or ecstasy?

Heavy rain before kick off cast a grey outlook on the day but by kick off the traditional Cup Final sunshine had returned. We had the same end of the ground as for the League Cup Final so we were in the shade, a happy thought after the broiling I experienced back in '79. And there was a nice touch before kick off as the unfortunate Steve Morrow finally climbed the 39 steps to the Royal Box to collect his League Cup winners' medal.

We started well and midway through the first half Ian Wright, hanging in the air at the far post, nodded us into a 1-0 lead. After that Wednesday appeared to have lost their early threat. But a different Wednesday emerged for the second half and they took the game to us, forcing us onto the back foot, and around a quarter of an hour in they equalised. The rest of the game, however, failed to spark into life. There were probably no more than two meaningful attempts on goal as the teams cancelled each other out through the rest of the 90 minutes, and on through the 30 minutes of extra time. No penalty shoot out in the Final then, there would have to be a replay on the following Thursday.

Thoughts immediately turned to the inevitable scramble for tickets which went on sale on the Monday to personal applications only. This required logistical planning on a military scale and a very creative use of the term 'lunch hour'.

So, come Thursday, I was on my way back to Wembley. This time I had a ticket sitting with Steph. It was a miserable day; it rained and rained, then rained some more. The evening was prematurely grey as we arrived at the ground and when we got into the stadium we discovered that kick off had been put back half an hour; an accident on the M1 motorway causing a major hold up and delaying Wednesday fans coming to the game. We went to have a look at our seats and the vast empty spaces at the Wednesday end were genuinely shocking. There were still great gaps in the crowd when the game eventually kicked off on a night more autumnal than spring-like.

The game sparked into life after about 18 minutes when a shocking challenge by Wednesday's Mark Bright, leading with his elbow, resulted in a broken nose for Andy Linighan. It seemed to spur us on; we began attacking with some conviction, and a few minutes later Linighan almost scored with a header. That *must* have hurt! Then, on 34 minutes, we scored, the goal one of efficient simplicity. From a Wednesday goal kick a header sent the ball back towards Alan Smith whose deft flick allowed Ian Wright to run on and chip into the net. Those Wednesday fans who had only just taken up their seats would probably have preferred to be back on the motorway. The red half of the stadium began pumping out all the old favourite songs.

The second half proved quite feisty with some crunching tackles, but we were holding our own until, with 68 minutes on the clock, Wednesday equalised – the shot from Waddle squirting in off Lee Dixon. Having led for over a third of the game I'd begun to believe that a cup double was on, but now we had to do it all over again. It was draining. And then Wednesday almost scored again. I was stunned. But we were a tough team; we wobbled, regained our composure and settled back into the intense rhythm of the game. All square after 90 minutes meant extra time. I don't know how the players felt but I needed that break. Just one mistake, one slip, meant the end of a dream. The tension of those last 10 minutes was unbearable.

Although a penalty shoot out did not apply at the end of the first game it would come into play if scores were level after the replay. With no further goals in extra time and just the final few seconds of injury time left to play it seemed I was about to witness the first FA Cup Final to be settled by the arbitrariness of penalties – the success or failure of the individual in what is a team sport. It is a process much loved by the media and the neutral fan, but hated by those directly involved – unless you win!

Then, as I began to prepare myself for the inevitable, a shot from John Jensen ricocheted off a defender and we had a corner. There was no question, this was the last chance. Merson took the corner out on the left, swung the ball high into the penalty area and there, rising above everyone, appeared Andy Linighan – broken nose leading – to power it towards the net. Chris Woods in the Sheffield Wednesday goal got his hands to the ball but couldn't stop it. YES!! It was in the net. We'd won the Cup! As had been the case at Anfield in 1989, a last minute winning goal is one of the great adrenaline-packed emotional rushes that you can experience in life. It was a night to cherish – for not only had we just won the Cup, we'd made history too – the first team ever to win both the League Cup and FA Cup in the same season.

When we finally emerged from the stadium after being part of the Gooner celebrations it was still raining but I didn't care. I did, however, experience a fleeting flicker of sympathy for the Wednesday fans. We watched as some of their coaches exited the stadium, their fans peering glumly through the grey, condensation blurred windows at the beginning of their long journey back to Yorkshire. They'd had a bad, really bad week and I understood their pain - I'd been there, done that – but it was just a fleeting moment of sympathy. We'd just won the Cup; on a wet night in Wembley it was not a time for reflection, it was a time for celebration. Perhaps the old stadium was winning its way back into my affections.

13

The Birth of an Anthem

The prize for winning the FA Cup in 1993 was a place in Europe the following season, in the now defunct European Cup Winners' Cup. Nowadays winners of this prize take part in the bloated Europa League, a competition clubs strive all season to qualify for and then more often than not seem reluctant to take part in. While in England the FA Cup is always fiercely contested, other European countries do not necessarily value success in their own national cup competitions as highly. As such, around this time it was often felt that the UEFA Cup provided a stiffer test – but this was most definitely not the case in 1993/94. The Cup Winners' Cup was a streamlined competition with just 32 teams qualifying for the 1st Round, but that season we were joined in the line-up by such European luminaries as Real Madrid, Ajax, Benfica, Torino, Besiktas, Beyer Leverkusen, Standard Liege, Hadjuk Split, Ferencvaros, Panathinaikos and the holders of the cup, Parma.

We started our European adventure against Odense of Denmark in September. Playing the away leg first we secured a 2-1 win after some nervy moments and I, like most Gooners, expected the home leg to be a formality. But we rarely do things the easy way and although we scored early in the second half Odense made the score 1-1 on the night with five minutes to go, leading to a nerve-wracking finale. But we held on and scraped through to next round where we drew Standard Liege of Belgium. A 3–0 first leg win at home set up a comfortable return in Belgium but I don't think anyone expected the extraordinary performance that resulted in a stunning 7–0 victory on the night and 10–0 on aggregate. Such was our

91

performance that even the Belgian fans were applauding us at the end. Yet it rankled with me that we never got the credit we deserved for our performance that night, the game getting just a few seconds coverage on the TV news. That night Norwich City grabbed most of the headlines as, incredibly, they knocked Bayern Munich out of the UEFA Cup. Other coverage that night focused on terrible scenes from Istanbul where fans and police clashed at the Galatasaray/Manchester United European Cup tie. This lack of recognition festered away in me for a long time and, as we prepared for the quarter-final ties in March, I wrote to the Arsenal programme who printed my letter under the heading "Credit where it's due." The press had made much of the weakness of Liege's defence in contributing to our victory – but I felt the need to point out that in the Belgium League, in the 22 games Liege had played they had let in just 16 goals – and we'd scored 10 against them in our two games. I felt better having got that off my chest.

The cream had floated to the surface by the time the last eight gathered for the quarter-final draw. Alongside us stood Real Madrid, Bayer Leverkusen, Parma, Ajax, Paris Saint-Germain and Torino. We drew Torino and after a four-month winter break the European challenge was back on.

With the first leg played in Turin it meant I was able to spend my 37th birthday glued to ITV watching a match described by one newspaper as "this tepid, torpid, goalless, guileless encounter." Personally I've seen worse.

The return at Highbury two weeks later was another tense affair – both games had been so tight that it became clear that just one goal would probably settle it. Then, just over an hour into the game, Paul Davis floated in a free-kick from wide on the right towards the far post as Tony Adams charged through a gap between two Torino defenders to powerfully head the ball home. 1–0, game over, and we were in the semi-finals.

The draw took us to France to play Paris Saint-Germain, a top side at the time, featuring in their line-up such luminaries as George Weah and David Ginola. A semi-final in Europe, I had to go. Steph was keen too so we signed up for the Travel Club's one day air tour which, for £167, promised a match ticket, flights and coach transfers to and from the Parc des

Princes. I had foolishly presumed that would also allow a little time for a bit of a stroll around Paris; I was very wrong.

After the obscenely early start and endless delays that go hand in hand with following your team into Europe, we finally landed in Paris. But after we landed we began to taxi, and taxi and then taxi some more. We eventually rolled to a halt at some long-forgotten corner of the airport and, looking through the window, I saw men of the CRS, the notorious French riot police, ringing our aircraft, and even an armoured car drawn up. No passport control, no airport lounge – we descended from the aircraft and, like captured international terrorists, were guided directly onto waiting buses and exited the airport by a side entrance led by a police motorcycle escort. With their sirens blaring, our escort led us rapidly through the Paris traffic, but we were not heading for the city, we were being bussed straight towards the ground hours before kick-off.

We finally came to a halt near the Roland Garros tennis stadium. Here the police herded us all into a side street, amusingly – well, initially at least - named the Rue de Gordon Bennett. Once there the police closed the road off with crash barriers and held us in a tactic similar to the 'kettling' which has recently earned much notoriety when employed by the Metropolitan Police. Eventually the police released us from this holding area one by one, after checking our match tickets, conducting body searches and even confiscating the belts of some individuals. I think we passed through two more holding areas before finally gaining entrance to the stadium. It appears that as far as the French authorities were concerned, every single English football supporter, man, woman and child, was a hooligan just waiting for the chance to rampage through their city. As a football fan you surrender your rights when you travel abroad, you accept this abuse when it happens or you are dealt with harshly and unceremoniously by the police.

The atmosphere inside the stadium was quite something, the acoustics causing the music and the chanting to reverberate through your body as the stadium announcer worked up the home supporters. PSG fans have quite a reputation and a fierce rivalry exists between those gathered behind the opposite goals. But what surprised me, and most other Arsenal fans too, was the blasting out of the Pet Shop Boys' hit, "Go West", on the PA, and the whole stadium responding, roaring "Allez, Paris Saint-Germain" during the chorus. It was quite unexpected – and impressive.

Once the game started we settled well and by half time a beautifully timed glanced header by Ian Wright had given us the lead. Then, after the teams left the pitch the stadium PA started blaring out "Go West" again to stir up the home fans; but this time the Arsenal fans took up the tune, changing the chorus to "one nil to the Arsenal!" In no time the whole Arsenal section had taken up the song and an anthem was born. The French were a little bewildered. My seat was at the end of a row and a policeman spoke to me in broken English and asked what we were singing. I explained to him that we were singing the score; he looked at me quizzically, shrugged – as only a Frenchman can - and walked away shaking his head.

PSG equalised in the second half with a headed goal from Ginola after a defensive howler, but we played out the rest of the game without any further mishap. A 1–1 score looked promising for the second leg, and allowed me the opportunity to dream of a European final.

The second leg at Highbury two weeks later took place on a horribly wet April evening, but there was a fantastic atmosphere – the ground was buzzing with anticipation. The club placed coloured cards on every seat for us to hold high when the teams emerged. As they jogged out onto the pitch Highbury instantly turned red and white.

After one very early scary moment Kevin Campbell rose at the Clock End to head home a Lee Dixon cross from the right. Cue an explosion of joy and a deafening chorus of "one nil to the Arsenal" – it was the song that defined a season. There was no better place to be right then. The game remained tight. Ian Wright was distraught when he received a yellow card for a silly tackle, which meant he'd miss the final, but we couldn't get a second goal, making the last 15 minutes hellish as PSG did all they could to level the scores. Ear splitting whistles screeched from the crowd urging the referee to call the match to an end and when he finally did the whole stadium erupted in a communal ecstatic celebration – a mixture of relief, joy and delirium – garnished with an endless chorus of "one nil to the Arsenal." It was one of the great Highbury nights.

When the celebrations finally subsided I turned my attention to the final. Our opponents were Parma, one of Italy's leading teams and current holders of the trophy. They boasted in their line-up such stars as Gianfranco Zola, Tomas Brolin and Faustino Asprilla. It was going to be tough.

To support your team in Europe at a major Cup Final is without doubt one of the greatest experiences a football supporter can have. The aggressive policing in Paris quickly forgotten, I spoke to Steph, and we were back to the Travel Club to join the multitude heading to Denmark, determined to be present at this great occasion in the club's history – the date 4 May 1994.

Visiting Copenhagen was a delight; low-profile policing and the chance to see some of the city – watch and learn, Paris. It is hard to explain the feeling one gets on occasions such as this, when a vast number of people sharing a common cause descend upon a foreign town – it is perhaps like being a part of an invading army. Wherever you went in the city that day you encountered great clusters of Arsenal fans, bedecked in red and white and draped in flags, in great spirits, singing their hearts out. There was no trouble and it made you feel proud that you too were part of this buoyant, exuberant and good-humoured occupation. I pitied the Parma fans that I saw, wandering disconsolately around the city, so overwhelmingly outnumbered. In the face of this Arsenal invasion they appeared to have already conceded defeat. And everywhere in the city one song filled the air – "One nil to the Arsenal!"

At the ground it seemed like the Parken Stadium had become Highbury for the night as the towering stand at our end of the ground rippled like a great red and white waterfall – and again, that song. Surely any other score would be a travesty. In fact the opening exchanges were scary as the skilful Parma side came streaming forward with Brolin putting a header over the bar and then minutes later smacking a shot against the foot of post. But after twenty minutes the game changed. Dixon fired in a cross which a Parma defender

95

bizarrely attempted to clear with an overhead kick, but instead it fell to Alan Smith. The unassuming Smith controlled the ball on his chest, let it drop to his left foot and volleyed it home off the upright. Now it really was "one nil to the Arsenal."

What followed was a demonstration of the discipline, organisation and collective spirit that George Graham had imbued in that team. Parma had not made a significant breakthrough as my watch showed that ninety minutes were up, but still the game carried on with Parma pushing forward all the time. They had the ball in the net during almost five excruciating minutes of injury time but the referee clearly signalled it offside. And then we won a corner, that was it, we all knew then that there would be no more time for Parma. Seconds later the referee blew his whistle and I shot up into the air like a cork from a champagne bottle – the song had worked its magic – we'd won the Cup, one nil to the Arsenal. These are the great moments, shouting yourself hoarse, celebrating victory as part of a great collective, as part of the team.

That is the highlight of European football; travel is always the low point. Coaches held back for missing fans, endless airport delays, waiting for trains back to London, then waiting for a night bus or taxi back home. I think I got home about four in the morning. But I was up for work four hours later, in a happy daze, and drifted in to the office. I found a large Parma flag draped forlornly across my desk, left there by a Tottenham supporting colleague who'd taken it to the pub to watch the game on TV, anticipating a Parma victory. I smiled a satisfied smile. I don't think I contributed much to the company profits that day, but I did acquire a full set of newspapers!

14

Paris is a Gas!

While some seasons remain in the memory for all the right reasons others endure for the complete opposite. 1994/95 was one to forget on so many levels, but in particular for a return to Paris. In the League we finished in twelfth place, just six points above relegated Crystal Palace and our FA Cup run was over almost before it began as we lost to Millwall in a 3rd round replay. Hopes of a crack at the League Cup (Coca Cola Cup) ended at Liverpool in the quarter-final and our one and only attempt to win the European Super Cup failed as we lost 2-0 on aggregate to AC Milan. In November Paul Merson publicly declared his addiction to alcohol and cocaine and missed three-months of the season on a rehabilitation programme. He returned in February just as George Graham, at that time the club's most successful manager, received his marching orders and subsequently a ban from all football for a year when it emerged that he had taken a 'bung' – an illegal payment – during transfers arranged through a Norwegian agent. It was not a great time to be a Gooner – only Europe offered a chance to dispel the gloom that surrounded everyone connected to the club.

As we'd won the Cup Winners' Cup the previous season we gained an automatic right to defend the trophy. We started in September against the Cypriots of Omonia Nicosia, having a comfortable opening, winning 3–1 away and 3–0 at Highbury. Cup Winners' Cup matches had now moved to Thursday nights and so less than 48 hours later we were playing again – losing to Crystal Palace at home in the League. Much discontented muttering emerged from the club that soon there would be football played every day of the week – they got that right.

The second round provided tougher opposition in the shape of Brondby, one of Denmark's top sides. We took a 2–0 lead in Copenhagen, but Brondby got a goal back making for a tense finale. But having secured a 2–1 lead I anticipated a comfortable return game at Highbury, but that thought was destroyed after just a minute of the second leg when Brondby scored to bring the aggregate scores level. We came back and scored twice but then in the second half Brondby levelled the scores on the night meaning we were 4–3 ahead on aggregate as the clock ticked down. Then in the dying seconds the Danes had a good penalty shout as the whole of Highbury held its breath. A goal for Brondby and we'd be out on the away goals rule. But the referee waved aside the appeal, the whistle blew, the crowd breathed again and we were through. I like a nice relaxed game of football.

Like the previous year, we now had a four-month break before the quarter-final, against Auxerre of France. By the time we returned to European action George Graham had departed and Stewart Houston, the first team coach, found himself occupying the manager's seat for the remainder of the season. The games against the French Cup holders proved anything but easy. We played the home leg on a freezing March night – my birthday again – with snow falling at kick off. An Ian Wright penalty gave us the lead but Auxerre came straight back and equalised giving them the advantage of an away goal for the second leg. It meant that to have any chance of progressing we would have to score in the away leg and, considering our League form, that looked a big ask. But there was always Ian Wright. Wrighty the goal machine benefited from a slip up by two defenders and turned with the ball before unleashing a curling thunderbolt into the Auxerre net. From then on it was backs to the wall, but we held on; it was a magnificent performance. It would need another to get us through the semi-final.

Unfortunately the semi-final draw meant we would play at Highbury in the first leg again, which can be a disadvantage in Europe – our opponents, one of the top Italian teams,

Sampdoria. Managed by Sven-Goran Erikson, Sampdoria featured renowned goalkeeper Walter Zenga with Attilio Lombardo in midfield and current Manchester City manager Roberto Mancini up front. It proved to be quite a contest.

Unexpectedly we raced to a 2–0 half-time lead in the first leg, with both goals from the unlikely source of central defender Steve Bould. But a mistake by Tony Adams allowed Sampdoria to pull one back, before Wrighty scored and restored our two goal advantage. But Sampdoria wouldn't lie down; they came back and scored again. With the match ending 3–2 they had the crucial away goals. I left the ground that night subdued and fearing elimination in Genoa.

Before the second leg kicked off the odds appeared to be heavily stacked against us. Although Wrighty scored again, ceaseless waves of Sampdoria pressure ensured we were 3–1 down on the night with just seven minutes left to play – trailing 5–4 on aggregate - and about to drop out of the competition. Then, with just three minutes left to play, the referee awarded us a free kick almost 30 yards from goal. From the way the game had developed I felt sure this was our last chance. Up stepped Stefen Schwarz, a pre-season signing from Benfica, to blast a guided missile of a shot along the ground, through the wall and into the corner of the net. Delirium! All square and both sides had two away goals; we were back in the game.

Thirty tense minutes of extra-time came and went with neither team creating a decent chance. It was clear that the dreaded penalty shoot-out would settle the tie. Memories of the 1980 final against Valencia immediately flooded my mind – not again…please! I was watching the match on TV with Steph and David. I felt sick. But the tension of the game was nothing to what followed. Lee Dixon took the first penalty and scored, Sampdoria took theirs and David Seaman saved it - muted excitement. Next up was Eddie McGoldrick, who sent his kick flying over the bar. But instead of the Italians drawing level with the next kick, Seaman saved again - tense celebration. John Hartson and Tony Adams both scored with their efforts as did the next two Sampdoria players. The score sat 3–2 to us with one kick each left. Merson stepped forward, if he scored we'd win the game – but he didn't, the 'keeper saved. Disaster.

Lombardo then prepared to take his and force the game into sudden death penalties. David Seaman's brilliance had already seen him save twice and I recognised the odds must be against him pulling off another. Lombardo struck the ball to Seaman's left; Seaman dived the right way, thrust out his right arm and punched the ball away from goal. We'd done the Italian job; cue an explosion of celebration loud enough to blow the bloody doors off.

Penalty shoot-outs are an unsatisfactory way to end important matches, but when you win them you don't think about that – and it is not just about scoring the goals, the sheer adrenaline rush of your own goalkeeper saving the last kick to give you victory is something you never forget. David Seaman is the best Arsenal goalkeeper I have seen during my time – we've had some other great ones, and some shockers, but for me Seaman was the best. Always so calm, and always there to make the great saves seem effortless. With a 'keeper like that behind you defenders play with confidence and are able to concentrate on their own game without worrying what the 'keeper is going to do next.

While we were emerging victorious against Sampdoria there had been a very real chance that our opponents in the Final would be Chelsea. They had reached the other semi-final and were playing Real Zaragoza. However, a 3–0 loss in Spain in the first leg proved too much to overcome in the return at Stamford Bridge, giving Zaragoza a place in the Final. It meant a return for the team – and me – to the Parc des Princes in Paris.

Happily our reception in Paris appeared to be more relaxed than on our previous visit, although the CRS were everywhere in intimidating numbers. I travelled out with Steph and we arranged to meet David in Paris as he went out early to stay with a mate who lived in the city. Always keen on 'signs' we agreed to meet at the Arc de Triomphe. We met up easily enough. There were many other fans from both sides there too, all happily chatting together until the CRS moved in and ushered the fans away in opposite directions - so unnecessary, so typical. Later we met up with David's friend in a bar in the St. Germain district for a beer or two before the game. We met the CRS again at the stadium. They controlled a strict cordon, only allowing fans to enter the stadium area after everyone went through a body search. There was a lack of female officers to search women fans.

Real Zaragoza's star player was an Argentinian forward, Esnaider; they also had Gus Poyet and the irritation of a former Tottenham player, Nayim, in midfield. As Arsenal fans reading this will know, there is no need to dwell on the match any longer than necessary.

Zaragoza took the lead after 68 minutes when Esnaider lashed in a curling volley that caught Seaman wrong-footed, but we came back and equalised through John Hartson nine minutes later. The score was 1–1 at full time and remained so through the 30 minutes of extra time. Dreaded penalties loomed as the teams played out the final moments, but after Seaman's heroics against Sampdoria we could face them with real confidence. With less than a minute left to play, however, Nayim picked up the ball in our half of the field (no, not from the half-way line as Tottenham fans would like to remember it) and launched a speculative sky-bound effort from about forty yards. No danger. But then I saw that Seaman seemed just a bit too far off his line. As the ball began to drop the scene switched to slow-motion as Seaman desperately back-pedalled, throwing up an arm in a despairing attempt to flick the ball over the bar. He failed. Seaman, the ball and my hopes crashed into the back of the net. The emotion of a last minute winner is a moment of ecstasy; conversely, a goal conceded at that time drives you to a dark place of misery and pain. I visited that place that night; it was a place that had so much pain to give. And the night was in the mood to keep on giving.

The CRS had been an intimidating and provocative presence in the build up and during the game, clad in helmets and body armour, carrying shields, batons, sub-machine guns, and I saw one man armed with a rifle. But I think some may have become bored as there had been no crowd trouble for them to over-react too. When the final whistle blew moments after Zaragoza's winning goal, we discovered that we, along with all other fans, were unable to leave as steel gates closed off all the exits from the seating areas. It took 40 minutes before the first sections of Arsenal fans gained their freedom, ensuring we all had to watch the entire Zaragoza post-match celebrations. But the process was excruciatingly slow with sections only released one at a time. It then became clear that while our section remained locked in, the police began allowing Zaragoza fans to leave. Frustration mounted in our section as the ground had now almost emptied; some fans were shouting for the gates to open, one or two began kicking angrily at the immovable steel barriers. No explanation was offered as to why our section – and by now no other – remained locked in. Then, without warning, officers of the CRS appeared behind the gate and began indiscriminatingly spraying canisters of CS gas into the milling crowd: men, women and children. It was an appalling, dangerous and unnecessary over-reaction, as fans panicked in their rush to get clear and people fell over seats in their haste to escape. I was unable to see properly for about five minutes and suffered eye irritation for over an hour. All around me I could hear people coughing and choking. Although I couldn't see it, people were on their hands and knees vomiting. A few minutes later the steel doors opened and through my streaming eyes I saw the grinning faces of four armed officers of the CRS, happy, no doubt, with the culmination of a fine evening's work. As we left the ground we funnelled through a narrow corridor formed by two lines of menacingly assured and armed CRS men. A comforting end to a miserable evening.

So incensed was I by the treatment we received, when I returned home I wrote to Tony Banks, MP, and described my experience. He had appeared on television the weekend before the Final, highlighting recent incidents of unprovoked thuggery by some European police forces against English football fans who just wanted to support their teams. I also wrote to Lennart Johansson, then Chairman of UEFA, asking for his views on the behaviour of the CRS at this match. UEFA showed little interest. The reply I received did nothing to address my grievances. I was informed,

> ...the overall evaluation of the final in Paris was, on the whole, excellent and that the handling of more

than 30,000 supporters travelling from England and Spain passed off extremely smoothly.

We regret that English supporters, are generally speaking, received with a certain reserve when travelling abroad. This is in close relation to the part conduct of English spectators at matches abroad involving English teams.

However, we should always keep in mind that all those "constraints" are primarily made for *your own security*.

That was a nice touch, UEFA added italics to ensure I realised that the CRS had kept me locked into the Parc des Princes for well over an hour after the final whistle and tear-gassed me for my own security. Thanks UEFA.

UEFA concluded by informing me that they would pass on my letter to the French Football authorities so they could comment on my "specific experience." Unsurprisingly I'm still awaiting their thoughts.

The response I received from Tony Banks was far more interesting. He included a copy of Hansard – the printed transcripts of parliamentary debates – covering a debate on "The Treatment of English Football Supporters Abroad" that took place on 8 June 1995. It is now freely available on the internet. It makes shocking reading, mainly focusing on the mistreatment experienced by Chelsea and Arsenal supporters in Europe, but even more shocking for me was the response from the government by the Under Secretary of State for Foreign and Commonwealth Affairs, Tony Baldry, MP. His response was pompous, uninformed and an insult to those many innocent supporters who had suffered at the hands of foreign police forces for years. Less than a month later Mr Baldry became Minister for Agriculture, Fisheries and Food in John Major's Conservative government – his attention instantly realigned to the plight of mad cows rather than the concerns of angry football fans. I don't suppose he ever gave another thought to the problem. It seems somewhat ironic to me then that Mr Baldry later went on to serve as Chairman of the Conservative Party Human Rights Commission, because I, like many other football fans, feel our human rights received scant respect in Europe in the mid 1990s.

My anger at the way we were treated in Paris has mellowed over the years, but the memory of that ball dropping out of the night sky, over David Seaman's head and into the net remains another open wound.

The season had been a great disappointment, but things were about to change. A new Arsenal was gestating. In June 1995 the club appointed Bruce Rioch as manager. Rioch had performed miracles, bringing Bolton Wanderers from the second division all the way to the Premier League, and then stunned everyone by making Dennis Bergkamp his first Arsenal signing; Bergkamp, one of the world game's iconic players. A month later he signed David Platt, English football's most internationally recognised player. This was high-profile stuff, we were making the news for the right reasons; it demonstrated a refreshing ambition. We were about to embark on a new adventure and I was looking forward to seeing where the journey would take us.

15

A Unique Treble

That summer – 1995 - a work colleague, Dickie, decided to apply for a season ticket. With no endless waiting list back then the club invited him up to Highbury to choose his seat. I'd presumed he'd get the seat next to me which sold on a match-by-match basis the previous season, so I was surprised to discover it had gone. We went up together one lunchtime, arrived at the famous marble hall entrance, met a guy from the box office who led us all around the stadium and up into the Upper West stand; the plan being to find a seat as close as possible to mine. Amazingly they offered him the row behind me, one seat to the left. I had got to know a lot of people sitting in the seats around me over the years, but since my grandfather had died twenty years earlier I had sat 'on my own' as such. I always met Steph and Gerry before the game and again at half time, but I was looking forward to having a mate close at hand.

And after years when the occupiers of the seats next to me regularly changed, I now had a permanent neighbour too. And strangely I thought I recognized the face that had pipped Dickie to the seat, but couldn't immediately put a name to it. Then it clicked; my new neighbour, Andy, appeared on television a couple of times a week in the long-running TV police drama *The Bill*, playing the role of PC Quinan. I've got to know Andy well over the years and he was quick to make sure I knew of his all-encompassing hatred for Chelsea. A number of the crew and cast on the show were Chelsea fans and life on set was no fun if Chelsea beat us. That pain only increased for Andy when Roman Abramovich changed the fortunes of that club with his vast wealth. Some 17 years later, despite moving stadiums, we still sit together. And while *The Bill* is long gone, Andy's dislike of all things Chelsea remains undiminished.

With no European football on offer due to our poor league season – and defeat in the final of the European Cup Winners' Cup – 1995/96 was a season to focus on domestic competition. Rioch did improve the way the team played, resulting in a significant improvement in our league position; we ended the season in fifth place, only missing out on fourth as we'd scored three fewer goals than Aston Villa. But fifth place earned a return to Europe, in the UEFA Cup.

Our annual assault on the FA Cup failed miserably with a 3rd Round exit to Sheffield United, while Aston Villa brought an end to an encouraging League Cup run in the semi-final. It was a promising start for Rioch, but that's as far as it got.

In August 1996, five days before the start of the new season, the club surprised everyone when they sacked Rioch after a dispute with the Board – although it appears the club were already sealing a deal with his replacement. Stewart Houston again stepped forward to steer the ship in the interim, but a month later he resigned to become manager of QPR, with Rioch - in a role-reversal - joining him as his assistant. The club turned to Pat Rice to take up the caretaker role while we awaited the arrival of Arsène Wenger, a manager well respected in France and Germany and at the time earning plaudits in Japan – but little known to the English media. They should, like me, have read *World Soccer* magazine, that would have put them right. He officially took up the managerial reins on 1 October 1996 – and changed the club forever. Even before he officially began work he recommended the purchase of a young French player by the name of Patrick Vieira, a fringe player at AC Milan. Vieira went on to become one of the most influential players – and captains – of the club ever.

Our latest European adventure ended with huge disappointment even before Arsène Wenger arrived in North London. Defeats home and away by German club Borussia Moenchengladbach sealed our early exit. Events like that are always huge disappointments. When you have battled all season to secure qualification to European competition, then throw it all away in the first match it seems such an anti-climax. I guess that is what the group stage of the Champions League now protects against. Domestically we bowed out of the FA Cup after Leeds United – managed by George Graham (who returned to football management in September 1996) – did a very 'George Graham' job on us at Highbury, scoring early and holding out for the rest of the game. We fared little better in the League Cup, going out to Liverpool at Anfield in the early rounds of the competition.

In the League, though, Wenger was building a team and a new way of playing – and putting an end to the booze culture well-established amongst the players at the club. With four games left to play we maintained a great chance of claiming second place, which for the first time since the revamped competition launched in 1992, would give access to the elusive Champions League – but we blew it. We drew against Blackburn and Coventry and then the real killer, a 1–0 loss at Highbury to Newcastle in the penultimate game. It was an extremely frustrating match. We had plenty of the ball but Srnicek had one of those games that visiting goalkeepers often have at Highbury and saved everything we fired at him. Newcastle scored in injury time at the end of the first half – from a corner – and despite their having a player sent off with ten minutes still to play, we could not beat Srnicek. We won our final game, away at Derby, but finished third in the table, level on points with Newcastle but behind them on goal difference. If we'd got just a point against Newcastle we would have claimed that second spot and Champions League qualification. I was massively disappointed. Champions League matches received major TV coverage and I had watched enviously as the likes of Manchester United (mainly) and Blackburn Rovers played in the premier European competition. It had always seemed a far-off dream to see Arsenal take part because for the first five years of the revamped competition it was, as the name suggests, only open to champions, and that had been beyond us for a few years now. We had come mighty close to qualification this time but fell at the final hurdle. My ambition to see Arsenal play

Europe's best remained on hold. In the meantime we focused our European attention on the UEFA Cup once more.

The summer of 1997 proved a very interesting time as Wenger – in a move away from how we generally see him these days - embarked on a spending spree, bringing in a number of new players, and by new I also mean players that in most cases few fans had heard of. In came French starlet Nicolas Anelka who had in fact joined towards the end of the previous season and had already made a few substitute appearances; he was joined by Emmanuel Petit, Marc Overmars, Giles Grimandi, Luis Boa Morte, Alex Manninger and Chris Wreh. It proved a busy summer, but the legendary defence of Dixon, Winterburn, Adams and Bould/Keown remained untouchable. At the same time he cleared out a number of players, remnants of the Graham years. The question all Arsenal fans were asking now, though, was "Could so many new players gel into a team?" There are no gentle games in the Premier League; it is an unforgiving place.

That summer my little group of fellow fans grew again as David joined us as a season ticket holder in the Upper West stand. As when Dickie had applied there was no problem getting one. I went up to the ground with David and again they showed us available seats near mine. David secured a seat in the row in front of mine, about six or seven along to the right. It was David who was later responsible for the phenomenon of the lucky lawnmower!

I also made a momentous decision that summer. Part of the ritual of attending a football match is buying the programme. I had done so for every game I had ever attended, which after 30 years meant an awful lot of programmes! In a small flat a collection like that takes up a lot of room. But with the decision made, my relationship with the Arsenal matchday programme ended in August 1997. I have only occasionally bought one since but I can't say I've really missed it.

As the new season – 1997/98 – got underway we started well but there were still questions. By the end of October we'd played twelve games in the league and were undefeated, having won six and drawn six. Those draws included a remarkable 3–3 at Leicester in August when Bergkamp scored a magnificent hat-trick. His final goal, deep into injury time – to make the score 3–2 in our favour - was of such quality as he juggled the ball and bamboozled the Leicester defence, that it deserved to be remembered as a special match-winning moment. The referee, however, played on, allowing Leicester to snatch an equaliser right on the final whistle. Such a sudden descent from ecstasy to agony was harrowing. Also during this period Ian Wright became our leading goal scorer of all time. After weeks of anticipation, Wrighty finally equalled Cliff Bastin's record of 178 goals. It had stood unchallenged since 1939 but against Bolton Wanderers, and fittingly at Highbury, the record was his. Caught up in the emotion of his first goal that day Wrighty pulled up his shirt to reveal a sponsors t-shirt with the words "179 – just done it!" He'd sparked his celebration just a little early but he only had to wait another five minutes before the simplest of tap-ins meant he did indeed reach 179 goals – equalled and then broken the record in the same match. The ground erupted in celebration; Ian Wright was a player who clearly loved the club and seemed to be one of us, a fan, too. We loved him. He scored again late on, a hat-trick on his special day – that was Ian Wright. Substituted near the end of the game, the crowd stood as one to salute our hero – his chant, "Ian Wright, Wright, Wright", echoing from every corner of the stadium. Drinking in the adulation, he left the pitch having created another truly memorable moment and milestone in the long history of Arsenal Football Club.

But while we'd been playing well in the league, we took another early exit in the UEFA Cup, losing to PAOK of Greece in the first round. A friend who went to the away game said he'd never before in his life felt so intimidated by opposition fans.

Then, after the good solid start in the league we encountered the autumn slump, something that has regularly plagued us since. In November and December, although we enjoyed a memorable victory at home over Manchester United, the winning goal coming from a superb David Platt header, we lost four games in that period. I felt huge relief when floodlight failure at half time in our game at Wimbledon, just before Christmas, caused the abandonment of the game; I had no confidence that we were going to get a victory from that fixture.

By the end of the year we were in sixth place, 12 points behind the leaders Manchester United, having been in top spot in early October. It looked like any dream of a tilt at the title had faded away.

Europe and the League may have gone, but after struggling through the first two rounds of the League (Coca Cola) Cup we had reached the quarter-finals and our FA Cup campaign had yet to start. There was still much to play for. The second half of the season proved to be a truly remarkable – and historic – time for everyone connected with the club.

A mounting injury list, rather then sending us on an increasingly downward spiral, seemed to galvanise the team. As we had proved when the FA docked us two points back in 1991, we seemed to play better with our backs to the wall. Three months later, by the end of March, we'd played ten more league games, winning eight and drawing two. Those eight victories included a 1–0 victory in the rearranged game against Wimbledon at Selhurst Park fortuitously abandoned back in December during our poor run of form. It was that victory which finally made me believe once more that we had a chance. Another victory by the same score three days later – at Old Trafford – the goal scored by Marc Overmars ten minutes from the end of a fantastic performance, meant that chance had become very real. In a publicity stunt a Manchester bookmaker had already started paying out on Manchester United winning the title; it proved a little premature.

During this same period our assault on the League Cup ended against Chelsea in the semi-final at Stamford Bridge. With Vieira sent off in the second leg, Chelsea eventually overtook our 2-1 lead from the first game at Highbury, gained control and the tie.

Meanwhile our FA Cup run stuttered along unconvincingly. In the 3rd Round we needed a replay, extra time and penalties to dispose of Port Vale, but won away at Middlesbrough in the next round. Then in the 5th round we required a replay to beat Crystal Palace before West Ham put up more stiff resistance in the quarter-final. A 1–1 draw at

Highbury and another in the replay at Upton Park meant extra time and penalties again before we emerged victorious from the tie.

During this period a hand injury to David Seaman saw our young Austrian goalkeeper, Alex Manninger, step up and play six league games – keeping a clean sheet in every one and making a number of outstanding saves. He also played five FA Cup games, seeing us safely through to the semi-final, and David Seaman's return. His contribution that season was crucial but often overlooked.

Back in the League, by the end of March we had reeled Manchester United in; we were still three points behind but had two games in hand. Having clawed our way back into contention the title was now ours to lose.

April began with the semi-final of the FA Cup at Villa Park, our opponents, Wolverhampton Wanderers. I travelled up by car with Dickie and 'Prinders', another Gooner who had recently joined the company I worked for. It proved to be a nightmare journey with massive delays on the motorway as kick off edged ever closer. We were still in the car as the game started, but another colleague from work, a Villa fan, had given us some 'local knowledge' for parking so we were not as late as we could have been. But we were late enough – Christopher Wreh scoring the only goal after 12 minutes. If he'd held back for a few more minutes we'd have been comfortably in our seats. It remains the only goal I've ever missed when attending a game. But that single goal meant we'd reached the FA Cup Final – to play Newcastle. Now the heady scent of a Double filled the air.

We returned to the League like a team possessed. We began April in rampaging style: 3–1 against Newcastle, 4–1 against Blackburn and 5–0 against Wimbledon. Two more moderate wins later in the month – against Barnsley and Derby Country - meant that at the end of April we steamed past Manchester United who had just two games left to play. They trailed us by four points and we still had three left to play. It meant that a win against Everton at Highbury on Saturday 3rd May – a gloriously sunny Bank Holiday weekend – and the League was ours.

A great sense of anticipation pervaded the streets around the ground and in the bars that day – yet as a football fan you always have doubts too. But I needn't have worried – the team ran out that day with only one thing on their minds. An hour of play later and we were 3-0 up, playing out the rest of the match in a sunshine celebration. But the team had one final treat for us – a goal that provided one of the truly iconic images of my years as a Gooner. With just a minute left to play Steve Bould chipped a long pass over the Everton defence and there, charging down on the Everton goal in a most unaccustomed role, was Tony Adams. I think I held my breath as Adams galloped forward in the shadow of the West Stand. You could sense a collective anticipation from the crowd. Fans behind the goal stood up, surely not, can he, he must! As he emerged from the shadow Adams took one touch with his chest then, as the sunlight touched him like a spotlight, he lashed the ball into the net from the edge of the penalty area. Tony Adams, 'Mr Arsenal', a stalwart survivor from the 'old' Arsenal scored the sort of goal that had thrilled me in the pages of my childhood comics. He strode towards the fans in the North Bank and held out his arms like a conquering hero before his people; that is the image that for me says '1998'. It perhaps demonstrated better than anything else the changes Wenger was bringing to the club. And now all that remained was for Adams to lift the trophy: Arsenal, Premier League Champions! At the end of a brilliant day and numerous choruses of "We Are The Champions" I retired to the *World's End* at Finsbury Park with Steph, Dickie, David and Prinders – to drink in something other than the glory of the moment!

All attention then turned to the FA Cup Final and a chance to clinch a second Double. Steph's dad, Gerry, couldn't make the final so we gave his ticket to Paul, yet another work colleague. We only gave it to him on the understanding that he would paint his face for the Final – he did. My ticket in 1998 cost £30 and the programme had risen to £6 for a large, 116 page magazine. It seemed totally inappropriate for carrying around at a football match; I made a mental note, if there was to be a next time I wouldn't bother again.

The day of the Cup Final was gloriously sunny, as always (that's not true, it isn't always sunny, but it seems like that in my memories!) Both Dennis Bergkamp and Ian Wright were absent through injury which meant another chance for 19-year-old Nicolas Anelka to impress. It seemed he had a great future with the club, but it was not to be and he has proved to be a player unable to settle for much of his career. But on that sunny Saturday the only club that mattered was Arsenal.

Winning any Cup Final is a fantastic moment for a football fan, but the matches do not always live up to the hype generated by the media. We took a while to settle down but then, after 20 minutes, Anelka had a great chance to head home a cross but put it over the bar. Three minutes later another attack met with success. Petit hit a perfectly weighted pass into the path of Marc Overmars. He shrugged off the attention of a Newcastle defender, nudged the ball forward with his head and stoked the ball home. We were sitting right behind the goal and the ball seemed to come straight toward me as it ran through Shay Given's legs. A perfect start. Midway through the second half Alan Shearer had a great chance to equalise after a mistake by Keown presented him with the ball just outside our box. The Newcastle forward ran on with the ball and fired in a shot. Again, from my seat, the ball was coming towards me; it beat Seaman's outstretched arm and seemed destined for the net – but no, it hit the foot of the post and rebounded clear. At that point I thought, "That's it, they're not going to score today." About five minutes later, with 20 minutes still to play, it was all over. Anelka burst through the Newcastle defence and clipped the ball home from 19 yards. It was a double Double, 1971 and 1998 - a glorious achievement on a glorious day.

We returned to Finchley Road to celebrate at the *North Star* pub. There were a group of Newcastle fans in there, they didn't have tickets for the game but had come down anyway and watched it in the pub. They couldn't understand why we weren't bouncing off the walls! It was interesting really, I had wanted to win the League so much that – and I shouldn't say this – the FA Cup just seemed to creep up unnoticed that year. I think it took a beer or two before it really sank in – we'd won the Double. The Geordies were magnanimous in defeat - oh how they wanted to see their team win something, anything - and chose to enjoy a few beers with us that evening before heading off.

I guess we got a little louder as the evening wore on. We were out on the terrace at the side of the pub and as it got later there were only a couple of other people outside. We were indulging in a 'tuneful' rendition of Patrick Vieira's chant, "He comes from Senegal, he plays for Arsenal, V-i-e-i-r-a", at which point our fellow drinker told us he came from Senegal. That was a big mistake. Having had one or two beers by then, we began to serenade our new friend and repeat the chant over and over and over again for him. I even mentioned to him that I had been to Senegal for the 1992 African Nations Cup and offered him the only local phrase I could remember at that moment, which I also repeated over and over again – "Awma xalis, awma xalis." I was impressed with myself, but I think my enthusiasm for the Wolof language wore a little thin on him, but then if someone keeps repeating "I don't have any money" at you, it would, wouldn't it!

That summer, while continuing to bask in the glories of the season just past, we had the distraction of the latest World Cup tournament – France '98. Generally World Cups and other international tournaments prove a huge anti-climax for England fans after the media build the team up as all-conquering heroes – and then drop them from a great height as soon as things go wrong. And I always get a bit hacked off when people who have never shown the vaguest interest in football - 'Eileen from Accounts' shall we call them - suddenly become leading experts on the world game. Then once England are knocked out these 'experts' disappear and are never heard from again…until the next tournament. For England, 1998 was pretty standard fare; a struggle through the opening games then out on penalties in the knock out stages – this time to Argentina. But 1998 had an added interest for Arsenal fans. With the arrival of French influence at Highbury we had a number of players – present and future too - in the French squad. France, of course went on to win the tournament; the final goal in France's 3–0 victory over Brazil scored by our own Emmanuel Petit who ran onto a Vieira pass. The headline in the following morning's *Daily Mirror* said it all: "Arsenal Win the World Cup." That was some Treble!

16

My Fantasy Nightmare

So, there was heightened anticipation ahead of the new season. West Ham fans must have felt the same when Moore, Hurst and Peters returned to their club after the 1966 World Cup win. Sadly, Ian Wright would not be part of any future glory. An injury ruled him out for much of the run-in towards the Double at the end of the previous season and his relationship with Wenger seemed awkward at times. Wenger left him on the substitute's bench at the FA Cup Final and in the summer Wrighty moved on to West Ham.

Having won the Double and with our players having a hand in winning the World Cup it seemed that we were in a position to build on this recent success. Wenger began to strengthen the squad for the future, adding Freddie Ljungberg and later he brought in Kanu. Both went on to earn their place in the club's folklore.

Something else was new that year. After years of waiting, we had finally qualified for the Champions League. But it came with a huge disappointment. The club took the decision to play our home games, not at Highbury, but at Wembley. UEFA regulations regarding pitchside advertising hoardings meant a reduction in the crowd capacity at Highbury, and the club said that they wanted as many supporters as possible to see the games. They therefore decided to set up 'home' at Wembley. It is hard to ignore the fact that the club would also make a huge increase in revenue by doing so - but the decision backfired horribly. Visiting teams seemed to take great inspiration from playing at the famous old stadium and any home advantage we would have enjoyed at Highbury evaporated. The club went to great lengths to try and move fans to similar areas at Wembley to those they occupied at Highbury but this didn't disguise the fact we had given up home advantage. Our three home games resulted in a win (Panathinaikos), a draw (Dynamo Kiev) and a defeat (Lens). What was so frustrating was that both Kiev and Lens scored late goals. And a similar sequence of results away from home meant that was that, we didn't progress beyond the group stage. The only abiding memory I took away from our first attempt at the Champions League was of the long, long, wait along Wembley Way, endlessly queuing for access to Wembley Park station. But for the club the sell out attendances of 73,000 for each game focused attention on the limitations of Highbury's 38,000 capacity, this was a revenue source they desperately wanted to tap into on a regular basis.

In fact, in the League, the season developed along very familiar lines but proved, ultimately, agonisingly frustrating. Our regular autumnal slump saw us play five games between mid November and mid December which resulted in us depressingly and frustratingly dropping 12 of the 15 points available. But we regained our form, fought back and a great run through spring saw us on equal points with Manchester United at the top of the table with just two games to play. We were in a strong position: incredibly the defence only let in 17 goals all season, we were on an unbeaten run of 19 games and had beaten Manchester United at home and drawn at Old Trafford. However, the dream died at Elland Road. The demands of the Sky TV contract meant we played our next game – against Leeds United - a day before Manchester United played. Both sides made chances and we kept pushing, knowing that we needed to win. A heart-stopping moment came on the stroke of half time when the referee awarded Leeds a penalty, but the resultant kick cannoned off the bar and back into play. I was watching the game in a pub on Finchley Road with Steph and Gerry; it was unbelievably tense. There is no pleasure in watching games like that on TV when it is your team that has everything to lose. We had two attempts cleared off the line and Leeds made chances too. Then, with just four minutes left on the clock, they scored. A sickening, gut-wrenching goal from which there was no return. The Arsenal-haters in the pub loved it. The following day

Manchester United, knowing that just a point would now give them a huge advantage on the final day, duly drew 0–0 at Blackburn.

Our final game was at home to Aston Villa while United were at home to Tottenham. Everyone knew Tottenham never win at Old Trafford. It was a rather subdued atmosphere at Highbury as we kicked off; we had to win, the rest was beyond our control – for once in my life I was willing a Tottenham victory, but didn't believe it could happen. Briefly there was a glimmer of hope as Tottenham took the lead midway through the first half. The word spread rapidly around Highbury, but everyone muttered the same thing, "It won't last!" And it didn't. Manchester United equalised before half-time and then scored again at the beginning of the second. We beat Aston Villa but it didn't matter, Manchester United won the League by one point – I couldn't help thinking back to our autumn of despair and what might have been. Manchester United ruined my year – again.

Manchester United ended my dream of the FA Cup that year too. We'd enjoyed a reasonably straightforward march to the semi-finals, except for the 5th Round tie against Sheffield United, which proved to be one of the most controversial FA Cup ties ever played. Midway through the second half one of the Sheffield players put the ball out of play to allow an injured colleague receive treatment. When play resumed we took the throw-in and directed the ball back towards the Sheffield United goal. Kanu, however, intercepted it. He'd only just come on as a substitute, making his debut in English football and, perhaps overawed by the occasion, failed to follow the unwritten rule and allow the ball to reach a Sheffield player. He crossed to Overmars who put the simple chance away. The Sheffield players and their manager Steve Bruce went mad, imploring the referee to disallow the goal, but no official rule had been broken. It proved to be the winner. A media frenzy followed but the club acted quickly, and, with FA blessing, sportingly offered to play the game again, declaring the first game void. Ten days later the two teams met again, but there was no change of fortune, the score remained the same, another 2–1 victory.

An uncontroversial last minute Kanu goal gave us victory at home against Derby County in the 6th Round, our reward, a semi-final at Villa Park against Manchester United. The game took place on Sunday 11th April and was not a memorable one, ending 0–0. The replay - the last ever FA Cup semi-final replay - took place three days later on the Wednesday evening. It meant a mad scramble for tickets and a train up to Milton Keynes to meet David who was working there and then on by car to Villa Park. Although now considered one of the FA Cup's classic encounters, I don't it that way. For me it was another miserable occasion when we had victory in our grasp and threw it away.

We sat high up in the Holt End with a good view over the length of the pitch. There was an excited atmosphere and confidence seemed high around me. That steadied my nerves a little. But after 17 minutes Beckham scored for Manchester United with a long-range shot at the far end of the ground and that remained the score at half-time. I was subdued. In the second half, however, we came right back into the game and with about 20 minutes to play Dennis Bergkamp lashed the ball home from the same distance as Beckham. We continued to press. Bergkamp fired in another shot which Schmeichel pushed away only for the rebound to fall to Anelka who tucked it away. For a moment every Arsenal fan was up celebrating, as was the team, but then followed the dark realisation that the assistant referee had flagged Anelka offside. But we kept pressing. And then, a marvellous moment: Roy Keane, the Manchester United captain and serially unloved figure to all Arsenal fans, slid into Marc Overmars and brought him down. A second yellow card and he was off. United were down to ten men and our tails were up. We kept pressing and then in the dying seconds of injury time a United foot shot out and tripped Ray Parlour in the box. As he hit the turf every single Arsenal fan was up, screaming "Penalty!" The referee concurred. This was it. Score and it was game over.

The penalty was at the far end of the ground to us. Bergkamp stepped up to take it. As everyone focused on Bergkamp and Schmeichel in the United goal, I thought I could see Schmeichel standing just off centre of his goal line and leaning a little to his left, Bergkamp's right. To me there seemed a much bigger gap to the Bergkamp's left and as he began his run up I involuntarily – and pointlessly - screamed "to the left!" Bergkamp hit it to the right and Schmeichel saved. In extra time Giggs wriggled through our defence to score and win the game and, apparently, celebrated by swirling his shirt in the air revealing an unfeasibly hairy chest. I've never witnessed the moment. Instead, I've made an art form of managing to avert my eyes whenever the goal appears on TV. Football is a cruel, cruel game. The gap between ultimate success and failure is narrow. *If* Bergkamp had scored that penalty and *if* we'd taken one more point during our autumn slump there is a very strong chance that we would have gone on to win the Double two years in succession. Instead, we achieved nothing and Manchester United claimed that prize for themselves. And they still had one more final twist of the knife in store for me that year.

I have always enjoyed taking part in fantasy football competitions and have had reasonable success over the years. That year I won one run by a football magazine, the prize, a trip for two to Barcelona for the Champions League Final. I gave the other to Tony, a work colleague, who had also been in with a chance of winning the competition until the final games; we'd made a pact, if either of us won we'd take the other. We travelled out with a representative of the magazine, checked into our hotel, which was rather a long way out of town, and then headed into the city. We had a good day; the down side now was that I was going to have to watch Manchester United play in the Champions League Final. They were not particularly high on my 'like' list – they had ruined my season.

Our seats were in a neutral section of the Camp Nou, giving us a towering view of the pitch. And I soon began to enjoy the game as United's opponents, Bayern Munich, took the lead after just six minutes. And so it stayed. Bayern had other chances to increase their lead but failed to score, although they looked the better team on the night. It seemed the effects of a long season had finally caught up with United. Then, with the fourth official already indicating the game had entered injury time, Manchester United equalised and then, unbelievably, scored again. The stadium was in uproar, the neutrals around me suddenly leaping about like life-long United fans. I alone remained seated, my head in my hands, my mind despairing, disbelieving, while all around me was madness. I had just seen Manchester United win the Champions League, and with it a Treble. I was in the wrong place at the wrong time - I did not want to be there. But there was still one final insult. After the game we visited a few bars and had a few – quite a few – beers. When it came time to head back to our hotel there was not a single taxi in sight. We walked around for over an hour desperately trying to find one. Eventually, so tired after a very long day, we sat down on a traffic island and went to sleep. All in all, it was not a great prize!

17

Paying the Penalty

If I thought all my disappointments were over for a while at the conclusion of the season then I was wrong. There were many more disappointments waiting in the wings over the coming months as the 1999/2000 season unfolded, although the summer signing of a 22-year-old French forward called Thierry Henry looked promising. Certainly he was someone Wenger had known for a while as he gave him his first professional contract while managing Monaco. Henry moved from Monaco to Juventus in January 1999 but it didn't work out for him and seven months later Juventus were happy to let him go, allowing Wenger to bring him to Highbury and the rest, as they say, is history.

The League Cup, having changed its sponsor again, now paraded as the Worthington Cup. The change in name, however, made no difference to our recent runs in the competition as we went out at Middlesbrough on penalties in the 4th Round. In the Champions League the curse of Wembley continued to haunt us. In spite of creditable draws away at Barcelona and Fiorentina, defeats at Wembley by the same teams saw our participation brought to an end by early November – and our relegation to the UEFA Cup. I hated those Wembley nights. At least the club did not prolong the misery any longer and the rest of our European games that season reverted to Highbury.

Our FA Cup run ended as quickly as the League Cup, when we went out – on penalties again – at Leicester in a 4th Round replay. Things, however, were going much better in the secondary European competition. In the UEFA Cup we disposed of both Nantes and Deportivo La Coruna by 6–3 on aggregate. The symmetry was almost perfect as we saw off Werder Bremen 6–2 in the quarter-final. Next up was French team Lens in the semi-final, tough opponents who had beaten us at Wembley the previous season in the Champions League - but not this time. At Highbury in the first leg a Bergkamp goal after two minutes got us off to a great start that I presumed we'd build on, but Lens didn't crack and we were unable to increase the advantage. In the second leg, however, we shone. Suspended for the first game, Henry returned for the second leg scoring a superb goal, and a confident performance saw us triumph 3-1 on aggregate. While we at home celebrated, in France the CRS were doing their best to create chaos out of calm and spoil the night for many of our supporters. Free of this distraction I was able to contemplate a return to the Parken Stadium, our happy hunting ground in Copenhagen. But the news that we were to play Turkish side Galatasaray in the Final was not so comforting. The fatal stabbing of two Leeds United fans in Istanbul prior to the other semi-final had cast a dark shadow over the competition and confirmed the intimidating and menacing reputation that the Turkish fans revelled in.– something the football authorities seemed disinclined to deal with.

Before the final, though, there had been much to be disappointed with in our League campaign. Having come so close the previous season to claiming the title, we finished second again. But while for many clubs that would be a mark of success, for us, at this time, it was not. Instead of pushing Manchester United all the way, yes, we came second, but this time we trailed them by a massive 18 points. Manchester United had run away with it. There was, however, one real highlight to our season, back in October at Stamford Bridge – Kanu v Chelsea.

Although we started well, Chelsea got the goals. Early in the second half we were two down and I was just praying we wouldn't let in any more. I listened to the commentary on the radio; I was miserable. However, with 15 minutes left, Overmars fired in a hopeful shot through a crowd of players. It hit Kanu, who stuck out a leg and poked it along the rain-soaked turf into the net. Interesting! Come on Arsenal. Eight minutes later Overmars again caused problems for the Chelsea defence when he fired a low cross into the crowded penalty area. With his first touch Kanu made space, with his second he slammed the ball into the net. Now I was up and bouncing around the room! What an incredible recovery, but there was more. On 90 minutes we were still pushing forward but a pass intended for Kanu was badly misplaced. A Chelsea defender on the touchline went to hoof it clear but Kanu got in the way, charged it down and set off towards the goal line. Suddenly the Chelsea 'keeper came flying out of his box, but with a swing of the hips that should have earned him a place on the BBC's *Strictly Come Dancing*, Kanu left him for dead. At that point Kanu was well wide of the goal and maybe no more than a yard from the goal line with six Chelsea defenders in the box as cover. It seemed an impossible angle and the sensible money was on a layback to the onrushing support. But without any hesitation he struck the ball over the heads of two of the Chelsea defenders and, seemingly defying the rules of geometry, it flew into the far corner of the net. In the last 15 minutes of the game Kanu's hat-trick had taken us from 2–0 losers to 3–2 winners. No longer content with just bouncing around the room, I was now ricocheting off the walls too. There are some days in each season when you just can't wait for *Match of the Day*, you feel like a child on Christmas morning, knowing that wonderful things are coming your way. That was such a day. I recorded it too; I just couldn't get enough of those goals.

But with the League title long out of reach it was to the UEFA Cup I looked for a last chance of glory that season. I travelled over to Copenhagen with Steph, Dickie and David on a trip organised by the Arsenal Travel Club. But the news ahead of the game was not good. Trouble had flared in the centre of Copenhagen the day before the final between groups of Arsenal and Galatasaray fans. Arsenal supporters had travelled to Europe for years without any hint of trouble, but now, Galatasaray's notorious fans piled into Copenhagen from all over Europe and it seemed they were not coming to soak up the culture. The night before we departed for Copenhagen, images of fighting had filled TV news reports. At the airport representatives from the Travel Club were assuring supporters that things were not as bad as they looked on TV and that the trouble was restricted to just one area of the city. I think they even offered to refund money if anyone chose not to go. Needless to say, we went anyway. A coach took us from the airport to the city and our rep. spelt things out very clearly. When we got off the coach, if we turned left we would be in the area where the trouble had been on the previous day, if we turned right we would have a pleasant day in Copenhagen. We turned right, and he was right, we enjoyed our day in the city. Others were not so lucky and stories later circulated about groups of Turkish fans armed with knives and broken bottles attacking Arsenal fans. Fortunately we were unaffected.

We returned to the coaches to travel to the stadium at the appropriate time but the traffic was at a standstill. Eventually we got off short of the stadium and decided to walk the rest of the way. Close to where we got off we spotted a bar which didn't look packed and dived in. Moments later we realised we were in a gay bar – but it was certainly a lot less packed then any of the bars in the city and there was something to be said for not having to fight our way through the Arsenal hordes to get a beer!

Unlike '94, when Arsenal fans had ruled the Parken Stadium, this time it was the mad, intimidating atmosphere of Istanbul that dominated. It did not boost my confidence before kick off. Like us, Galatasaray had started the season in the Champions League, but failed to qualify from their group. We did not play well on the night but created chances that on another occasion we would have put away. Inevitably the Galatasaray goalkeeper, the Brazilian Taffarel, was outstanding. With the score level at 0–0 after 90 minutes, we entered the stressful extra 30 minutes, with a twist. UEFA were using the short-lived 'Golden Goal' rule – the game would end after the first goal. Almost immediately the advantage seemed to swing to us as Hagi, one of our opponent's best players, was red-carded after he thumped Tony Adams. We created three clear chances after that but couldn't break the deadlock. And so it was penalties again. What a disaster. In front of a hostile, smouldering, baying wall of their own fans Galatasaray scored their first four; they didn't need to take the fifth. Davor Suker smacked our first against the foot of the post, Ray Parlour scored but then Vieira cracked his against the crossbar. Knocked out of the League Cup, FA Cup and UEFA Cup on penalties all in the same season, that has to be some sort of miserable, unwanted record. There, in the city where Hans Christian Anderson wrote many of his fairy tales, I found no happy ending.

18

New Century – Same Result

August 2000, here we were at the start of the first full season of the 21st century. When I was young I read a comic called TV 21, it was kids science fiction, set – you guessed it - in the 21st century, with space ships and satellites zapping all over the place. Strangely I've never noticed any spaceships in the sky when I emerge from the tunnel at Arsenal station following my regular crushing on the Piccadilly Line, but the satellites are out there, although they're not firing death rays at the planet. Instead they're feeding the Earth's population a 24/7 diet of televised football. That summer did show me the future in another way though; Emmanuel Petit and Marc Overmars left us for Barcelona, twelve years on and we still haven't managed to seal that particular air-lock.

That summer saw change. The club finally accepted that playing our Champions League games at Wembley was working against us and decided to return to Highbury, a move much appreciated by all. There were additions to the playing squad too as Arsène Wenger invested in Robert Pirès, another French player who went on to become one of Highbury's heroes, along with Sylvain Wiltord, who also made a lasting mark. Wenger was building a new team.

In spite of any hopes I had that we would knock Manchester United off the top spot in the league, the season followed a now well-established path. We finished second to them for the third year in a row, ten points behind – and had our customary November wobble. The familiarity was depressing.

The switch to playing our Champions League games at Highbury, however, paid immediate dividends. In the first group stage we won all three home games, against Sparta Prague, Shakhtar Donetsk and Lazio. Things were a bit tighter in the second group stage, in the over extended format employed at the time, and despite a thumping by Spartak on a dismal November night in Moscow, we eventually squeezed into the quarter-finals where, although we beat Valencia 2–1 at Highbury in the first leg, we lost 1–0 in Spain and crashed out on away goals – but a definite European improvement.

So, with the league offering no chance of success, the door to European glory slammed shut and an instantly forgettable League Cup campaign – where Wenger was now blooding teams of mainly young inexperienced players – all that remained was the dream of a FA Cup run to keep the interest bubbling. But Wembley was no longer the goal, the FA were building a new stadium on the site. In the meantime the Final relocated to another country, to Wales!

Wins at Carlisle and QPR gave us a home tie in the fifth round against pre-Abramovich Chelsea, and, despite injuries forcing us to field an unconvincing central defence pairing of Oleg Luzhny and Igor Stepanovs, two late goals from Wiltord gave us a 3–1 win and the reward of another home game in the sixth round – against Blackburn Rovers. The match proved to be a stroll; we were 2–0 up after five minutes and played out the game to win 3–0. However, our semi-final draw promised a much fiercer encounter, our opponents Tottenham – and the venue for two rival teams from North London? Why, Manchester, of course.

Strangely, after all my years of following Arsenal, I had never been to Old Trafford so this was a first. I went up by car with Dickie and Steph, and a Sunday 1.30 kick off meant an early start. But we followed advice to park in Altrincham and caught the tram to the stadium, which worked out fine. Sadly I couldn't say the same about the return journey, having to queue forever to get a tram back. I can't say I was that impressed with Old Trafford as a ground – it was just incredibly tall - and the vertigo inducing climb up to our seats was more akin to an assault on Mount Everest than attending a football match. But, as they say, no pain, no gain, and we certainly gained that day.

Before the game Tottenham fans were full of "when the year ends in one" nonsense, but had major injury concerns over their captain and talisman, Sol Campbell. However, he made the starting line up. Amazingly for such an important North London derby, we were well on top from the start and it was really one-sided, but Tottenham took the lead! A wayward shot was heading for the corner flag when it hit one of their players on the head and rebounded into the net. After that it was just one-way traffic with the Tottenham goalkeeper saving them time after time. A crude foul by Campbell, was the key that finally unlocked the door. Campbell injured himself making the challenge and was off the pitch when the resultant free-kick floated into the box and Vieira soared above the undermanned Tottenham defence to score. Our joy increased even further when Campbell limped off for good. Irony is ever-present in football and here was another example. The next time Sol Campbell pulled on a football shirt it was one of ours – and he'd already made his first contribution to the club by giving away that free-kick. In the future there would only be cheers, not jeers for Campbell – who in a role reversal became a victim of an appalling hate campaign by his one-time fans for crossing the North London divide. But that was still a few months away.

We kept pummelling the Tottenham goal in the second half and finally got our reward when the new boys combined; Pirès slotting home a simple chance from a Wiltord cross. There is no better feeling then beating Tottenham – convincingly - in an important game. And so to Wembley – sorry, I mean Cardiff – where we were to meet Liverpool.

Having given the travel options some consideration I, along with Steph, Dickie and Prinders, elected to take the train. Cardiff greeted us with blistering sunshine – a surprise, I thought it always rained in Wales. As it turned out it was the only thing that illuminated the day for me.

Early in the game Thierry Henry broke through the Liverpool defence, rounded the 'keeper and fired the ball goalwards at the far end of the stadium. Then, just as the ball was about to enter the net a Liverpool player shot out a hand and pushed it around the post. "Handball!" we screamed. No, nothing given. Seconds later Dickie's mobile rang. The text was simple and clear, "definite penalty." And as well as being denied a penalty Liverpool should have been reduced to 10-men, but the referee waved play on and the crime passed unpunished.

Despite this injustice it was all Arsenal from then, but decisions like that tend to haunt you, and when the goals don't come, doubt starts to creep in. Frustration and nerves increased, but then…glorious release. With less than 20 minutes remaining to play Freddie Ljungberg, with his Arsenal red stripe in his hair, darted on to a Pirès pass, rounded the 'keeper and crashed the ball into the net, right in front of the wildly celebrating massed ranks of Gooners. Moments later it should have been 2–0, but Henry fluffed his lines. We were in command and there was no hint of what was about to happen next.

With just eight minutes left and Liverpool having offered little all game, our defence failed to deal with a free kick (sounds familiar) and Michael Owen was on hand to fire home. In an instant the game turned on its head and two minutes from time, as everyone was preparing for an extra 30 minutes, Owen ran through and scored again. How do you deal with such unbelievable shock and disappointment? Me? I go very quiet and sullen, tortured by my inner pain. I had plenty of time to ponder the injustices of football as we joined the never-ending queue that snaked, immobile, around Cardiff station waiting for a train back to London. They call the Northern Line of the London Underground the Misery Line. I dispute that, I found another where personal suffering was far more acute.

Once on the train I was appalled to find a group of Liverpool fans in our carriage, although considering how many expat Scousers there are loose in London I shouldn't have been surprised; but why hadn't they stayed to watch their team celebrate? In a vain effort to lighten the mood Steph went off to the buffet to get some beers. When she returned I could tell from the look on her face that all was not well. In her hands were four cans of Carlsberg – the sponsors of Liverpool.

19

One Beautiful Week

I had one simple overwhelming concern as season 2001/02 dawned; would we ever overhaul Manchester United again. However, other than a surprising home defeat by Leeds, we made a solid start to the season before the regular autumn wobble arrived in October. In a run of four games we took just three points, including a stomach-churning home defeat by Charlton, when the south Londoners scored four times in a 20 minute period either side of half time to win 4-2. That result, in early November, left me stunned and had the media already writing off our title challenge. At the same time we were scraping through the First Group stage of the Champions League in second place on goal difference – having finished behind Panathinaikos and level on points with Mallorca. This and the rude awakening from Charlton meant my mood could best be described as hopeful but not confident. There was no hint of what was to come as the chill winds of November heralded the beginning of the serious part of the season.

While playing in the Champions League was the icing that year, I desperately wanted my cake too: the League. I like cake! Sadly the icing soon crumbled when we failed to progress through the second group stage of the Champions League. But it did leave one outstanding memory, Freddie Ljungberg's second goal against Juventus in a majestic 3–1 win at Highbury, set up by the mesmeric close control of Dennis Bergkamp. Simply breathtaking.

In fact, rather than the defeat by Charlton having a negative effect on the team, it seemed to spur them on. And, with no pun intended, the next game was at Tottenham, which ended 1–1, their equaliser in injury time following a mistake from our stand–in goalkeeper Richard Wright. It was the game when Sol Campbell first faced the bitter hatred aimed at him by his former fans. Then, after the Tottenham game, things just kept getting better, starting with a 3–1 home victory over Manchester United on a cold and wet November Sunday afternoon. With ten minutes to play and the score evenly balanced at 1–1 Fabian Bartez in the United goal made two horrendous gaffes in the space of five minutes. Each time Henry calmly took advantage and scored in front of the North Bank to send Highbury bouncing into ecstasy. And the joy of that moment heralded even better things to come by the time we played United again in the return fixture at Old Trafford in May.

In the meantime we started our FA Cup run with a comfortable win at Watford followed by a feisty 1–0 win victory over Liverpool at Highbury. With memories of Cardiff the previous May fuelling the fire before kick off, we had Keown and Bergkamp sent off in the second half, quickly followed by Jamie Carragher - for indiscriminately hurling a coin thrown at him back into the crowd – all within a four minute spell! Further victories, against Gillingham and Newcastle meant it was back to Manchester for the semi-final, this time against Middlesbrough. We followed the same routine up to Old Trafford and, with a later 4.00pm kick off, there was enough time for a beer in Altrincham this time. The game, it has to be said, was completely forgettable – but a Middlesbrough own goal was enough and we were back to…Cardiff – no chance to sing the semi-final winning team's favourite song – "Wem-ber-ley, Wem-ber-ley!"

Although it was clear that the M4 from London was going to be busy as our opponents in the Final were Chelsea, after the endless queuing and delays with the trains the previous year, we decided to drive – Dickie, Steph, Prinders and me. But we had a good omen on our side. The date of the game, played the week before the end of the league season, was May 4th, the eighth anniversary of our European Cup Winners Cup victory back in 1994. May the fourth be with us – again.

The journey down was fine until we passed that English-fleecing barrier, the Severn Bridge. Shortly after that we found ourselves on a barely moving car park all the way to Cardiff. Fortunately a mate of mine, Bill, lived in the city at the time and we had arranged to park at his house. After a trip to the local chippy, Bill squeezed us all into his car and dropped us off near the stadium. My ticket set me back £55 and the programme that year sold for £7 – it was far too big for carrying around at a football match – and who actually reads the programme *at* the game anyway - I bought one later on eBay; it was cheaper too.

I must admit, while I never enjoyed the travelling to Cardiff, I thought the stadium really knew how to crank up the atmosphere. I didn't need any help, however, in cranking up the tension; I was managing that pretty well on my own. But we sensed another omen at the ground – we were sitting at the other end to the previous Final, perhaps it would be lucky for us as it had been for Liverpool.

It was not an outstanding first half but we created two good chances that should have produced goals: headers from Bergkamp and the right-back, Lauren. Another chance fell to Thierry Henry right at the beginning of the second half, but while Henry is one of the greatest players ever to pull on an Arsenal shirt, he rarely seemed to have any luck on the big occasions; this time Cudicini saved. The second half livened up as Chelsea came back into the game. But that just prepared the stage for Ray Parlour - the 'Romford Pele'. Parlour, better known as a midfielder of boundless energy and doggedness rather than a scorer of outstanding goals, was about to stamp his name on the Final.

With about 20 minutes left to play Parlour picked up the ball in midfield but his way forward appeared blocked. However, as the Chelsea defenders stood off him, watching the runs of players they deemed more dangerous, Parlour created a little space for himself then hit a tremendous curling shot from 25 yards that rocketed into the top right hand corner of the net. The massed ranks of Arsenal fans behind the goal - us included - went wild. Surely it couldn't get any better than that, but it did. Nine minutes later Freddie Ljungberg picked up the ball just inside our own half of the pitch. He burst forward and darted past three Chelsea players, the last one,

John Terry, desperately trying to claw him down. Ljungberg shrugged him off and as he reached the edge of the penalty area he looked up. I seemed to be in line as he struck the ball with precision, and watched, mesmerised, as it curved out to the right beyond the dive of Cudicini and then curled back and into the net. Ljungberg had already become the darling of the crowd that season, the red streak in his hair cementing his place in our hearts – helped not a little by the six goals he'd scored in the last five games prior to the Final. There was no way back for Chelsea.

As the players paraded the Cup, the stadium sound system cranked up the volume and began blasting out the 1960's hit "Can't Take My Eyes Off You" – it was Freddie's song. What an extraordinary feeling that must be, to have tens of thousands of fans singing to you. "We love you Freddie, because you've got red hair, etc.etc." It was a magical moment. Yet we were not just deliriously happy because we'd won the Cup; our amazing run of form in the League meant that the Double was on again too. But before that, we had to get out of Cardiff – it proved to be the toughest part of the day.

Our extraordinary run in the League – unbeaten since December, unbeaten entirely away from home and on a run of eleven consecutive victories – meant that after the Cup Final we had two games left to play; and just one point would secure the title – and the Double. The fact that the first of those games was against Manchester United at Old Trafford added extra spice. If we lost that and our final game against Everton we'd fall at the final hurdle. That didn't bear thinking about.

We played the Manchester United game on the Wednesday after the Cup Final, which meant another deeply distracted day at work before meeting Steph and Gerry at a pub on Finchley Road to watch history in the making. I was nervous – so much to lose – and Manchester United came out playing the rough stuff like they so often do against us. But this was a tough, resilient Arsenal and they weren't intimidated. Our time came 10 minutes into the second half. Ljungberg – again – burst through the middle only to see his shot saved by Bartez, but he could only push it into the path of Sylvain Wiltord who slotted it home. Pub pandemonium. The Double was ours – for the third time: 1971, 1998 and now 2002. And if we couldn't seal the title at Highbury, well what better place could there be to claim a treble Double than Old Trafford.

All this meant that the final game, at home to Everton, had a crazy carnival atmosphere, and this festival feeling was reflected in the final score, a 4-3 victory. Thierry Henry spent a part of the second half more focused on teeing-up Francis Jeffers for a goal against his former club rather than scoring himself – I guess you can afford to do that when you've already netted 24 in the League and become the winner of the Golden Boot. But it was almost as though the result was irrelevant – we all just wanted to see the trophy handed over. When it came, and Tony Adams lifted it high, we in turn lifted the roof of the stadium with the now traditional chorus of Queen's "We Are The Champions." The players took it in turns to step forward and lift the trophy, but perhaps the most memorable moment on a memorable day came when Robert Pirès stepped up. After a great first season he had missed the last two months due to a cruciate ligament injury. When he lifted the trophy the whole squad knelt and bowed, paying homage to one of the season's most outstanding players. Special moments, a special team and a very special season.

20

For The Record

Around this time the club announced plans to introduce a new badge, the vague copyright nature of the existing one threatening the club's ability to maximise its merchandising revenue. When the club revealed the new design they invited fans to post their comments via the website, but it was pretty clear they had already adopted it and were just going through the motions. I, like many long-term fans, had grown up with the previous crest, it said tradition, history and it had class, so I told them. I pointed out that the existing crest featured a cannon that was a real piece of artillery, one that carried a threat, whereas the cartoon-like gun on the new badge reminded me of one of those comedy cannons whose wheels fall off when the clowns drag it into the circus ring. An automated reply thanked me for my interest and comments, but realistically I'd be surprised if anyone ever read it.

Disappointment at the passing of the old club crest aside, this was now a really special time to be an Arsenal fan. Under Arsène Wenger opposition fans could no longer assail us with the chant "Boring, boring Arsenal", he had consigned that image to the history books. Now it was Arsenal fans who sang the same song - ironically - as we regularly cut through the opposition to score our third or fourth goal with aplomb. This was a special, wonderful and breathtaking team emerging. From my second home up in the West Stand at Highbury I watched Patrick Vieira, Robert Pirès, Freddie Ljungberg, Dennis Bergkamp and, of course, Thierry Henry cast their magic spells, ably supported by David Seaman, Ashley Cole, Sol Campbell, Kolo Touré, Sylvain Wiltord, Gilberto Silva and the one-name warriors Edu, Kanu, and Lauren. There was much to look forward to during the summer of 2002 – as another World Cup came and went - and I waited for the new season to start, feeling sure we'd carry on from where we left off at the end of the last season. And it seemed we would.

On day one of the new season we broke a record! Playing Birmingham at Highbury on a hot summer's afternoon we completely overwhelmed our opponents although we only won 2–0. But that result meant we had won 14 consecutive League games stretching back to early February – a record for the top flight – and particularly satisfying as the previous joint record holders were Tottenham on 13, which they'd achieved twice over 40 years earlier, and Preston and Sunderland who managed it in the 19th century! There is always a special pleasure in taking Tottenham's records away. During that incredible run we'd scored 31 goals and let in just six – and Everton scored three of those in the carnival match on the last day of the previous season. Of course the reason I mention this now is that we drew the next game at West Ham, with Wiltord bringing us level at 2–2 with just two minutes left to play, thus bringing that particular run to an end. But there were more records to come.

In September, a month after the draw at West Ham, we remained unbeaten in the new season and in a press interview, according to the tabloids, Wenger claimed we could go the whole season unbeaten. He was, of course, misquoted and his actual comment was rather less arrogant. He had actually said, "I know it will be difficult for us to go through the season unbeaten. But if we keep the right attitude, it's possible we can do it. It was done by Milan in Italy [in 1992] and I can't see why it's shocking to say that we can do it this season…It's everybody's dream to go through a season without losing, so let's give it our best shot." People, however, preferred to misquote him – but Wenger and every Arsenal fan would eventually have the last laugh.

At the end of September we played Leeds at Elland Road and put on a scintillating, spellbinding, performance to win 4–1 – and broke two more records. The goals meant we had scored in 47 consecutive League games, breaking a 71-year old record held by Chesterfield, which we extended for another nine games before we lost 2–0 at Old Trafford in December. The victory at Leeds also confirmed we had surpassed Nottingham Forest's run of 22 away games undefeated. That run ended two games later when a 16-year-old kid called Wayne Rooney came on as a sub for Everton with 10 minutes to play and scored the winner in the last minute. Rooney's goal also ended our stunning run of 30 League games unbeaten – 12 short of equalling Nottingham Forest's incredible all-time record of 42 unbeaten. And of course that defeat, our first of the season, meant every Tottenham and Chelsea fan recalled Wenger's 'unbeaten' misquote with delight and ridicule and missed no opportunity in reminding Arsenal fans of it. But our time would come.

Having been undefeated for so long, it came as a major shock when we lost the next game too, at home to Blackburn, with another defeat at Highbury in between those two games, by Auxerre in the Champions League. And then, in our worst run of results since 1983, we lost again the following week away at Borussia Dortmund in the same competition. Our annual autumnal slump was right on cue, but we still qualified from our Champions League group in first place. Thankfully, as the calendar flipped over into November, the crisis ended. We returned to winning ways against Fulham and then, on Saturday 16 November 2002, Tottenham came to Highbury. The game produced an unforgettable moment, one that will forever burn brightly in my memory.

Games against Tottenham always occupy the mind for days in advance. You turn over the permutations of victory or defeat throughout the working day, and at night when you go to bed and want your mind to clear they are still there gnawing away. You accept you will be happy with any victory no matter how it comes, no matter how well or badly you play, but it must be victory, defeat is just too painful to contemplate. Thierry Henry understood how the fans feel about these games.

Right from the start we assaulted the Tottenham goal with Sylvain Wiltord slotting home after just four minutes – but a flag ruled it offside. As the game developed Tottenham had no legal answer to our swaggering attacking play. In his match report in *The Guardian* Ian Ridley wrote that "Tottenham Hotspur resorted to the snarling spite of the inadequate, and Arsenal responded with a quick, slick show of appropriate disdain, including an exhilarating goal by Thierry Henry." It was a goal to feature in every Arsenal fan's top three Henry goals of all time.

With just 13 minutes on the clock, Vieira rose to send a towering header clear of our penalty area. It fell to Henry who took the ball, twisted away from his marker and left him gasping in his wake as he crossed the halfway line. The speed of Henry's run had the Tottenham defenders pouring back, but as he closed on their penalty area three formed a solid barrier in front of him. Making the slightest feint to suggest he was about to shoot for goal with his right foot, instead, Henry touched it to his left across the line of Tottenham's backtracking defenders then smashed it into the bottom corner of the net. While I and every other Arsenal fan in the stadium that day went wild, Henry was in the mood to make a point too as he sprinted back the other way, running the entire length of the field to slide on his knees and pose arrogantly in front of the Tottenham fans. At that moment he became every Arsenal fan. While recalling this moment, I wondered how Tottenham fans viewed this posturing. I checked a few of their websites and found this amusing and honest summing up on one.

> The Frenchman then ran all the way back to his own half to taunt the Spurs contingent at the Clock End with his celebrations. Spurs struggle to find the energy to run up the field once, never mind there and back again.

It was an iconic moment, a moment not lost on the club either. Nine years later, as part of the 125th anniversary celebrations in December 2011, a statue was unveiled capturing it forever in bronze. Erected outside the stadium it ensures no one will ever forget that delicious, delirious, joyous moment – as if we could. And in years to come, when future generations of Gooners not yet born come to the ground for the first time, their fathers, mothers, brothers, sisters, uncles, aunts, grandfathers or grandmothers will relish the chance to stand in front of the statue, tell them about that goal and proudly say "I was there!"

After that defeat at Manchester United early in December, which ended our record run of scoring in consecutive games, we remained unbeaten for the rest of 2002 and ended the year five points clear of Chelsea and Manchester United at the top of the League. I began to dream the impossible dream, the dream of retaining the title.

Two months later, at the end of February, it not only looked like we were well placed to retain the League title but another Double was on the cards too. On 16 February we'd knocked Manchester United out of the FA Cup in the 5th Round at Old Trafford and ended the month with an irresistible 5–1 victory away at Manchester City – the real City, before they found money. We ended the month five points clear of Manchester United with just 10 games to play and an FA Cup 6th Round tie against Chelsea awaiting. But we stumbled in March when Blackburn Rovers beat us for the second time that season. With our lead at the top scythed to just two points, we then exited the Champions League after the second group stage, losing at Valencia and having drawn all three home fixtures. But a stirring 3–1 defeat of Chelsea at Stamford Bridge in a 6th Round replay left all Arsenal fans dreaming – or at least hoping – that the Double was still up for grabs. But as every football fan knows, it's the hope that kills you.

In April we played four League games and drew three of them, including a must-win home game against Manchester United which ended 2-2. With the battle at the top always so tight a draw is the new defeat. Dropping two points in a game when your rivals win is often critical, while to draw matches from winning positions by conceding late own goals, as we did at Aston Villa and Bolton, is shattering and means confidence suffers. At the end of February we had a five point lead over Manchester United, by the end of April we had fallen five points behind them. We, however, had three left to play while Manchester United had just two, and with two of our games at home there was still hope, but my mood was downbeat. The glorious days of the first half of the season were gone, the crucial thing now was to secure a win, any sort of win, in our next game, at home to Leeds, and then see what was possible. However, by the time the game was played, Manchester United had extended their lead to eight points while we had nine left to play for - so, mathematically anyway, there was still an outside chance, but I didn't believe anymore. And Mark Viduka painfully extinguished that slim hope when he smashed the ball home two minutes from time to leave me feeling devastated, just as they had done four years earlier when a late goal at Elland Road had realistically ended our dreams of winning the League that year. And so the shoots of hope nurtured in the winter withered and died in the despair of springtime. I shed no tears when Leeds United were relegated at the end of the following season, they had caused me much pain over the years, but I feel sympathy for my brother-in-law, Rob, and nephew David, committed and now long-suffering Leeds fans both, their club ripped apart by financial mismanagement.

Free of the pressures of the title-run in the team suddenly remembered how to win again, beating Southampton 6–1 at Highbury then winning 4–0 at Sunderland in the last game of the season. But where had that same confident dominating style of play been against Leeds or in the previous games when we'd drawn at Villa and Bolton? My genuine belief – and hope – that we would win the League in 2003 shattered in games like that – against three teams who'd spent the season striving to avoid relegation. Even so, the Southampton game was fabulous to watch, but no one at the time could have realised its later significance; that would only become clear 15 extraordinary months later.

But there was still a chance of a prize, a reward for the way we had played the beautiful game for much of the season: the FA Cup Final beckoned. The 6th Round victory over Chelsea meant a return to the now familiar venue of Old Trafford for the semi-final, and, with a 1.30pm kick off, another very early start for the drive to Altrincham; this time our opponents were Sheffield United. The game itself was completely forgettable as semi-finals often are, except for one astounding moment – a piece of goalkeeping by David Seaman - just returning from injury and making his 1,000[th] senior appearance at the age of 39.

We'd gone ahead in the first half with a goal by Freddie Ljungberg in a game of few chances and seemed to be happy to settle for 1–0. Then, with just over five minutes remaining to play, Sheffield United pumped a panic-inducing ball into our penalty area. It rebounded and ricocheted around until it reached a player standing on the six-yard line. He swung wildly at the ball but managed to redirect it towards Paul Peschisolido who found himself no more than five feet from a wide gaping goalmouth. He twisted his neck to power it into the net. To every spectator in the ground and every viewer watching on TV it was a goal. The ball had already passed Seaman who was a little off his line when he threw his arm out behind him and made contact with the ball. For a split second time seemed to stand still, then his giant hand flicked the ball up and away. The Sheffield United players were stunned. Watching from the far end of the ground I just stood in disbelief - it had so clearly been going in the net, but it didn't. With that one touch Seaman secured the win. There is no doubt in my mind that that is the greatest save I have ever seen in 45 years of watching football – and yes, I include Gordon Banks' save against Pelé in the 1970 World Cup.

The win over Sheffield United ensured we would return to Cardiff for the FA Cup Final for the third year in a row, as we had done previously in 1978, 1979 and 1980. Then the sequence had been lost, won, lost. I tried to banish the thought from my mind but the current run was lost, won, and …? And that third loss in 1980 held particularly bad memories as we went on to lose two Finals in the less than a week. It was not a sign I was comfortable with. Now we were playing in our third consecutive FA Cup Final having lost out on our challenge to retain the League. This parallel gnawed away at me as we made the journey to Cardiff again. I know everyone is supposed to get excited about the FA Cup Final but that year I didn't. It seemed to me there was too much to lose, from a season that promised so much we could end up with nothing – after a season of 57 games in all competitions everything now balanced on how we fared in the 58th and final game.

We followed our same ritual as previous years but once in the city I could sense that the fans of our opponents – Southampton - were 'up' for the occasion. My mood was subdued while the grey and brooding rain-laden skies did not help lift me. Inside the ground too (ticket £60 – programme £8.50) the Southampton fans were clearly in the ascendancy, but then it was their first FA Cup final for 27 years while it was our third in three years. It was almost becoming an expected end of season game. I think many Arsenal fans felt like I did that day, having lost out on the League this was now the consolation prize. I know it is wrong to think like that about watching your team play in the FA Cup final. As a child, winning the Cup Final seemed the highpoint of sporting achievement to me, but after our spring of despair, it was not the glory of a Cup win I sought. My motivation was just the desperation not to end the season empty-handed.

As things turned out we were the better team overall and won 1–0 with a goal that fittingly combined the skills of Henry, Bergkamp and Ljungberg before Pirés slotted home. Southampton just did not have players of that calibre. It was great to win the Cup, to be the first team to win it in consecutive years since Tottenham did it in 1982, but I think my overwhelming emotion that day was one of relief. I could now lay the season to rest as we – with great relief - added another trophy to the cabinet. I could now look forward to a football-free summer – I needed the break, precious time to ease the twisted knots of anguish that had held my stomach in a vice-like grip for weeks on end.

21

The Invincibles

The summer of 2003 heralded the beginning of a massive change in football. It was the summer when the Russian billionaire Roman Abramovich bought Chelsea Football Club, relieving them of their massive debts, and opened his cheque book wide. Football finances were about to change forever.

When season 2003/04 kicked off I didn't know what to expect after the collapse at the end of the previous season. We had been in a strong position and blown it at the crucial moment – it hinted of a weakness in the mentality of the team. Yet four straight wins in August – three against tough opposition - suggested another strong season, while the 4–0 victory at Middlesbrough showed we hadn't forgotten how to demolish teams with incisive attacking play. September, however, brought a little reality check as Portsmouth played out a hard-fought draw at Highbury before we suffered a crushing 3–0 home defeat by Inter Milan in the Champions League; not the ideal preparation for a visit to Old Trafford which was next on the fixture list – and inevitably the result could have a crucial impact on the season ahead.

That game turned out to be a tightly-fought battle with neither side daring to take a risk. And so it seemed the game would end all square, until Martin Keown brought down Diego Forlan in the penalty area in the very last minute. I held my breath in disbelief and then to my horror the referee pointed to the spot. Ruud van Nistelrooy, who had been involved earlier in an incident that saw Patrick Vieira red-carded, stepped up to take it the spot-kick. In goal for us was Jens Lehmann, a summer signing after David Seaman moved on to Manchester City following a magnificent 13 seasons at Highbury. Lehmann danced backwards and forwards along his goal line like a 'keeper in one of those early football video games, trying to unsettle van Nistelrooy who then, incredibly, smacked the ball against the crossbar and away. Seconds later the referee blew the final whistle. Wildly excited, Keown descended upon the Dutchman like an avenging angel, leaping high above him with outstretched arms claiming retribution for his part in Vieira's sending off. It probably did look a little unsavoury to outsiders as other Arsenal players surrounded van Nistelrooy too. He looked genuinely scared, but I loved the photos of the moment in the following day's newspapers. Passion for the cause was clear to see and we left Old Trafford having survived a stiff test with our unbeaten start to the season intact.

The run continued through October with 2–1 victories in the League over both Liverpool and *nouveau riche* Chelsea, followed by a draw at Charlton. In the Champions League, however, a draw in Moscow and defeats by Inter Milan and Dynamo Kyiv suggested our participation would be short in Europe's premier competition. On a more positive note, the month also saw the full debut in the League Cup (now sponsored by Carling) of a 16-year-old Spanish boy called Cesc Fabregas who showed great promise. But, as November approached, the talk among my group of Gooners was, "Is this it, is it time for the autumn stumble?", and what made that feeling slightly worse was that Tottenham were due at Highbury that month. Thankfully, however, the stumble came a little later that year. Tottenham were beaten 2–1 with the winning goal, 'scored' by Freddie Ljungberg, coming after an outrageous up and under deflection – which made winning even more fun. That win came sandwiched between superb victories at both Leeds and Birmingham at a time when our Champions League campaign experienced a dramatic change of fortune too.

After three games in Europe we sat firmly rooted to the bottom of our group with just one point, having scored only one goal and conceded five. This made the fourth game, at home to Dynamo Kyiv, absolutely critical: win or bust. Our performances against sides from eastern Europe generally left much to be desired and as the game wore on, although we created chances, we could not beat the Ukrainian goalkeeper. With the game at stalemate it looked like we were about to make an early exit. That is until just two minutes of play remained. Wiltord pumped a high ball into the Kyiv penalty area, it flicked off a defender's head and there, rushing in to send a diving header into the net, was the unlikely figure of Ashley Cole. An explosion of joy – and relief – swept over Highbury like a tidal wave; what a fantastic stadium it was at moments like that. I hugged Andy as he hugged his son until we were a mass of entwined madness. We had won the game and although we were still bottom of the group, we'd given ourselves hope – oh, hope again… Now all we needed was to beat Inter Milan at the San Siro, who'd already stunned us at Highbury when they won 3–0. Oh well, it was fun while it lasted.

When the day – 25 November – dawned the enormity of the task seemed insurmountable. We hadn't won away from home in Europe for a year – although that was in Italy, against Roma – and injuries weakened our starting line-up as we missed Vieira, Bergkamp, Wiltord and Lauren. But from this position one of the greatest Arsenal performances of all time emerged. I watched the game in the *North Star* on Finchley Road with Steph. It was like an out of body experience, I could not believe what I was watching. We were 1-0 up after 25 minutes, the goal scored by Henry, but a wicked deflection saw Inter equalise eight minutes later and that, I imagined, was the end of that. The score remained the same at half time. But early in the second half Henry teased the Inter defence before setting up Ljungberg on the edge of the six-yard box to give us a 2–1 lead. We continued to play well and our defence seemed to be coping as Inter upped the pressure. With five minutes to go we cleared a corner out to Thierry Henry. He picked up the ball in our half then sprinted with it to the other end, bamboozled his marker and lashed the ball low into the corner of the net. An incredible, unbelievable moment – yet there was still more to come. That third goal shattered Inter and we took full advantage. As the clock ticked down we scored again, Henry setting up Edu, and then again, when Robert Pirès slotted home after good work by the substitute, Jérémie

146

Aliadière. The final score, a 5-1 victory at the San Siro comes from the world of make-believe, but it happened, I saw it and it left me with a feeling of euphoria and a fixed smile that remained unmoved for at least a week.

The result meant that we climbed from bottom to second in our group, one point behind the leaders, Lokomotiv Moscow, who were our final opponents – at Highbury. Again, great tension before kick-off but we were on a roll and were not about to be denied. Early in the first half Pirès received a pass from Henry, broke into the penalty area and shot low past the Russian 'keeper; the perfect start. I began to feel a little nervous when a second didn't come quickly, but eventually, with about 20 minutes left, a delightful flicked pass from Henry found Ljungberg who chipped the ball over the 'keeper and into the net. It was all over and the phoenix had completed its remarkable rise from the ashes, from bottom of the table after three games to top of the table after six. Our reward, a last-16 tie against Celta Vigo of Spain: that seemed winnable.

While we had been completing a remarkable European turnaround, things had not gone quite so well in the Premier League; our delayed autumnal wobble had finally arrived. In a run of four games up to Christmas we grabbed a narrow victory over Blackburn amongst draws against Fulham, Leicester and Bolton, with both Leicester and Bolton scoring late equalisers. The outcome of this poor run was that Manchester United leap-frogged us into top spot. Thankfully the wobble ended there and we returned to winning ways. It meant we had reached the halfway point of the season unbeaten; now that was something special, something to be really proud of. And so it carried on.

Across January and February we played eight games, we drew the first at Everton but won the other seven in some style. By 10 January we were back in top spot – and never surrendered it again. In fact we continued to win; we won every League game until Manchester United held us to a draw at home on 28 March. By then we'd cast United adrift and opened a 12 point gap over them; our closest challengers now were Chelsea, trailing us by seven points. Within this period, with perfect symmetry, Thierry Henry scored his 100th League goal; his victims, Southampton, the same team he'd scored his first goal against back in September 1999. Everyone in the crowd celebrated the moment, yet it seemed that every goal we scored was something special, with Henry, Pirès, Bergkamp and Ljungberg bewitching opponents with their vision, passing and positioning. This was a joyous time to be an Arsenal fan, this was one of the truly great football teams – and they earned the ultimate accolade, supporters of other clubs enjoyed the way we played too. Our progress in the League appeared unstoppable and other competitions offered hopes of glory too.

By then we had exited the Carling Cup, being beaten in the semi-final by Middlesbrough, but had strolled majestically to the semi-final of the FA Cup having swatted aside Leeds United, Middlesbrough, Chelsea and Portsmouth, scoring 15 goals and conceding just 4 in the process. In Europe we by-passed Celta Vigo to be rewarded with a quarter-final against Chelsea, a team we'd already beaten home and away in the League and knocked out of the FA Cup. The first leg at Stamford Bridge ended 1–1 and it seemed that advancement in Europe and the ultimate dream of winning the Champions League remained very much alive. That draw gave me hope – and belief – but when that is taken away, oh how it hurts.

On Saturday 3 April I travelled up to Villa Park for the FA Cup semi-final against Manchester United and was dismayed to find, with Wenger mindful of the packed schedule ahead, Henry named only as a substitute. The game was another of those overly-physical approaches by United and they won 1–0. It was not a great performance and, in the process, challenges by United players left Reyes battered and bruised and Ljungberg with a broken hand. After this roughing up the talk on the way home turned to the second leg of the Champions League only three days away and the feeling that the effort made today would surely have a draining effect on the players on Tuesday.

I travelled to the Chelsea game from work with Dickie and Prinders and we met Steph, Gerry and Andy at the ground. Prinders and I had already probably spent just a little too long talking about the game that day at work. At the ground our conversation veered between excitement and nerves, anticipation and fear – at stake a place in the semi-final of the Champions League.

We made the breakthrough right on the stroke of half-time when Jose Antonio Reyes latched onto a ball headed down by Henry and slashed it into the net from close range. Highbury went wild, the goal encouraging excited half-time conversations – the beacon of hope burned brightly. But six minutes into the second half it dimmed a little. Lehmann fumbled a long range shot allowing Chelsea to equalise when Frank Lampard swept the loose ball into the net. Both sides created chances after that but neither got on top as the game appeared to be heading for an extra 30 minutes. I felt sure that with home advantage this would tell in our favour, but, with just three minutes of the 90 remaining, Wayne Bridge, the Chelsea full back of all people, popped up to play a one-two on the edge of our penalty area. He took the return and fired home. It was all over, the match and the dream. I sat with my head in my hands while others vented their anger. I couldn't bear to watch Chelsea celebrate.

As the whistle blew I left the stand immediately. The snatches of conversations I heard were angry and disbelieving; I retreated into my shell trying to make sense of it all, while Dickie, Prinders and Steph aired their frustrations. Andy had gone, lost in his own personal hell. The following day at work Prinders and I remained angry and sullen. At lunchtime we walked the streets of Clerkenwell turning the game over and over. We had thrown away such a great chance to reach the final, and perhaps even win it, for in the semi-final Chelsea, who spent £120m of Roman Abramovich's money that season, lost to Monaco who in turn lost to Porto in the final. There was no Barcelona or Real Madrid barring the way that year. It was a massive loss.

The worry now was whether the two defeats, to Manchester United in the FA Cup and Chelsea in Europe, would affect our assault on the League title. Two possible trophies had disappeared in the blink of an eye. What if our form now collapsed in the League? The possibility of ending the season empty-handed was simply unthinkable.

We returned to League action three days later, for a Good Friday lunchtime kick-off at home to Liverpool, and all I wanted was a win – any win – it didn't matter how it came. But at half-time the spectre of Chelsea catching us in the League loomed large as we went into the break losing 2–1. I would not describe my mood at half-time as buoyant. But there was always Thierry Henry. He'd scored in the first half and a few minutes into the second half he combined passes with Ljungberg to allow Pirès to level the score. From then on there was no looking back – a minute later we took the lead with a breathtaking goal by Henry which is my personal favourite of all the 228 goals he scored for the club.

Picking up the ball just inside the Liverpool half of the field, Henry burst forward, leaving Dietmar Hamann sprawling in his wake as he approached the penalty area, but further forward progress appeared barred by a road block of four Liverpool defenders. But Henry was special. A minute change of direction threw the defenders into confusion and they parted, like the Red Sea, as Henry strolled through leaving the defenders crashing into each other before he calmly slotted the ball home beyond the reach of the diving goalkeeper. Unforgettable. It was a goal that, for me, summed up the brilliance of the man. But he wasn't finished and went on to complete a hat-trick for a stunning 4–2 victory. Our lead over Chelsea remained seven points with seven games to play – and an incredible 15 ahead of Manchester United. Nerves calmed again; I knew I was watching something special.

A week later, having drawn away at Newcastle on the Easter Sunday, we had another Friday game, this time the opposition was Leeds United. It proved to be another perfect game with Henry scoring four times as we won 5–0. Such was his performance that he appeared untouchable. He scored his final goal after a trip by a Leeds defender, but he managed to adjust his body as he was falling to poke the ball into the net before he hit the ground. I have never seen a footballer so on top of his game as Henry was at that time. As he said later,

"You don't want the ref to blow the whistle. You want to play that game all your life."

What it all meant was that if we won our next game – at White Hart Lane against Tottenham – we'd be Champions. There is a delicious pleasure in winning the League at the ground of your local rivals and memories of my trip to the ground back in 1971 when we'd claimed our first Double came flooding back. But this time I would have to be content with coverage via the media. However, Prinders was there – something I have never let him forget! Prinders' wife-to-be was from a family of Tottenham season ticket holders. She had a spare one for the game so Prinders grabbed at the chance. Now Prinders likes his stats and he was our fount of knowledge on all things Arsenal, but that day he made a terrible unthinkable mistake.

In the build up to the game, the certainty was that if we won we had enough points to ensure no one could catch us even though there were still another four games to play after this one. However, Chelsea had an early kick off and their game finished before we started. They lost at Newcastle which meant just a draw now would be enough to clinch the title. For everyone watching or listening in pubs or at home it was very clear – but to Prinders, who'd left the pub with the Chelsea game still level and now amidst a throng of hostile Tottenham fans, that important little fact got missed.

We started the game brilliantly and by half-time had coasted to a 2–0 lead, making it look easy. Tottenham fans must have feared things could get even worse for them in the second half. Prinders, with much difficulty, was fighting to suppress any outward signs of joy. Annoyingly, however, Tottenham pulled a goal back after around an hour of play and the game became more even, but the win looked secure as we entered three minutes of injury time. Then, inexplicably, Jens Lehmann had one of his mad moments and ended up in a needless shoving match with Robbie Keane after the danger from a Tottenham corner had passed. Following much confusion, the referee awarded a penalty and Keane scored to equalise. Tottenham's fans celebrated like they'd won the League themselves; to Prinders it seemed worse, our expert statistician convinced himself that goal meant the title was still on hold, while in fact Tottenham's celebrations were a mixture of joy at not losing to Arsenal and the fact that the point guaranteed they had averted an end of season relegation battle. When the whistle blew moments later, he stormed out of White Hart Lane and headed home. He was well on his way before he encountered celebrating Gooners and the truth dawned on him – and he'd missed the chance to watch the players celebrating winning the League title on the White Hart Lane pitch. Oh Prinders – you missed a glorious moment!

The title was ours, we were League champions but now we wanted more – we wanted to go the whole season unbeaten in the League, a goal Wenger had spoken of the previous season only to face ridicule for his ambition. Now, that incredible achievement was just four games away. Yet it was not a comfortable ride. After the glories of White Hart Lane we were held 0–0 at home by Birmingham, followed by a 1-1 draw at Portsmouth with Lehmann making up for his antics at Tottenham by saving in a one-on-one situation near the end of the game. A resolute away performance against Fulham secured a 1–0 win in the season's penultimate game and so we approached the final game of the season – against Leicester City at Highbury – still unbeaten after 37 games. To go unbeaten for a whole season was impossible, unbelievable. No one had achieved it since the 'Invincibles' of Preston North End way, way back in 1888-89 over just a 22-game season. And now that 'impossible' prize was within reach.

The day of the Leicester game was warm and sunny which added to the carnival atmosphere around the game before kick-off. Smiling faces everywhere. But completely against the script a former Gunner, Paul Dickov, scored for Leicester in the first half leaving us trailing at half-time. Cue nerves. But we'd come too far to lose now, and within two minutes of the restart, Henry slotted home a penalty and a weight was lifted off everyone in the stadium. It was impossible to think anything could go wrong now and, sure enough, we scored again when Dennis Bergkamp sent through a slide-rule pass for captain Patrick Vieira to side-step the Leicester goalkeeper and pass the ball into the net in front of the adoring North Bank. The players knew it was all over and so did I. It is an incredible feeling in football, playing out a game knowing the ultimate prize is yours. When the referee blew his whistle and brought the season to an end we were Champions, eleven points clear of Chelsea in second place, and had entered the history books as the new Invincibles: Played 38, Won 26, Drawn 12, Lost 0 – football doesn't get any better than that. Simply incredible.

Having immersed myself in the post-match celebrations as the team finally received the Premier league trophy, it eventually came time to move the party on and so we headed for the *World's End* at Finsbury Park – a very popular venue that day!

We had been there a while when Prinders, now recovered from his White Hart Lane shocker, suddenly exclaimed, "That was Jens Lehmann!", as a car drove by. We didn't really believe him but without another word he sprinted off up the road clutching his inflatable League trophy - a popular accessory at Highbury that day. It seems Prinders caught up with Lehmann at the next set of traffic lights and proceeded to jump up and down brandishing the trophy and yelling incoherently. Herr Lehmann, seemingly a little bewildered by the antics of this madman beside his car, nervously waited for the lights to turn green before accelerating away to safety as fast as he could.

All around us that night I saw only smiling faces; a remarkable day at the end of an incredible season. But while we celebrated, conversations turned to the changes that were coming. In February the club announced that finally they had secured the funding needed to build a new stadium. Having considered a number of options, in 1999 the club identified a potential site at Ashburton Grove, just 500 yards from Highbury. However, securing funding had proved difficult, as had negotiations with the council, local residents, businesses and the police. But in February 2004 the stadium project received the go ahead, with a completion date set for the start of the 2006/07 season. I knew I would be sad when the time came to leave Highbury but the confirmation that the new stadium was on our doorstep was the best possible news.

22

Jekyll and Hyde

With season ticket renewed for 2004/05 I had to ask myself how we could possibly improve in the new season. Elsewhere Roman Abramovich made it clear he wanted to win at any cost and spent another £90m on players over the summer and brought in José Mourinho, the manager of Porto who had just won the Champions League, to replace Claudio Ranieri. We could not compete with Abramovich's limitless money supply, but we did bring in a young Dutch striker, Robin van Persie who went on to do much to irritate Chelsea over the years.

We began the season having extended our unbeaten run to 40 League games, with the all time record of 42 held by Nottingham Forest now within our sights. We started the season in blistering style, equalling the record in a pulsating game at Highbury against Middlesbrough in which at one point we were 3–1 down, before winning 5–3. Then, three days later, following victory over Blackburn Rovers, the record, which had stood for 26 years, was ours. And the run didn't end there. On 16 October we played our ninth League game of the season and beat Aston Villa 3–1 at Highbury, taking the run, which started with the 6-1 thrashing of Southampton in May 2003, to an incredible 49 games. Yet I felt the run was becoming a burden. I went into every game worrying about it coming to an end. And if I felt like that, how was it affecting the players? There was predictability about the end when it came, in the 50th game, at Old Trafford. On the Wednesday before the game we'd played out a competitive 2–2 draw in Greece against Panathinaikos in the Champions League, while

Manchester United had an extra day to recover after their trip to Prague.

The game itself remained evenly balanced until the 73rd minute when Wayne Rooney, who had controversially left Everton for Manchester United that summer, threw himself to the ground as Sol Campbell pulled back from a tackle in the penalty area. The referee was taken in and Ruud van Nistelrooy celebrated enthusiastically after he slammed the penalty home, no doubt remembering his failure from the penalty spot a year earlier. The misery was complete when Rooney scored again in the last minute and the run was over – but what a run, the envy of every other club, no matter how much money they had to spend. There was no love lost between the two teams at the best of times, but this game gained further notoriety later when it was revealed that the team's sense of injustice boiled over as the players of both sides clashed in the tunnel after the final whistle, the incident becoming known as 'The Battle of the Buffet' and 'Pizzagate' as a slice of pizza thrown by one of our players hit the United manager Alex Ferguson in the face during the scuffle. Obviously you can't condone that sort of behaviour…but I had to laugh!

What I wanted now was a quick return to winning ways, but it didn't come. The defeat seemed to set the players back. Only a last minute goal by Robin van Persie secured a draw at Highbury against Southampton, and that was followed by another at Crystal Palace; our annual autumnal wobble was right on cue. That weekend Chelsea took over at the top of the League, a position we were unable to reclaim.

At this time, while we were struggling to get back to winning ways, the fixture list decreed we were to play Tottenham at White Hart Lane. The timing I felt could have been better. But what an extraordinary game it turned out to be. If ever a game warranted the term 'a roller-coaster of a match' then this was it; it was a match when both teams forgot how to defend. Tottenham took the lead late in the first half but Henry levelled the scores in stoppage time at the end of the half. Ten minutes into the second half we scored from the penalty spot and five minutes after that Vieira strolled through the Tottenham defence to give us a 3–1 lead. I settled back to

155

enjoy us play out the game. But just a minute later Tottenham embarrassed our defence and brought the score back to 3-2. I was at home pacing up and down while listening to the commentary on BBC Five Live; it was not a comfortable experience. Back we came again, a delightful pass from Cesc Fabregas deceiving the entire Tottenham defence leaving Freddie Ljungberg in space to make it 4–2 and restore our two goal lead. With 20 minutes still to play, I just hoped we'd start defending properly and I wished desperately for the end. But five minutes later Tottenham scored again. It was now 4–3. I felt sick, as if I was aboard a real roller-coaster. We'd been drawing games recently; now all I could think was that this was about to become another. Arsenal/Tottenham games were not supposed to be like this. Then, with just nine minutes left on the clock, we scored again, Pirès slotting home from the narrowest of angles; surely now, with the score at 5–3 we were safe. Unbelievably Tottenham then scored again: 5–4 with two minutes still to play. I was in turmoil and had worn a groove in the carpet by the time the referee ended my torment. I felt shattered, as though I'd been playing myself - and we'd won! I can not imagine how I would have felt if they had drawn level. It was perhaps a game better suited for the neutrals.

Having remembered how to win – just – I felt we would now start challenging Chelsea again for top spot. But then we draw our next game at home against West Bromwich Albion before losing at Liverpool, the winning goal coming in injury time at the end of the game, leaving us five points adrift. It was hard to accept the change – unbeaten for 49 games then finding it a struggle to win again. That defeat at Old Trafford seemed to instil doubt in the team and expose a hitherto unseen mental fragility.

In December we started putting a run back together and won all our games except a 2-2 draw at home with Chelsea in a game we had to win. But our chances of retaining the Premier League finally evaporated early in the New Year. Manchester City held us to a draw at home before a defeat in the next game at Bolton, and then the final nail in the coffin when Manchester United came to Highbury on 1st February. There was a huge build-up to the game, even more so than usual, following the 'Battle of the Buffet' in October. Even before the players got out on to the pitch Vieira and Manchester United captain Roy Keane had been squaring up to each other in the tunnel. It proved to be an ugly, spiteful game, with Rooney escaping punishment after clearly abusing the referee, having already been booked earlier for persistent fouling, and with Silvestre later sent off for a head-butt on Freddie Ljungberg. But from leading 2–1, we lost the game 4–2. It was another of those dark moments that have punctuated my relationship with the team.

Somewhat surprisingly our performances improved after that, recovering well this time from disappointment. We remained unbeaten for the rest of the season, until the last game when we shockingly lost 2–1 at Birmingham City having levelled the score at 1–1 with just two minutes left to play. Fortunately it did not affect our final League position, second again, this time 12 points behind big-spending Chelsea but, happily, six points ahead of Manchester United. And in that final run-in there was the pleasure of beating Tottenham and Liverpool as well as enjoying a festival night of brilliant, breathtaking football resulting in the 7–0 demolition of Everton in our final home game of the season. Send them home wanting more seemed to be the motto that night. And there was still more to come.

As each season goes by the domestic cup competitions seem to lose the influence, the importance, they once enjoyed. Everything now is focused on the Premier League, and then within that, qualifying for the Champions League – not winning it, just qualifying, for the financial rewards are great, and without money it becomes impossible to finish high enough in the League to repeat the process. Regularly now we see teams fight all season for a Champions League place only to finish one place below and qualify for the Europa League instead. This secondary European competition does not offer the same financial rewards and often sees English teams viewing participation as a drain on their strength as the next League season gets underway. At home the lesser of the domestic cups, the League Cup, sees the top clubs often put out young teams with little or no first team experience, while lesser rated Premier League teams will also put out weakened teams to ensure they are fully prepared for the next Premier League fixtures. Yet, with only three domestic trophies available each season you would think more teams who know they are not going to win the Premier League would make an all out effort to win it. But they don't because of the fear of getting distracted in the League and finding themselves battling against relegation, because with relegation comes a vast reduction in revenue.

Under Arsène Wenger we have consistently put out young teams in the early rounds of the League Cup. They have built a remarkable record of beating apparently stronger teams in the competition before more experienced players are fed in as the competition progresses. However, in this season, early promise brought about by victories over Manchester City and Everton disappeared at the beginning of December. The draw sent us to renew our edgy rivalry with Manchester United at Old Trafford, where a 1-0 loss ended our progress in the competition for another year.

Away from domestic issues things initially progressed smoothly in Europe. Following our final Champions League group game in early December - a 5–1 home win over Rosenborg of Norway a week after this loss in the Carling Cup - we topped our group after a generally unspectacular campaign. The eagerly awaited draw for the last 16 of the competition then paired us with Bayern Munich. We had a poor game in the away leg, 3–0 down as the match approached its conclusion. But with two minutes left on the clock we clawed one back giving a final score of 3–1. Immediately I thought back to the 1970 European Fairs Cup final against Anderlecht when a late Ray Kennedy away goal set us up for ultimate victory. Now, if we could just beat Bayern 2–0 at Highbury we'd be through – it was game on. But actually it wasn't. Henry scored shortly after the hour of the return leg but we could not grab the all-important second goal. With our season unravelling our only chance of a trophy now rested with the FA Cup.

We moved through the opening rounds efficiently but not spectacularly, disposing of Stoke City and Wolves before

158

meeting Sheffield United at Highbury in the Fifth Round. The first game ended 1–1, with Dennis Bergkamp sent off in the first half and our opponents equalising in the final minute from the penalty spot. That hurt. That hurt a lot. But after a couple of scary moments in the replay we took control but couldn't score. The game ended 0–0 and went to penalties from which we emerged, with a huge sigh of relief from me, as winners.

In the quarter-final draw we landed Bolton Wanderers away, which was never going to be easy. After just three minutes, however, Freddie Ljungberg struck and we then dealt well with everything Bolton had to throw at us and even had time for Ljungberg to sky one over the bar in front of an empty goal in the final minute. Of course I wouldn't be quite so generous in my description of his miss had it cost if us the game!

The semi-final draw paired us with Blackburn Rovers and, for reasons best known to the FA, both semi-finals took place at Cardiff's Millennium Stadium. Then, to add further insult they decided our game would kick off at 12.15. The discussions did not take long. I didn't enjoy the trip to Cardiff at the best of times but the thought of needing to be there for a 12.15 kick-off screamed "No!" at me and my mates. And besides, if we won, we'd need to go back to Cardiff for the final a month later, and if we lost, well I wouldn't have wanted to witness it anyway. We weren't the only ones who turned our backs on the game – the attendance was only 52,000, meaning 20,000 empty seats.

As for the game, Blackburn, under Mark Hughes, set out to make it a bruising encounter. I can only presume they accepted that if it came down to football alone they could not compete. A goal by Robert Pirès in the first half gave us the lead which looked like being the final score – until Robin van Persie came on as a late substitute. By the time the referee blew for full-time eight minutes later Van Persie had netted twice and we'd won 3–0.

So Cardiff called again; our fourth FA Cup Final in five years. There was some irony for me in that. I lived just one stop away from Wembley on the Metropolitan Line, now our amazing sequence of appearances in the Cup Final coincided with the rebuilding of Wembley and the relocation of those games to Wales. So, with Cardiff back on the menu who would be our dish of the day? Why, Manchester United, of course. After victory way back in August in the FA Community Shield, two tense and tetchy defeats in the League and one in the Carling Cup had followed, and we were now about to complete our clean sweep of domestic dating. We just couldn't bear to be apart.

We followed our normal Cardiff preparations (ticket £65, programme £8.50) with one minor change. My friend Bill had left Cardiff but even in his absence he arranged parking for us. Cardiff was rainy and damp, which matched the mood of the majority of Manchester United fans that day. News had emerged during the week that American businessman and sports magnate Malcolm Glazer had taken over their club, securing ownership by settling massive debt on it. As football fans rarely let an opportunity to taunt rivals go by, all Gooners at the Final amused themselves as they took up their seats – at our 'lucky' end again - by riling our opposite numbers with chants of "USA! USA!" It was the same end we'd occupied when beating Chelsea and Southampton – a 'lucky' tag and an omen rolled into one.

With Thierry Henry injured we lacked a cutting edge up front and, as the game unfolded, it soon became clear that this was not going to be a pleasant experience. Manchester United attacked us from all angles while we, with our backs to wall, offered little threat. At times it appeared we were in danger of being overwhelmed but made it through to the respite of half-time without conceding a goal.   If I'd hoped for a change of fortune in the second half I was quickly disabused. Manchester United continued to create chances while we generally did not. Somehow, however, we were still in the game when the referee blew at the end of 90 minutes.

The general consensus of opinion now was that our only chance of winning would come if we could hold on for penalties. And so it proved. At the end of the additional half an hour the score remained unchanged; the official match statistics show we managed just one shot on target in the 120 minutes –a Robin van Persie free kick in extra time – and four

160

wide of the mark. Manchester United, meanwhile, racked up 20 shots with eight on target, keeping Lehmann on his toes throughout. Now, for the first time since 1912, the FA Cup Final had ended goalless (Barnsley v West Bromwich Albion should you need to know) and the match was to be decided by penalty kicks for the first time ever. Psychologically it seemed to me the team would not be overawed by this. Having been so outplayed in the game we were now on level terms with Manchester United, who themselves must have been troubled that it had come down to this.

Manchester United won the advantage and as the players prepared to take the penalties at 'their' end of the ground we looked on from high up behind the goal at the opposite end of the stadium. Just five kicks from agony or ecstasy. First man up to take a penalty was the man we loved to hate – Ruud van Nistelrooy. Boos and whistles rang out from the Arsenal end, but he scored. Then Lauren stepped forward for us and lashed the ball home. Next, Paul Scholes took the ball and hit it hard to Lehmann's right, but the 'keeper leapt the right way, got two hands to the ball and blocked his shot, prompting wild celebrations at our end of the ground. The pressure was now on Freddie Ljungberg, our next penalty taker, but Freddie scored with ease; cue more celebrations. Two penalties taken and advantage Arsenal. Manchester United scored from their remaining kicks, as did Robin van Persie and Ashley Cole, meaning that as Patrick Vieira prepared to take our fifth and final penalty the score was 4–4; if he scored we'd win the Cup, miss and it would be down to 'sudden death'. No pressure then. I think I was silently begging, pleading, repeating over and over again, "score, score, score!" And he did. Playing the captain's role to perfection, and facing the taunts, jeers, boos and whistles of the mass of Manchester United fans behind the goal, he calmly placed the ball on the spot. As the referee give him the signal he strode forward on those long legs of his to fire home the perfect penalty, just inside the post and beyond the reach of the diving, despairing 'keeper.

Both on the pitch and up in the stands anyone with Arsenal blood in their veins erupted as the tension of the occasion evaporated in an instant, to be replaced with joyous, bouncing, hugging, hysterical celebration. It was the 10th FA Cup win in Arsenal's history and I felt proud to have personally witnessed seven of those victories. Later though, as we walked away from the ground having enjoyed the celebrations, I couldn't help thinking about how we'd been outplayed and won on the lottery of penalty kicks. It mirrored our Jekyll and Hyde season. I didn't feel the same height of satisfaction and pleasure I had taken from those previous six triumphs. It was a strange feeling and it unsettled me a little. Now, in hindsight, I wonder if perhaps I sensed the team was coming to the end of its cycle. But at the time my overwhelming emotion was relief, relief that we had not ended the campaign empty handed having played such stunning, beautiful football at times during the season; that alone deserved its reward.

23

Leaving Home

The summer of 2005 is probably the first time I questioned how much longer I would continue as a season ticket holder. Rising costs and weekend disruptions were making me think. Something that in the past which would have been unthinkable was now allowed some consideration. I knew it wouldn't be now, but I recognised that time may come. I would certainly want to be a part of the move to the new stadium at Ashburton Grove, now confirmed that it would bear the name Emirates Stadium for 15 years, following the signing of a naming rights deal with Emirates Airlines. One wonders – and worries - what name it will bear next.

So, the season ahead – 2005/06 – marked the end of an era. At the close of the season the club would leave Highbury, home of Arsenal Football Club since 1913, and move to the new stadium, increasing our crowd capacity at a stroke from 38,000 to 60,000. To mark this occasion the club chose to change our now traditional red shirts with white sleeves to a solid dark 'red currant' colour to represent the dark red shirts originally worn when we first moved from Woolwich to Highbury. Personally I would have preferred if the team had played out the final season at our spiritual home in red and white, but selling replica shirts makes football clubs a lot of money, so why wouldn't they?

To be honest it was not one of our better seasons in the League, but it did give us a rousing end to send us away from Highbury on a high. That season we lost 11 games, the highest total in any season under Arsène Wenger and the highest total for 11 years. Things had changed a lot since the 'Invincibles' just two years earlier. There were of course outstanding

163

matches and moments through the season that made it all worthwhile, matches like the 7–0 humbling of Middlesbrough at Highbury in January. Henry notched another hat-trick that day and in the process equalled Cliff Bastin's record of 150 League goals which had stood since 1939, a record he claimed outright ownership of two weeks later. He had already taken Ian Wright's record of being highest goal scorer in the club's history when he netted twice in the Champions League in October away at Sparta Prague. He was legend. The 5–0 beating of Aston Villa at home in April also sticks in the mind, which included two glorious goals from Henry and one from Van Persie.

While we had been inconsistent in the League there would also be no domestic cup glory, our runs in the League (Carling) Cup and FA Cup both ending in the last week of January. Fielding an under-strength team at Bolton in the 4th Round of the FA Cup we paid the price, losing 1–0 to a late goal, while in the Carling Cup we lost the two-legged semi-final against Wigan on away goals after Wigan scored a minute from the end of extra time at Highbury in the second leg. Fortunately I was out of the country at the time. Dumped out of the domestic cups and inconsistent in the League, all my thoughts now turned to the exciting distraction of the Champions League.

Progress through the group stage was efficient although generally unspectacular, as evidenced by the two games against Champions League minnows FC Thun of Switzerland. We won the home leg 2–1 with a last minute goal from Dennis Bergkamp and the away leg 1–0 with a penalty two minutes from time. But we disposed of Sparta Prague comfortably home and away, and an away win at Ajax early in the competition meant the return leg, which was the final group game, was of little consequence. It ended 0-0, we topped the group and both sides progressed through to the knock-out stage. The days when we played our games at Wembley and struggled to register a win in the competition, seemed a distant memory. But a rather daunting obstacle now barred further progress; an appointment with Real Madrid for our first ever competitive pairing.

The run up to the game was less than ideal, held, as we were, to a home draw by Bolton and losing to Liverpool at Anfield. Now we were off to the Bernabéu to face a Madrid team that included Zinedine Zidane, Roberto Carlos, David Beckham, Ronaldo (the chubby Brazilian one), Raul and Casillas. As we prepared to face these giants of the game circumstances forced us to field an unconvincing defence which included Eboué, Senderos and Flamini, aware also that no English team had ever beaten Real Madrid on their home patch. The youthful bench reflected the threadbare nature of the squad that night too, with Walcott, Djourou, Diaby, Song and Lupoli making up the numbers. Madrid must have felt confident. Yet we also had Reyes and Fabregas in the starting line-up, two players who knew what it was to face Madrid, and of course we had Thierry Henry.

I always think watching a game on television is far more stressful than being there, but TV it was that night. Incredibly we came roaring out of the blocks, creating a number of good chances in the opening 10 minutes. Then the nerves kicked in again and I started to think, was that it, will we get another chance? We needed to take one of those, but we continued to play well and just a couple of minutes into the second half Henry received a short pass in the centre circle, looked up and started a run towards the Madrid goal. Immediately three defenders closed in around him but he shrugged off two challenges and skipped over a third before switching on his turbo-pack and accelerating towards the goal as only he could. As he sped into the penalty area a fourth defender closed in, but before he could make his challenge Henry had struck the ball across the 'keeper and into the far corner of the net. Unbelievable, and 'one nil to the Arsenal' was the final score. A truly historic performance and result, and an overwhelming feeling of pride in what the team achieved that night, in becoming the first English team to beat Real in Madrid. The goal, the night, both will live long in my memories. But in the meantime, of course, there was still the small matter of the return leg at Highbury to come.

The return leg proved an enthralling encounter, with Real forced to press for a goal while we were not a team to sit back and defend. Both teams created chances, both goalkeepers made saves but when the final whistle blew the score remained 0–0 and we were through to the last eight. Elsewhere Barcelona beat Chelsea and Benfica knocked out Liverpool, meaning we were the last English club still involved in the competition.

The draw for the next round paired us with Fabio Capello's Juventus who at the time were proudly sitting clear at the top of Serie A. Within their ranks they now had our former captain and inspiration Patrick Vieira. Vieira's last kick for us had been scoring the winning penalty against Manchester United to win the FA Cup. Now he was about to return to Highbury, in a Juventus shirt. Vieira had been an inspirational figure for us, so I felt mixed emotions as the night of the first leg at Highbury approached; I looked forward to seeing him on the pitch again, but was also aware of his capabilities. I should not have been concerned. That night we were magnificent and 18-year-old Cesc Fabregas put in a performance that simply overshadowed Vieira and the rest of the Italian club's midfield. For Vieira it became clear it was not to be his night when Robert Pirès, never known for his tackling, slid in on Vieira as he advanced and emerged with the ball. With Vieira left on his backside and looking bewildered, Pirès raced away before slotting the ball through to Fabregas who, with a matador-like flourish, side-sidestepped a defender and scored. As we celebrated madly, everyone recognised the significance of that goal – the King is dead, long live the King. A second goal, scored by Henry and set up by Fabregas ensured a 2–0 victory. The frustration felt by the Juventus players boiled over in the last few minutes resulting in two red cards, meaning both players would miss the return leg. It was a fantastic night, and I began to believe, really believe, that we could reach the final. A lifetime's dream was within reach.

The return leg in Turin did nothing to destroy those dreams. We played out a relatively comfortable 0–0 draw and had chances to win it. We had reached the semi-final where we would play Villarreal of Spain. If we reached the final our opponents would be either Barcelona or AC Milan.

The first leg against Villarreal at Highbury was a tense, tight affair, nothing like the game against Juventus. In the end a goal from Kolo Touré just before half-time secured a 1–0 win, ensuring the second leg would be tough. And so it was. Villarreal had us pinned back on the defensive for long periods of the match as they strove to bring the tie level on aggregate. It did not make pleasant TV viewing. It seemed only a matter of time before they achieved their goal, but half-time came and went and the outstanding minutes slowly, very, very slowly, diminished. As the nerve-jangling tie edged into the final couple of minutes we were hanging on but it looked like we were going to make it; then Gael Clichy jumped with a Villarreal forward who crumpled to the ground as though shot with a .44 Magnum. The referee pointed to the spot. Penalty. No, not now, not that! As Juan Roman Riquelme placed the ball on the spot, close-up television pictures showed the Argentine midfielder narrowing his eyes like a Wild West gunslinger of old. Riquelme v Lehmann: at stake, a place in the Champions League Final. The moment seemed to be endless, elevating the tension to unbearable heights. Riquelme made his move but Lehmann was quicker on the draw. He threw himself to his left – and blocked the shot. And then it was over. We were going to play in the Champions League Final.

Ever since I'd watched grainy black and white images of Celtic winning the European Cup on TV back in 1967 I'd dreamt of Arsenal playing in the final. Every year since then I had watched the final and had even been to the match in 1992 and 1999. I looked on with envy when Liverpool and Nottingham Forest, Aston Villa and Manchester United brought the trophy back to England; and now my team, who I'd followed through the good years and the bad, who'd made me cry and made me deliriously, uncontrollably happy, had reached that pinnacle. It was hard to take in. But it was real: the venue Paris, the date, 17 May 2006.

Before then of course there remained the small issue of saying farewell to Highbury. I felt I needed to mark the occasion in some way, to help preserve my memories, so decided I would go up to the ground early before each game as the season drew to a close to photograph the stadium and match day atmosphere inside and outside the ground. I made my first photo-call before the game against Aston Villa on 1 April, taking photos around the East Stand, North Bank, Avenell Road and Highbury Hill, as the crowd built up. Two weeks later, before the game against West Bromwich Albion, I included Arsenal station, inside the West Stand and then the stadium itself as the crowd began to take up their seats and the team warmed up on the pitch. Then finally before the very last game, against Wigan on 7 May, I strolled down to *The Gunners* pub, then back to the ground. In Highbury Hill residents had strung lines across the road from the upper windows of their houses from which they hung Arsenal shirts and flags, it looked really festive; everyone was smiling and, like me, taking their final photographs.

Inside, the stadium looked fantastic. On each seat the club had laid a t-shirt – red or white bearing the legend "I was there...", and even blue ones for the Wigan fans in the corner. When pulled on we painted the whole stadium in broad living stripes of red and white. Even the pitch received special attention with the word Highbury and 1913-2006 revealed in the rolling of the turf. This was all great, but we could not forget the importance of the match. Besides it being the last match at Highbury we actually found ourselves in fifth place, one point behind Tottenham of all teams, and therefore outside Champions League qualification. In order to claim that important fourth place we had to achieve a better result than Tottenham who were playing at West Ham.

Rumours were rife since lunch time that Tottenham were trying to get their game postponed, claiming their players had food poisoning through eating a dodgy lasagne, much to the outrage of the hotel where they had their meal. This was really worrying news. If our game went ahead and they played theirs at a later date it would give them the advantage of knowing exactly what they needed to do to finish above us. The general consensus among Arsenal fans was that Tottenham had 'bottled it' – knowing that fourth place was theirs to lose. When the news finally came through that the FA had told Tottenham they must play there was huge relief – and much humour – around the ground. And so the time had come, the very last match at Highbury began.

It was clear right from the start that the team was focused, determined to do their bit and go for the win. We made a great start with Robert Pirès poking home after just eight minutes; a great start that quickly became perfect when news spread rapidly around the stadium that West Ham had taken the lead against Tottenham. But even before we had settled down again Wigan equalised. Surely that had no place in the script on our special day. The team seemed a little shaken by this development. Then, just after the half hour, Wigan scored again. A deep audible groan of 38,000 tortured souls resonated from all sides of the ground. At times like that you turn to Thierry Henry; cometh the hour, cometh the man. Two minutes later Henry raced through the Wigan back four and slotted the ball home. Emotions in the stadium immediately cranked back up, only to come crashing down again as we heard that Tottenham had equalised at almost exactly the same moment that Henry scored. At half-time both games were level meaning Tottenham were still one point ahead of us, and holding on to fourth spot.

The fears we all held as the second half began became reality for a moment. Word sped excitedly around the stadium that West Ham had a penalty, but then we heard that former Tottenham hero Teddy Sherringham was about to take it. Would Sherringham destroy the dreams of his former club? Moments later a groan announced that the Tottenham keeper had saved the kick. Although no one in the stadium had seen the penalty there wasn't a person there who didn't think 'fix!' Then, however, just before the hour things took a far more positive turn. A shocking back pass from a Wigan defender left Henry alone with just the 'keeper in front of him. A sidestep to the right removed his opponent from the equation and Henry walked the ball into the net. Now we were buzzing again; if the scores remained like this we'd claim fourth from Tottenham. Henry, however, wasn't finished. About 20 minutes later the referee awarded us a penalty for a foul on Ljungberg. Only one man was going to take that. Henry placed the ball on the spot in front of the North Bank, then dispatched it comfortably into the net to make the score 4-2, scoring a hat-trick in the final game. Henry knelt, kissed the turf then raised his arms to the crowd in salute. Rumours were rife that Henry would leave for Barcelona that summer and many took this gesture as his way of saying goodbye. I preferred to think he was saying "That's it, no more; the honour of scoring the final goal is mine." And so it was. Just five minutes later, a murmur grew into a roar as the news surged around Highbury – Tottenham were losing 2–1. The final ten minutes of play were a joy. Wigan had nothing left to offer, Dennis Bergkamp came on as substitute and played his final game before retiring, and we almost scored twice more. Tottenham were unable to get the two goals they then needed. We'd won our very last game at Highbury, gained our place in the Champions League and denied Tottenham their dream of qualifying for the competition for the very first time. Not a bad 90 minutes work, and what better way to bring down the curtain on 93 years of football at Highbury.

After the game the club laid on a farewell celebration which included a parade of numerous former players and legends from years gone by as well as the current squad and management. Roger Daltrey of The Who sang to the crowd and other celebrity fans appeared too while four giant images of the club's badge – past and present – were laid out on the pitch. Then, an electronic clock that had been running all season counted down the last seconds of the stadium's life and as it reached zero an explosion of fireworks shook the old stadium to its foundations.

The end had come and it was time to go. Before I left the stadium for the last time I couldn't help thinking back on the memories it had given me. I remembered my Dad bringing me for the first time and how he paid for my early season tickets, and I remembered my grandfather who I sat with at every home game for seven years before he died. They had made everything possible. I thought about the friends that had become part of 'my' Highbury over the years. And of course I thought of the great games, great moments and great players that I'd seen too. I'd been coming to Highbury since 1967 and had sat in the same seat in the West Stand for 37 years: from boyhood to middle age, through all life's ups and downs, Highbury had been a constant in my life. I was sad to say goodbye. As I finally left the stadium I looked across at the immense new stadium rising above the rooftops. A helicopter swept overhead trailing a large Arsenal flag bearing the words "Emirates Stadium…a bright new future." I hoped those words would prove right – starting with Paris in ten days time.

24

Springtime in Paris

The 2006 Champions League Final in Paris meant a first return to the French capital since the nightmare of Real Zaragoza back in 1995. This time the venue was the country's premier sporting venue, the Stade de France, built for the 1998 World Cup. I did my best to ignore the fact that the chosen date was the sixth anniversary of our miserable defeat by Galatasaray in the 2000 UEFA Cup Final. We applied for and got four tickets which meant I'd be going with Prinders, Steph and Dickie. A slight complication arose in that Dickie had booked a family holiday for that week in Italy, never imagining at the time of booking that we'd reach the Final. Dickie planned his own route to Paris while the rest of us booked with the Arsenal Travel Club. The news that we would need to check-in at Stansted Airport at 4.00am on the morning of the game was sobering. I caught an airport bus in the middle of the night, which Steph picked-up en route, and arrived zombie-like at the airport to meet Prinders who'd driven. It didn't take too long before things started to go wrong.

After a seemingly endless wait our time finally came and, packed onto buses, we drove across the tarmac to board our aircraft. But when we drew up alongside our plane nothing happened. No one had thought of supplying any steps for us to board the aircraft and so there we remained, crushed together in a situation familiar to any rush-hour Tube traveller. It took about 30 minutes to find some steps, only then were we granted release from our temporary prison; not a great start.

Once we landed in Paris we took the Metro and headed into the city, emerging into the daylight again at Notre Dame. From there we strolled down the Seine towards the Eiffel

Tower and stopped off at a bar for a beer. It was while we were there that we heard from Dickie; he'd left his match ticket with us so we could sell it on if anything happened to prevent him getting to the game. It was not good news. Dropped by his wife and kids at a local station in Italy he caught a 9.00am train to Nice where he was booked on a flight to Paris. His train was due to arrive in Nice at 11.00am allowing two generous hours for the four-mile onward journey to the airport. It all fitted together rather well – except that the 'two-hour' train journey took over three hours.

At Nice Dickie grabbed a taxi and explained his predicament to the driver, who turned out to be a football fan and had a soft spot for Arsenal. He recognised the urgency of the situation and responded accordingly. The ensuing journey to the airport was the stuff of Hollywood movies as the driver weaved through the Nice traffic at 90mph while looking backwards and explaining the recent injustice the local team had suffered in the final of the French League Cup. A shaken Dickie arrived at the airport in one piece just in time to see easyJet close the gates on his flight. His options were stark: buy a one-way ticket with Air France for £500 or wait five hours for the next easyJet flight. He took the waiting option, and that's when his call disturbed our pleasant beer in Paris. Dickie felt confident the timings would still work, but as we held his ticket any delays could impact on us too.

After our beer, and while we digested the news, we strolled to the Eiffel Tower which appeared to have been annexed by Spain that day, then crossed the Seine to the FanZone which UEFA always put on to amuse fans on the day of the Final. Again, it was mainly Barcelona fans there too, but you didn't need to be a genius to work out where the majority of our fans were! We carried on up to the Arc de Triomphe and finally began to find more Gooners. Perhaps we were all looking for symbolism in that monument. Then, as we started looking for food we thought we had seen a 'sign' – we found ourselves in Rue Arsène Houssaye! The Arc de Triomphe *and* the Rue Arsène close by; what could possibly go wrong.

Conversation was a little subdued during our meal as we pondered what we did not know. We'd heard nothing from

173

Dickie for some hours, although during the last contact we'd agreed to meet him at our entrance to the stadium. We must have reached the ground around 6.30pm, with kick off set for 8.45pm. In fact we had just arrived when we next heard from Dickie; he'd only just landed at the airport. But he calculated that the Metro journey - one train, no changes - would take about 30 minutes, then a final mile from the station to the stadium. As he said, "What could possibly go wrong?"

An hour later there was still no sign of him; we were getting more concerned and stressed. Prinders couldn't reach Dickie on the phone and Prinders, in particular, is a man who likes to savour the atmosphere of a big match build up. This was not what any of us wanted. And while we waited we watched the comings and goings of thousands of fans. Some, without tickets, unsuccessfully trying to talk their way past security guards, while one took his chance by climbing over the spiked perimeter fence. He was painfully unsuccessful. While attempting to breach the outer defences he fell or slipped, managing to firmly spear his thigh on one of the spikes in the process. It took a very long time before a medical team was able to cut him free.

At 8.00pm there was still no word. We all wanted to be inside the ground now but couldn't abandon our meeting point. Prinders was on telephone duty but desperately wanted a programme so I offered to go in and try and buy some while Steph and he continued to wait. Once inside, however, there was not a sign of a programme for sale. I took up a position on the outer steps of the stadium from where I could just see the others, both of them staring off into the distance, waiting and hoping. Dickie's Metro journey, delayed constantly by lengthy hold-ups between stations, took almost two hours. Fortunately, as a keen runner, the final mile didn't faze him. Phone working again, he told Prinders he was on his way so Steph left him and I met her on the steps. She looked distraught, Prinders was so angry she was convinced he was going to thump Dickie when he finally arrived. Steph and I took up our seats less than 10 minutes before kick off – Prinders arrived as the Champions League anthem faded and Dickie, bathed in sweat and looking like he was about to die, slumped into his seat next to me moments later almost unable to speak. I have never experienced a more stressful pre-match experience in all my life. Then, before any of us had a chance to draw breath, the game kicked off.

We started off well but 17 minutes in disaster struck. Samuel Eto'o broke through and, as Lehmann rushed out, the Barcelona striker pushed the ball beyond him leaving an exposed Lehmann to bring him down just outside the penalty area. The referee blew instantly for a foul, too quickly to see the move end in a Barcelona goal a split second later. So the goal didn't stand but we all knew Lehmann's continued presence on the pitch was very much in doubt. I held my breath. The referee then raised the red card high and, like a death sentence, appeared to kill my dream stone dead. As Lehmann trudged from the field Wenger withdrew Robert Pirès to allow Almunia to take over in goal. Pirès was about to leave the club at the end of his contract, this was his last game. He had been such a brilliant player for us, but this, he later admitted was the worst moment of his career. As distraught as Pirès must have been, I felt like I'd been punched in the stomach as we faced up to the prospect of playing over 70 more minutes with only ten men against Barcelona. I was desolate. Yet a storm did not break over the beleaguered team. In fact the complete opposite occurred. Having weathered some 20 of those minutes after the sending off we earned a fortunate free-kick outside the Barcelona penalty area on the right. Henry hit a cross into the box where Sol Campbell rose majestically above his marker to power the ball into the net. The Arsenal end of the stadium, bedecked in yellow, erupted – and to me, just for a moment, it reminded me of a great saucepan of bubbling custard! When half-time arrived the score remained 1-0. Now we had hope...oh.

As the second half wore on Almunia made a couple of good saves while we continued to create chances too. Then in the 70th minute Henry, in a perfect position, contrived to gently pass the ball straight at the Barcelona 'keeper. If he had scored I feel sure we would have held on to win the Champions League. But the score remained 1–0 and just five minutes later the Barcelona substitute, Henrik Larsson, flicked the ball out to Eto'o who scored, beating Almunia at the near post. Five minutes later Belletti, bursting forward, took a pass from Larsson and scored a second from a narrow angle through Almunia's legs. An amazing, resilient and heroic performance shattered in five cruel minutes. There was no way back. The descent from ultimate glory to the emptiness of defeat was complete. Devastated, I remember wondering if we'd ever get another chance. It hurt, it hurt so much.

After the game I headed straight back to the airport with Prinders and Steph, as instructed by the Travel Club; Dickie went off to find a bar and get a beer – his flight back to Nice wasn't until 6.30 in the morning. After much hanging around we eventually boarded our aircraft much later than scheduled, only to discover that a few people were missing and we wouldn't depart until everyone was there. And so we waited, and we waited. One group finally rolled up, having been for a beer in Paris, claiming, unconvincingly, that they didn't know they had to return to the airport straight after the game. But even then we weren't ready to go – there was still one person missing. He finally arrived after we'd been sitting on the aircraft for well over an hour. He looked like one of those people you hope doesn't sit next to you on the bus; he was not warmly welcomed.

Finally back in England I felt my ordeal must surely be over, but the day wasn't done with me yet. After we landed at Stansted the aircraft taxied to a halt and everyone made the usual rush to disembark. But nothing happened. Angry voices demanded to know why the doors didn't open; we were very late back, we'd all been awake for over 24 hours, we were tired, miserable and just wanted to get home. The reply, when it came, brought a groan of disbelief. As on the flight out there was a problem with the stairs. This time the ones provided were too short to reach the exit door! So desperate were people to get away that some wanted to jump down the six feet to the shortened steps, but the airline crew refused to allow it. With increasing frustration we remained trapped on the plane for almost another hour, until longer steps were located and finally we gained our freedom. Oh how we suffer for our team.

Back in Paris Dickie eventually got a taxi to the airport at 4.00am and grabbed a few minutes sleep on a bench before throwing up just prior to boarding his plane at 6.30am – doing a 'Tottenham' and blaming it on something he ate during his long wait. Eventually he got back to Italy a broken man. Exhausted, ill, unwashed and dishevelled he emerged from the railway station. There, oblivious to his sufferings, his happy and relaxed family welcomed him back with the cheery greeting, "Well, did you win?" It had not been a great day out for the fans.

25

Home Is Where the Heart Is

Over summer 2006 I worried about the direction the club was heading. I worried a lot. Pirès and Bergkamp were no more and Sol Campbell moved on to Portsmouth. Pascal Cygan left too and José Antonio Reyes went on loan to Real Madrid with Julio Baptista joining us on loan in exchange. Then followed an extremely unpleasant episode; Ashley Cole's acrimonious departure to Chelsea. At that moment it became clear just how far some players now distanced themselves from the supporters who cheered them on each week and sung their names in admiration. In the painfully drawn out transfer saga – as they always seem to be at Arsenal - Cole informed the football world of an offer Arsenal made him of £55,000 a week when he'd wanted £60,000. In his book *My Defence* he said that when his agent phoned him with the offer he "nearly swerved off the road…I was so incensed. I was trembling with anger." Now Cole may well have considered this was not a great offer in football terms but to the average member of the population these were fantasy figures. The average *annual* salary in this country is about half the sum the club were offering Cole for a week's work, so why should ordinary people – the people who paid to watch him each week – feel any sympathy for a man who in the real world was rich beyond comprehension. He handled the whole thing incredibly badly and became hated by Arsenal fans for it, earning himself the sobriquet 'Cashley' in the process and an enduring reputation for greed and self-interest. As a fan I felt badly let down that a player I had admired for so long and who had come up through the Arsenal ranks cared more about what he could earn elsewhere rather than playing for Arsenal. I know, I know, he was just doing a job and trying to maximise his earnings, but as a fan it is hard to be objective about things like that. But one thing was clear, football was changing and Cole brought those changes into the spotlight.

So, of the 18-man squad named for the Champions League Final in May, five moved on that summer. Besides Baptista the only other new faces to come in were William Gallas, who joined as part of the deal taking Cole to Chelsea, and Tomas Rosicky enrolled from Borussia Dortmund. The squad seemed weaker.

In preparation for the move to the new stadium, the club invited season ticket holders to view the seating plans and choose similar locations to those they held at Highbury. We took advantage to draw together the individual seats Dickie, Prinders and I held and Andy joined us, along with Bob and Neil who sat behind me. Steph and Gerry preferred to maintain their Highbury centre block status whereas we were in the 'cheap seats' of wing block.

My first visit to the new stadium came in July when it hosted a testimonial for Dennis Bergkamp, a fantastic, inspirational and loyal player who had thrilled Arsenal fans for 11 years. In every way he was the complete antithesis of Ashley Cole. As at the last game at Highbury, everyone received a commemorative t-shirt, in red, white or orange this time, which created bold stripes of colour around the Emirates, contrasting dramatically with the outside of the stadium and the public areas which all seemed rather grey and bland. But its sheer size made it an imposing, impressive sight and the playing surface looked fantastic.

The first half of the game featured current players of Arsenal and Ajax while the second half saw the introduction of a cavalcade of legends. They all came back for Dennis: Seaman, Dixon, Winterburn, Bould, Overmars, Petit, Parlour, Wright, Vieira, Kanu and many more, while Ajax fielded such giants of the game as Johan Cruyff and Marco van Basten. What other player could draw such a response? It was a great occasion, only spoilt for me by the fact that Dennis didn't score one final goal in the 2–1 win, but he was a giant of the game and we were privileged to have him as an Arsenal player.

I hadn't sat in my own seat against Ajax so the first league game of the season against Aston Villa introduced me to my new home, on the east side of the pitch directly in line with the edge of the six-yard box at the north end of the stadium. In choosing the seat we'd reckoned on the team continuing to play the second half of games attacking the north end, and it had the bonus of being closest to Arsenal station. So, we had the shiny new stadium, the pitch looked superb, now we just needed a win to make us feel at home.

As has often been the case since, we huffed and puffed but couldn't break the opposition down, taking one too many passes much of the time instead of shooting. And what's more, Villa recorded the first competitive goal at our new home when Olof Mellberg earned himself that honour, heading home after an error of judgment by Lehmann early in the second half. That was not in the script. Anxiety built as we struggled to get back on terms, then, with just over 15 minutes left to play Wenger brought on Theo Walcott for his League debut – Walcott, who Sven Goren Eriksen had bizarrely taken to the World Cup in Germany that summer, although he'd never played a first team game for us. Walcott's blistering pace had an immediate impact and in the 83rd minute his cross flicked off a defender's head and fell to Gilberto Silva, at the corner of the six-yard box, who lashed a rising drive into the net. The stadium roared into life, or rather it was a mixture of roar and - certainly from me anyway - an outburst of relief. Sadly we weren't able to push on and grab the winner that would have made it a perfect day. The new era had begun disappointingly.

It was in fact a rather strange start in general; we struggled to get our first win, then when it did come – in our fourth game – it was against Manchester United at Old Trafford. It was a well deserved win too; the crucial goal scored six minutes from time by Emmanuel Adebayor who'd joined us eight months earlier in January 2006 from Monaco. Like Cole, Adebayor was another who later seamlessly made the transition from hero to villain.

Our first home win in the League finally – thankfully – came at the third attempt when we beat Sheffield United on 23 September. But doubt, tension and anxiety were the emotions I

180

felt at half-time with the score still 0–0; we were playing well but couldn't break down the opposition's defence. Just after the hour, tension and anxiety were replaced by relief as first William Gallas lashed the ball home after an Henry chipped pass was flicked up by Fabregas, then, five minutes later, Henry's menacing cross diverted off a Sheffield United defender for an own goal. With all the tension dispelled we continued to attack and, with ten minutes left to play, Henry got the goal he deserved, heading home from a pinpoint Eboué cross. That day I went home happy from the Emirates stadium for the first time that season. I, like everyone else, hoped we had turned the corner but it proved a faltering start. Of the first seven League games at home we drew four by the same 1–1 score line, and in each of those games the opposition scored first. It was a very frustrating period. The last of those draws – against Newcastle in November – formed part of the annual autumnal League slump, along with consecutive away defeats at Bolton and Fulham, leaving us lying in sixth place. Happily the slump ended as we entered December and faced Tottenham on their first visit to the Emirates.

As I approached the stadium that day I walked in over the north bridge and found myself behind two Tottenham fans heading for the ground. For some reason their eyes were drawn to the flats built above the Arsenal Museum complex which, inexplicably, one of them thought was the stadium. He looked at it for a few moments before concluding, "Well it's nothing special is it," at which point his friend gestured silently in the other direction, towards the looming presence of the stadium. Now he could have reflected on the similarity of the stadium to Benfica's Estadio da Luz in Lisbon or how the metal and glass clad façade rises to surround a sweeping wave-like modern seating bowl, but he didn't. Instead, in awe, he uttered just one word. That single exclamation began with F and rhymed with truck!

As for the game, we were 2–0 up by half-time with a goal from Adebayor and a penalty from Gilberto Silva, who added a second penalty later to give us a joyous 3–0 win – and complete an extraordinary sequence of results. With eight

League games now played at the Emirates we had won four, all by 3–0 and drawn four, all by a 1–1 score line.

Yet, even this result didn't give the boost we needed to make the new stadium a place for opponents to fear. Portsmouth held on for draw in the next home game, having grabbed a two goal lead in a pattern that was becoming tediously repetitive. Blackburn, our next visitors, took an early lead too, but this time there was to be no mistake and with a late flurry of goals the team grew a 3-1 half time lead into a most welcome 6–2 victory.

By the end of December we were in fifth place, just outside the Champions League qualifying zone, but Manchester United were looking favourites for the title. In other competitions though, we were doing rather well. We topped our Champions League group and were through to the quarter-finals of the League (Carling) Cup.

In January the vagaries of Cup football presented us with two trips to play Liverpool at Anfield: on 6 January we met in the 3rd Round of the FA Cup, then three days later we returned in the Carling Cup. They proved an amazing few days.

The FA Cup game was remarkable, a unique collector's item in the form of a brace of goals of the highest quality from Tomas Rosicky, the first a curling volley and the second he smashed home after shaking off the attentions of six Liverpool players. Watching the game on television I was entranced. Liverpool came storming back in the second half and pulled one back with 20 minutes to go, and I felt it inevitable that they'd score another and maybe even go on to win. But thankfully Thierry Henry didn't think like me. With six minutes to play he embarrassed Carragher in a chase for the ball before strolling through three Liverpool defenders and stroking the ball home to win the game 3–1. A fantastic result and an exciting performance, but this was just the starter, we had the main course to follow on Wednesday.

As was Arsène Wenger's way in the League Cup, he made a number of changes for this game, but it didn't affect the result which was even more emphatic. A wonderful performance by Jérémie Aliadière, whose career had suffered through numerous injuries, and four goals by Julio "Beast" Baptista resulted in an extraordinary 6–3 victory.

After the excitement of Anfield our FA Cup run fizzled out in February at Blackburn Rovers, but the League Cup win at Liverpool led to a two-legged semi-final against Tottenham with us eventually coming out on top 5-3 over the two legs. That win gave us a place in the Final against Chelsea. I now faced a dilemma. I had been to every final we had qualified for since 1970 but now, for the first time, I questioned whether I wanted to go. The venue was Cardiff – again – and I really didn't enjoy the journeys to Cardiff. Then Wenger made it clear he didn't intend changing his policy - even in the final – of fielding a second string team against the experience of Chelsea. Here was a chance to win a trophy – albeit one that Wenger clearly didn't rate highly – but it was important to the fans. The club of course still expected the fans to be there but Wenger chose not to play on a level field – I thought that showed a lack of respect to us. I made the difficult decision not to go to the final, breaking a run that had extended for 37 years. I could not accept the fact that the club was not going to give it their best shot; I could not accept that mentality. The day of the game was difficult for me though, dominated by a feeling of guilt for not being there to support the team. As the afternoon wore on, Chelsea cancelled out our early goal and, although we played remarkably well considering the different experience levels of the two teams, Chelsea eventually scored a second and took the Cup. My only consolation on this rather depressing day came in knowing that I didn't have to face the frustration of sitting in the endless traffic jams queuing to get out of Cardiff after the game; it was, however, only a very small consolation.

Earlier that week we had played the away leg of our last-16 Champions League tie against PSV of Holland, and lost 1–0. It meant that our whole season now depended on turning that scoreline around in the home leg. That night, when it came, was one of cruel disappointment. The scores remained level at half time with the opposition goalkeeper Heurelho Gomes – who later moved to Tottenham – repelling everything we threw at him. Having seen us struggle to break down teams at the Emirates all season, I was left feeling nervous and uncomfortable during the break.

In the second half, just before the hour, luck took a hand when an Adebayor header hit PSV defender Alex and bounced off him into the net. With scores now level on aggregate we pushed on for a second goal which would give us the tie. The momentum seemed to be with us as the clock ticked down and I felt sure that if the match went into extra time we'd come out on top. However, with seven minutes left to play, Alexander Hleb stupidly got involved in a wrestling match with an opposing player by the corner flag. From the resulting free-kick Alex, on loan from Chelsea, rose above our defence to score his second goal of the night, this time, unfortunately, in our net. It was a sickening, gut-wrenching moment. In the space of ten depressing days we had been knocked out of the FA Cup, lost the final of the Carling Cup and then been dumped out of the Champions League. It was a very subdued journey home that night.

The rest of the season passed without note. It was plainly average; we won four games, drew four and lost three. One of those losses rubbed just a little more salt into the open wound of our first season at the new stadium. West Ham inflicted our first defeat at the Emirates – just as they had been responsible for the last defeat at Highbury. Although a hugely disappointing end to the season we did still manage to secure fourth place and so qualify for the Champions League once more – but finished a disconcerting 21 points behind Manchester United even though we had beaten them home and away. I looked forward to a summer break away from the Emirates, it hadn't won me over.

That summer, after a ceaseless public wooing, Thierry Henry finally decided to quit the club and move to Barcelona. It did not come as a surprise to anyone, but it still cast a dark shadow over me as I waited for the start of the new season. He will probably remain the greatest player ever to play for us. It is hard to imagine that we will ever have the privilege of watching a finer player. Freddie Ljungberg also left after an injury restricted season and moved to West Ham. With their departure just three regular starters from the 'Invincibles' of

2003/4 season, remained: Jens Lehmann, Gilberto Silva and Kolo Touré. We invested in three players at the same time: Eduardo, a striker from Dinamo Zagreb, Bacary Sagna, a defender from Auxerre and Lukasz Fabianski, a goalkeeper from Legia Warsaw. We paid out significantly less on new players than we made in the sales of our existing players, which was now the worrying norm. The financial demands of the new stadium were clear to see.

I renewed my season ticket, as I always did, but I doubted whether I'd see much improvement in the coming months. But improvement there was and in fact we should have won the League, but in the end the season became 'the one that got away.'

Despite early first day trauma at home to Fulham, going one down in the first minute to rekindle memories of all those dispiriting games of the previous season, we fought back and scored twice, to my huge relief, right at the end of the game. It was the beginning of a storming start to the 2007/08 season. Two League wins and a draw in August as well as comfortable progress through the Champions League play off against Sparta Prague boosted the spirits. Then, in September, we played six games, in the League, Carling Cup and Champions League, winning all, including a stirring 3–1 victory at Tottenham with a stunning goal from Adebayor to complete the scoring. That goal ultimately won the award presented by the BBC's *Match of the Day* for Goal of the Season. Adebayor then went on to register a hat-trick against Derby County in a 5–0 win in the next game. It seemed Adebayor had inherited the goal scoring boots so recently vacated by Henry and was about to elevate himself into the pantheon of Arsenal heroes. Or so it appeared at the time.

As we entered October I feared the traditional autumn slump would derail our early season promise, but we sailed through the month winning six of our seven games and drawing the other, ending the month on top of the League. That run featured a record equalling 7–0 pounding of Slavia Prague in the Champions League and a win at Sheffield United in the Carling Cup. We looked confident and dominant. Our excellent domestic form continued through November as we built up a three-point lead over Manchester United by the end of the month. Earlier though it looked like Manchester United would bring a halt to our unbeaten start to the season when leading at the Emirates in the final seconds of the game, only for William Gallas to grab a late, late equaliser and bring wild celebration around the stadium. Although it was just a draw, coming so dramatically late, it felt like a win. I left the stadium and became absorbed into a great buoyant crowd edging towards Arsenal station in a jubilant, celebratory mood. The team really looked like it meant business.

As December dawned the fixture list seemed daunting, with six of our nine fixtures away from home. We lost our first game in the League that month – away at Middlesbrough - but won four (beating Chelsea and Tottenham again) and drew two others in the League while winning our Carling Cup quarter-final as well as qualifying again for the last 16 of the Champions League. Our final game of the year saw us win 4–1 at Everton with two confidently taken goals by Eduardo, his first in the League. This was something new and it looked like he would offer an additional goal threat for the second half of the season. We ended the year on top of the League and two points clear of Manchester United. I felt that 2008 held the promise of great things to come.

January had generally gone well except for a slightly embarrassing defeat at Tottenham in the second-leg of the Carling Cup semi-final when Wenger rested a number of first-team regulars and we lost the game 5–1. Despite the nature of our team that day Tottenham fans celebrated as though they'd just won the League. So long had it been since they'd last beaten us – a run of 20 unsullied games - they even released a DVD in celebration. As far as many Tottenham fans I encountered were concerned, this appeared to be the greatest moment in their lives, and for some it was the first time they had ever seen their team beat us; the previous occasion, way back in November 1999, took place in another century! The month ended with two 3–0 wins over Newcastle United three days apart, first in the FA Cup and then in the League as we put the Tottenham game behind us. We looked unstoppable, and then we stopped – the date 23 February 2008.

As February began we continued to lead the way in the League with victories over Manchester City and Blackburn Rovers, before Cup commitments turned our attentions elsewhere. An injury-ravaged team, forced to play Justin Hoyte and Armand Traore at full back, experienced a contention-ending FA Cup fifth round defeat at Manchester United, while in the Champions League AC Milan held us to a goalless draw at the Emirates in the first leg of our last-16 tie. Our final League game in February was away at Birmingham City. That was the day we stopped.

Just three minutes into the game a horrendous miss-timed tackle by Birmingham defender Martin Taylor shattered Eduardo's leg, distorting it into inconceivable angles of agony. First on the scene, Cesc Fabregas recoiled, visibly shaken and distressed by what he saw, an emotion which quickly spread to rest of the team. So bad was the injury TV would not show a replay of the incident. Eduardo received treatment on the pitch for seven minutes before heading straight to hospital with questions as to whether he would ever play again on everyone's mind. When play finally resumed, and although we were now playing against 10-men, the team looked unable to put the incident behind them, going into the dressing room at half-time a goal down.

The break seemed to enable the team to refocus and within 10 minutes of the restart we were 2–1 ahead and looking for a third. The score remained like that until the dying moments of the game when an extraordinary lapse of concentration in our own penalty area gifted the ball to a Birmingham forward. Clichy stuck out a leg to poke the ball away, and although he appeared to get a toe to it before his momentum brought the player down, the referee awarded a penalty and the 10-men of Birmingham equalised right at the death. Instead of claiming the three points we surely should have taken, we left St. Andrew's with just one.

At the final whistle William Gallas, captain, chose to sit down on the pitch, alone, burnt up with frustration and apparently close to tears – I have often been left angry and frustrated at the end of a game, but it is rare you see that same raw emotion from a player. If nothing else it showed he cared, but it hinted at a lack of team spirit – the captain alone on the pitch, the rest of the players already in the dressing room. As for Eduardo, his horrendous injury meant he was out of football for 12 months. He did eventually recover and play for us again but didn't seem the same player. In summer 2010 Eduardo moved on, to Ukrainian club Shakhtar Donetsk, but returned to the Emirates later that year when the two clubs came together in the Champions League. He came on as a substitute during the game to a genuinely warm welcome from our fans and when he scored a late goal for his team Arsenal fans stood as one to applaud him. It was an emotional moment, although it probably helped that we were 5–0 up at the time!

The fallout from the Birmingham game seemed to last long after the game ended. We needed a strong leader but none appeared. The players' confidence had clearly suffered a setback, such as that which followed the ending of our 49-game unbeaten run, and took too long to shake off. It again questioned the mental strength of the team when things went against them. We managed only draws in the next three league games followed by defeat at Chelsea. It was a shocking and dispiriting collapse which saw us surrender top spot in the League. A last minute win at Bolton at the end of March gave me hope that the slump was over but another draw, at home to Liverpool, followed by defeat at Manchester United, hammered the lid of our coffin firmly shut. From the Birmingham game to that at Old Trafford we'd played eight League games and dropped 16 points. We went on to win our last four games of the season but by then it was too late; we eventually finished the season in third, five more points would have won us the title. The dramatic collapse in the League lessened the impact of an incredible 2–0 victory over AC Milan in the Champions League – when we became the first English team to have beaten both AC and Inter Milan at the San Siro - before we lost to Liverpool in the quarter-final. At the end of the season I felt badly let down by the team. They say that home is where the heart is. I think perhaps my heart was still at Highbury.

26

Increasing Frustration

The collapse of our League campaign that spring had been depressing and activity at the club over the summer months of 2008 did little to inspire me. The regular drain of players to Barcelona continued, this time Alexander Hleb followed the well-trodden path. Other high-profile departures included Jens Lehmann, Gilberto Silva and Mathieu Flamini, while the club brought in Samir Nasri from Marseille, 17-year-old Aaron Ramsey from Cardiff City, Carlos Vela returned from a loan period in Spain and, somewhat surprisingly, Wenger added the creaking 31-year-old Manchester United defender Mikael Silvestre. Nasri looked like an interesting signing, Ramsey was clearly one for the future but I struggled to see what Silvestre was going to add, particularly as he had missed most of the previous season through serious injury. All in all I didn't feel that the squad had improved and the loyalty of some of those who remained was questionable. Adebayor had just completed an incredible season in which he scored 30 goals in all competitions but now came the disquieting media gossip, encouraged by his agent, that Adebayor would be interested in possible moves to Barcelona or AC Milan. Fans appreciate loyalty from the players they support - Adebayor's relationship with the fans deteriorated rapidly after that.

As a season ticket holder, you commit to attending a whole season's games and the first thing you want and hope for is that the team plays well at home so you get to enjoy your – very large – financial outlay. Of course with a season ticket you pay your money in advance and have no idea what you will get back in return. Champions or relegation, the cost remains the same. Wouldn't it be wonderful if you paid by results! At

189

£50 a game there is no pleasure whatsoever in seeing your team lose at home to Hull City as we did early in the new season. Or to look on helplessly as they surrender a 4-2 lead to Tottenham with two minutes left to play and end up drawing 4-4 as managed in October. You know you should win games like that, so it continues to raise questions about the mental strength of the team. In a young, developing team we lacked experienced leaders to cope with situations like these. We had, of course, been gaining excellent wins in other games and in other competitions, but it is games like these that set the alarm bells ringing.

By the time we played that Tottenham game we had moved effortlessly through the Champions League play off against FC Twente of Holland and started the group phase unbeaten after three games with a draw at Dynamo Kyiv, followed by sound thrashings of Porto at home and Fenerbahce away, along with a 6–0 humbling of Sheffield United in the Carling Cup.

Defeat at Stoke City followed the Tottenham shambles, and then came a hugely disappointing 0–0 draw at the Emirates in the return match with Fenerbahce. Perhaps unsurprisingly, I approached the home League game against Manchester United three days later with mounting concern. Games against Manchester United always stoke up the nerves, but approaching the game after three poor results just added to the anxiety I felt. It was a miserable, grey and wet November day as I headed to the Emirates, but by the end it felt like glorious springtime!

Both sides played an attacking game but after 22 minutes Fabregas swung a free-kick into the Manchester United 18-yard box. The defence cleared the ball out to the edge of the area, to an unmarked Samir Nasri who lashed it back through the crowded penalty area and into the net. It was not Nasri's first goal – he'd got that in our first game of the season in the 1–0 win over West Bromwich Albion – but this was special. Then, just two minutes into the second half he struck again. Fabregas supplied the pass, into space created by an intelligent run by Theo Walcott, and there was Nasri picking up the ball on the edge of the penalty area before crashing a thunderbolt of a shot into the net. It was a stunning goal, full of intricate passing – a typical Arsenal goal – and even more so as it was against Manchester United. We gave away a goal in the last minute but it didn't deflect from what had been a fantastically uplifting victory. The win took us to third in the table, but any hope that gave me of a revived title challenge immediately fizzled out because we lost our next two. My frustration overflowed.

November, however, did end on a high. We secured three points in the return tie against Dynamo Kyiv and shocked everyone – including me – with a win at Chelsea, Robin van Persie scoring twice in two minutes after going one down to an own goal. Van Persie seemed to enjoy scoring at Stamford Bridge. But it was one step forward and two steps back again as the December fixtures unfolded and our traditional first half of the season run of poor form materialised: three draws in the League followed defeat at Porto in the Champions League. That month we also bowed out of the Carling Cup at Burnley. Only narrow wins over Wigan and Portsmouth prevented the complete cancellation of the season of goodwill. It was certainly not the stuff of champions.

It was therefore a relief to see Arsène Wenger return to the transfer market in January and sign the Russian midfielder Andrey Arshavin. He demonstrated his potential in a remarkable game at Anfield in April which really summed up our season. Arshavin, in a stunning personal performance, scored four goals, but, despite apparently securing the three points when he put us 4–3 up in the 90th minute, we still sickeningly managed to let Liverpool level the scores in the fourth minute of added time. It was a great game for the neutral – as the cliché goes - but I'm not a neutral.

In the meantime we had got back to winning ways in the League at the beginning of January, beating Bolton and Hull, but then comprehensively shot ourselves in the foot by drawing our next *five* games, including three soul-destroying 0-0 draws at home, against West Ham, Sunderland and Fulham. We had become too predictable. Visiting teams knew what to expect and made sure they effectively prevented us from doing it. A well-marshalled, determined defence generally did the job.

Dismally we went six weeks without a win in the League. I did, however, manage to stop myself becoming completely demoralised as we were still alive in the FA Cup after wins over Plymouth Argyle and Cardiff. The Cardiff win, in a replay, was particularly heart-warming as it marked the return of Eduardo, a year after his devastating injury at Birmingham. In an emotional night he scored twice, both goals greeted rapturously by all present. It was a very special moment. We also won our first leg home game against Roma in the last-16 of the Champions League. We had lost our way in the League but the cups still offered hope.

Further FA Cup wins, over Burnley and Hull, led us to the FA Cup semi-final, the game scheduled at the 'new' Wembley which finally, after endless delays, had reopened for business in 2007. I now faced a dilemma similar to the one I encountered before the 2007 Carling Cup Final when we lost to Chelsea. We were facing Chelsea again and, once more, I feared the worst. I still remembered how badly it affected me after Chelsea knocked us out of the Champions League back in 2004. I just couldn't bear the thought of watching us lose to them again in such an important game, so I chose not to go. I think perhaps Andy's dislike of Chelsea was rubbing off on me! In almost a carbon copy of that 2007 game Walcott scored early on, then Chelsea came back to equalise before Drogba scored the winner late in the game. And they say lightning never strikes twice.

The season was unravelling and the only competition left now was the Champions League. Having won our last-16 first leg tie against Roma by 1–0 it was clear the away leg would be tough. With just 10 minutes played of the return, Roma evened the score as I watched on TV, that familiar sick feeling in my stomach already churning away. It was not a good start but we dug in and at full time the score remained level on aggregate, and an extra 30 minutes failed to produce a winner either. Everything now depended on penalties, which got off to a bad start as Eduardo missed the first. Roma scored theirs, but in the second round of kicks Van Persie scored and Almunia saved the Italian's effort: scores level. At the end of five penalties the score stood at 4–4 and so, as the tension increased inexorably, it moved to sudden death. Denilson and Sagna both slotted theirs home and with the scores now level at 6–6 Diaby stepped up. His was not a great penalty, a bit too close to the middle, but fortunately the Italian 'keeper had started to move to his left and couldn't correct his movement: 7–6 to us. By now the tension was unbearable and at that moment I would have given anything for the Italians to miss. Fortunately I did not offer up anything too precious because miss they did; this final penalty soaring up and over the bar. After an incredibly even and tense pair of games the surge of relief was overwhelming. Two days later UEFA made the draw for the quarter-finals and paired us with Villarreal. I felt sure it was a sign; we'd beaten them in 2006 on the way to the Final.

The first leg in Spain was the classic 'game of two halves.' Villarreal went for the jugular in the first half, scoring after ten minutes and pressing for more. But then, after half time, we gradually got back into the game and another superb goal from Adebayor levelled the scores. We were pushing on for a winner at the end, but it didn't come and the game ended all square – with a valuable away goal in the bag if we needed it. We didn't. The second leg was a pulsating, exciting and emotional affair which we won convincingly in the end by 3–0. It was emotional because Robert Pirès was back 'home' playing for Villarreal. At last he received a proper farewell from the fans; one denied him by circumstances in Paris in 2006. There was great excitement around the stadium that night, but lurking behind the celebrations was the fact that we already knew that blocking our path to the Final now stood Manchester United. Our record against other English teams in the Champions League showed plenty of room for improvement.

Sadly, we failed to improve that dismal record and our Champions League quest came to a grinding halt. We lost the first leg at Old Trafford 1–0 and then, after just 11 minutes of the return at the Emirates, we had already conceded two more taking the tie out of our reach. By the time the final whistle blew we had lost 3–1 on the night and 4–1 on aggregate. It was a crushing, depressing defeat that emphatically ended our season.

Despite our indifferent performances in the League we still secured fourth spot, guaranteeing us a place once more in the play off round of the Champions League and the key to the vast riches that lay beyond. Rather dismally though we had finished 11 points behind third placed Chelsea and a massive 18 behind the winners, Manchester United. We couldn't compete with the pacesetters and, although the Emirates was full to the rafters each week, increasing the matchday revenue massively, the club continued to use this increased income to manage its stadium debt. But this commendable financial control meant we were unable to compete on a level playing field in the transfer market with other leading clubs. The club was securing its long-term future, which, when you see the depths some great clubs have sunk to, is obviously a good thing, but all the time the fan inside me howls out in pain, desperate to see my team competing at the very top each season.

27

The Harsh Realities

My personal work situation is unusual in that for six months each year – in spring and autumn - I have a 'proper' job in a London media agency and the for the rest of the year I write. In the spring of 2009, however, the downturn in the economy meant my earnings were seriously impaired when I found there was no work for me. By the time it came to renew my season ticket for 2009/10 this situation had not changed and I was also unaware as to whether things would improve later in the year. It meant I had to look at my finances and it raised a large question mark over whether I could, or should, commit the £1200 necessary to renew. After much deliberation I came to the conclusion that if I could sell on a number of games – at time of purchase – then I would get by. I put the word out but, as is always the case in situations regarding tickets, Steph came up trumps. Theo, a former colleague of hers – who I'd met a few times - is a devoted Gooner and has a large group of family and friends with similar tendencies. When Theo heard of my plight he stepped forward and without question offered to take the eight games I felt I needed to release to reduce my financial commitment. What a hero!

I was very grateful to Theo for making things possible so thought it only right to allocate the games fairly. To make it a bit more interesting I graded the games: A games were Manchester United and Tottenham, B Games were Chelsea and Liverpool, while C and D games were mid-table teams and those likely to be propping up the bottom. The deal was one A game, one B game, four C games and two D games, which we'd draw from an envelope, although I did insist on the Fulham game being one of mine; it was the last game of the season. I wanted that one in case we were in the battle for the title as the season drew to a close. It's not always obvious but there is still an optimist lurking very deep inside! I met up with Theo for the grand draw while Steph and Prinders came along too to see fair play. And although we also found time to fit in a number of beers, we still managed to allocate a season's worth of games in a fraction of the time it takes UEFA to make a Champions League draw. As I headed home that night I had mixed feelings. I was delighted to have overcome my immediate financial issues, but I also felt subdued; it felt as though I had surrendered my birthright.

The summer of 2009 heralded another major change in English football. Manchester City, perennial underachievers, were suddenly rich, immensely so. In September 2008 the Abu Dhabi United Group headed by Sheikh Mansour bin Zayed Al Nahyan, a member of the unimaginably rich Abu Dhabi royal family, bought Manchester City from Thaksin Shinawatra, the disgraced former prime minister of Thailand. They began spending vast amounts of money upgrading the playing squad. Overnight Manchester City became the richest club in football, upsetting the status quo and having a major detrimental effect on the transfer market for everyone else. There appears to be no limit on how much they spend on players. In July 2009 Emmanuel Adebayor couldn't pack his bags quickly enough when City came calling, although we had already recognised in the previous summer what appeared to motivate him most, and it certainly wasn't loyalty to Arsenal. Shortly afterwards Manchester City came shopping again and this time left with Kolo Touré as part of an estimated £120m summer spending spree. If figures in the media are correct we received about £40m for those two players, but, as has become our way, we re-invested only a fraction of that. But that money was spent well in acquiring central defender Thomas Vermaelen from Ajax who became an instant hero when he scored on his League debut – and has continued to do on a regular basis since.

Despite this somewhat unsatisfactory run-up, the season started well, amazingly well, with a 6–1 opening day victory at Everton, followed up with a sparkling 4–1 win at home against

Portsmouth. I had this one on my list of games so was able to see the first stage of the 'Arsenalisation' of the Emirates. This was a move by the club to tackle the fact that the majority of Gooners loved the new stadium structure but felt it didn't say "This is Arsenal." The process is ongoing and now includes the eight giant murals of club legends embracing each other and the stadium, while inside the old names of the stands have been resurrected: North Bank, Clock End, etc., and numerous other images, quotes, and historic moments decorate the formerly bland walls. It is an imaginative move and a much needed one – and at that Portsmouth game the club laid a woollen scarf on everyone's seat - a nice touch.

The positive start continued with home and away wins either side of the Portsmouth game against Celtic in the play off round of the Champions League which saw us safely into the group stage once more. But defeat at Old Trafford in the next game followed by an excruciatingly painful loss at Manchester City slammed on the brakes. At City, Adebayor, formerly idolised at the Emirates, scored against us. It is refreshing in football when you see players who score against their former clubs refusing to celebrate. It shows respect and acknowledges the position they once held in the affections of their former club's fans. Adebayor, who had already angered our fans by his enthusiasm to get himself a bigger payday elsewhere, did not take this option. Instead he chose to run the entire length of field – alone – to celebrate his goal provocatively in front of our fans, coming close to sparking a riot in the process. This was on top of raking his studs down Robin van Persie's face in a move the Dutchman believed was deliberate. Adebayor received a three-match ban for the Van Persie incident and a fine of £25,000 for his celebration, with a two-match suspended sentence – the FA suspended it because of abuse he received from Arsenal fans. And then, two years later, Adebayor went on loan to Tottenham! I can not think of another relationship in football that has passed so spectacularly from love to hate. It is safe to say fans will never pay homage to a statue of him outside the stadium.

Fortunately there was no negative reaction from the players after these two Manchester awayday defeats as we embarked on a seven match unbeaten run in the League which included spectacular wins over Wigan (4–0), Blackburn (6–2), Tottenham (3–0) and Wolverhampton Wanderers (4–1). I loved the Tottenham match – it was my 'A game' in the pre-season draw. The two teams started the day level on points and a tight, cagey affair seemed on the cards, as indeed it was until two or three minutes before the break. At that point Robin van Persie slid in at the near post to latch onto a cross from the right and score. No doubt having anticipated reaching half-time with the score level, our late goal seemed to stun Tottenham. They re-started the match in a daze and immediately allowed Van Persie to block a pass, the ball running to Cesc Fabregas still in the centre circle. Fabregas skipped passed two converging opponents and raced beyond a third before striking a low shot into the net from the edge of the penalty area. Just 11 seconds had passed since Tottenham restarted the game. The move was so quick I was still celebrating the first goal when the crowd exploded again in rapturous celebration. Those are the moments you never forget, the moments that make it all worthwhile, and a third goal coming in the second half confirmed our dominance and made it a perfect day.

The seven match unbeaten run came to a halt at the end of November when we lost a tight game by a single goal at Sunderland and then were humbled at home by Chelsea, leaving us 11 points behind them – which is exactly where we were at the end of the season. We started on another lengthy unbeaten run in the League, lasting 10 games, before losing two consecutive games at the end of January and beginning of February in a pattern that kept repeating itself. It was a pattern that firmly anchored us in third place throughout the second half of the season.

By then both our FA and League Cup runs were over but we had secured a place in the last-16 of the Champions League where we faced Porto. We lost the first leg in Portugal 2–1 which meant the return promised to be a big night. And it was, very big, as we crushed Porto 5-0 with Nicklas Bendtner grabbing a hat-trick and Samir Nasri scoring a solo goal of mesmerising beauty. Receiving the ball out wide on the right

Nasri tormented three Porto defenders, turning them inside out with the ball apparently stuck to his boots before unleashing a fierce low drive into the net from a narrow angle. It was the third goal on the night and it is the one that for me said 'game over'.

The win meant we faced the mighty Barcelona in the quarter-final. With the final taking place at the ground of their eternal rivals Real Madrid, they were even more obsessed than usual with winning the competition.

We played the first leg at home on 31 March 2010 and as soon as the game began Barcelona showed they meant business and only a string of fine saves by Almunia kept the scores level at half time. I felt a bit shell-shocked during the break and just hoped we could hold on. But within seconds of the restart Barcelona scored, and then repeated the feat on the hour. Things did not look good and, having made two enforced changes in the first half due to injuries, we had only one substitute left to play. Wenger made that change six minutes after Barcelona's second goal, bringing on Theo Walcott. Three minutes later he dashed into the Spanish penalty area to collect a perfect pass from Bendtner and fired low into the net. Despite our opponents' domination, we were back in the game and, although still trailing, the whole crowd stood to a man to greet the return of Thierry Henry who rose from the Barcelona bench for the last 13 minutes of the game. It was a great moment to see him grace the stadium once more. Henry, however, did not have an impact on the game, but his replacement as Arsenal captain did. With five minutes left Cesc Fabregas was brought down as he was about to fire a shot at goal. With Puyol sent off for the foul, Fabregas picked himself up to take the resulting penalty against the team he supported as a boy and had played for at youth level before joining Arsenal. He didn't realise it at the time but the challenge by Puyol had cracked a bone in his right leg. With adrenaline pumping through his body, he used the same leg to smash a rocket of a shot into the net, and only then did he begin to realise he was in pain. The stadium erupted in a mass of jumping, hugging, screaming humanity in celebration of a most unlikely comeback. Fabregas limped through the last few

199

minutes of the game and didn't play again that season, but he'd given us hope for the second leg.

By the time that game came around a week later Fabregas found himself sharing the treatment table with a host of regular starters, so an already difficult task became even more daunting. I watched the game on TV with Gerry and Steph, which had become the norm for away games in the Champions League, but viewed the coming match with some trepidation. Then, incredibly, we scored. Theo Walcott ran with the ball, out-sprinting the Barcelona defence and Nicklas Bendtner poked it home. Disbelief; we were leading 3–2 on aggregate. Then I looked at my watch and realised we still had 70 minutes to play. Three minutes later things got messy – or rather I should say Messi; Lionel Messi to be precise. It was the first of four goals he scored that night - completing his hat-trick before half time - to which we could muster no reply. Hope crushed. We were well beaten on the night but I was left wondering if the outcome would have been different if we had been able to field a full strength team; maybe not, but it made me feel a little better about the result. My dream of a return to the Champions League Final ended that night. Barcelona's dream of winning the Final at the home of Real Madrid was about to end too. Surprisingly, they lost to Inter Milan in the semi-final. All that effort for nothing.

What was important now was for the team to put the defeat behind them and turn their focus back to the League. We were on an unbeaten run of eight games and still in the running for the title; next up, Tottenham away. We lost it. And then, repeating the season's pattern we lost the next game too – at Wigan. It was a defeat that still haunts me today when I inadvertently allow myself to think about it.

Wigan were hanging on just above the relegation zone when we played them on 18 April. I remember the day well. It was a Sunday and I was at my partner Nicola's house. It was sunny and I offered to do a bit of work in her garden so I could focus on the radio commentary. We scored a goal either side of half-time to give a comfortable 2–0 lead and I anticipated more to follow. I got it but not in the way I expected. As I listened it became obvious that the team was happy to hold on to what they had, which encouraged Wigan to start pressing. With just 10 minutes left to play Wigan turned this pressure into a goal. Suddenly they were a team possessed and sensed they could rescue something from the game. I stopped what I was doing in the garden and while mentally I was in Wigan, physically, not really aware what I was doing, I began pulling stones from the soil and forming them into a pile as attacking waves bore down on our goal. I have experienced situations like this on numerous occasions over the years and inevitably they end with our opponents levelling the game in the dying moments. And so it was this time too. With two minutes left Fabianski flapped at a corner allowing Wigan to score the inevitable equaliser. My pile of stones was quite big by now. While I resigned myself to the draw, unfortunately Wigan did not. Just a minute later any remaining title hopes, encouraged just 40 minutes earlier, lay in tatters as a third Wigan goal confirmed a collapse of seismic proportions. I turned off the radio and threw it away from me, it was an unbearable moment. I was distraught, I felt shocked and humiliated. How could they do that to me? I left that pile of stones, a monument to my despair, and over the summer every time I saw it I felt the pain a little more. Eventually, mercifully, nature took it upon itself to break down that cairn and disperse my tormented memories.

From that point I just wanted the season to end. A draw at home to Manchester City and another defeat, at Blackburn this time, completed this depressing cycle before we finally returned to winning ways. That came at home to Fulham in the last game of the season; the game I had optimistically insisted on as part of my pre-season allocation. But that run of four games between Barcelona and Fulham, with a potential for 12 points, ended with us claiming just one. We finished the season in third place, ending up 11 points behind the winners Chelsea – the mathematics is simple. I was hurting again.

28

The House of Pain

After such a disappointing end to the season, the constant reminders in the media over the summer that we had now gone five years without winning a trophy were grating, while Barcelona's open pursuit of Cesc Fabregas was unsettling. And while the club continued to spend modestly on new players, signing Marouane Chamakh for free and Laurent Koscielny and Sebastian Squillaci for a combined outlay of about £12m, I watched Manchester City spend another £126m on star players. It was clear they were ready to upset the top table and qualification for the Champions League was about to become significantly more difficult. On a personal note, my work situation had returned to normal so I had the prospect of a full season ahead of me once more, but I held little genuine belief that 2010/11 would, or could, show much improvement upon the last.

Despite my pessimism, the opening to the season was dynamic and thrilling. We were unbeaten in the opening five games, recording a marvellously entertaining 6–0 win over Blackpool in our first home game, as well as victories over Bolton at home and Blackburn Rovers away. All seemed well, and then newly promoted West Bromwich Albion came to visit. The game was nicely set up. Earlier, in the Saturday lunchtime kick off, Chelsea had lost to Manchester City. That meant that if we beat West Brom and then did the same to Chelsea the following week we would be sitting on top of the table at the beginning of October. But that was as good as it got. In goal Almunia had a bad day and after 73 minutes I looked on, speechless, as West Brom went 3–0 up – having also failed to score from the penalty spot. We were missing

Fabregas, whose fragile hamstring had snapped again, and Van Persie remained a long-term injury problem, but this was shocking. Nasri pulled a goal back a couple of minutes after West Brom scored their third and, on full time, he grabbed a second, prompting a desperate assault in the five minutes of injury time, but it proved too little too late, and at the final whistle we'd lost. Then, at Chelsea, a week later we lost again. It was a hugely disappointing week.

The early promise shown in August faded as the season progressed towards the half-way point. A 2–1 victory over Birmingham, a 1–0 defeat of West Ham, with the goal coming just two minutes from time, and then defeats in consecutive home games to Newcastle and Tottenham was the level of the uncomfortable fare I watched. It was puzzling too, because away from home we'd recorded four consecutive League wins since the loss at Chelsea, including an extremely impressive 3–0 trouncing of Manchester City. The only game in the League in the first half of the season - after the wins over Blackpool and Bolton - that I felt really showed the team at its best and restored my faith was the 3–1 defeat of Chelsea on 27 December. We dominated and played confidently; I desperately hoped it was a turning point in the season.

While other Leagues across Europe take a winter break, in England we play on through those dark and dreary days. But the opening of the hunting season – sorry, transfer window - on 1st January offers plenty of distractions as the media churns out generally unfounded gossip and rumours about who's going where and for how much. In 2011, however, when the January sales opened there were no bargains. In an effort to strengthen their squads in the race for the title, Manchester City laid out another £27m on striker Edin Dzeko, Chelsea lost the plot and spent £50m on Fernando Torres and another £21m on David Luiz, while Liverpool reinvested the money they got for Torres by spending £35m on Andy Carroll and around £23m on Luis Suarez. As ever we took a back seat, and looked on enviously as others splashed the cash. Prudence remained the order of the day.

Once the dust of this transfer activity had settled we travelled to St. James' Park to play a Newcastle team stripped of their talismanic No.9, Andy Carroll. If Newcastle fans feared the worst, even they could not have envisaged what unfolded in the first half, and, in my worst nightmares, I could never have conjured up the horrors that awaited me in the second.

Less than a minute after the game commenced, Walcott put us one up and after ten minutes it was game over as we stormed to a 3–0 lead, adding a fourth before half-time. It seemed a perfect day. Newcastle were shambolic, some of their fans choosing to leave rather than witness any further humbling. Then, a few minutes into the second half, Djourou limped off, replaced in the centre of defence by Squillaci. Moments later Joey Barton made a crunching tackle on Diaby. Stupidly he reacted – lost it – grabbing Barton by the neck and shoving him to the ground, then pushing Kevin Nolan; it left the referee with no choice, Diaby was off. Even so, after a dominant first 45 minutes, even with 10 men, we could protect a four goal lead… Wrong. It was extraordinary – and inexplicable - but the confidence seeped away like water through sand. For no real reason the team suddenly looked nervous and shaken. Newcastle capitalised, with Barton scoring from the penalty spot on 68 minutes. Inspired now by the sending off and the goal Newcastle stormed forward. The game no longer bore any resemblance to the first half; it was a new game as Newcastle pressed us back, then scored again, and again, bringing the score back to 4–3 with eight minutes still to play. We appeared to have no answer, no one on the pitch was taking control and I feared the worst. I just knew what was coming next, and sure enough it did as Newcastle equalised in the 87th minute and came close to grabbing a winner. But finally the referee ended my torture. It was hard to reconcile what had just happened; I was too busy coping with the shock, disbelief, confusion, bewilderment and anger. Those painful dark memories still lurk within.

In the cup competitions in the first half of the season we had endured a nervous end to the Champions League group stage. Having started well with three straight wins we then stumbled to two defeats, meaning a win in the last game, at home to Partizan Belgrade, was essential, or we'd be out. With

Fabregas' recurring hamstring problems keeping him out of the game, I anticipated a tense night, but fortunately, despite Partizan levelling the score at 1–1 early in the second half, everything eventually came together as we recorded a 3–1 win. Yet, taking our eye off the ball after the three initial wins consigned us to finish second in the group. When the draw for the last-16 ties took place we knew we would play a group winner in the next round, and with a chilling sense of *déjà vu* the winner we drew was Barcelona, universal favourites to win the competition. It is of course the aim of every football team to pitch itself against the best, but as a fan – and you can call me old-fashioned - I must admit I'm rather keen just to see my team win.

A few weeks later, when the two games were over, it ended a 14-day period that brought the season to a shuddering halt, and heralded a collapse the likes of which I had never witnessed before. For me it raised a painful question - what direction was the team heading? But before that we faced Barcelona at the Emirates, without doubt the most memorable evening yet at the new stadium. On that night we went toe-to-toe with the best team in the world – and won.

That night as the teams emerged into the dazzling floodlit arena to a mass of swaying, waving flags – placed on every seat by the club – the atmosphere fizzed and bubbled prior to kick-off. Barcelona looked frightening and although they eventually went ahead midway through the first half, we kept battling, kept believing. In midfield that night teenager Jack Wilshire was simply magnificent, shining brightly among such luminaries as Iniesta, Xavi and Busquets – perhaps if he hadn't later suffered a long-tern injury Barcelona would have tried to buy him too.

As the clock ticked down it began to look like Barcelona would run the game down, but with 12 minutes left Robin van Persie wriggled clear of his marker. He ran onto a chipped pass from Gael Clichy and scored from the narrowest of angles. Revitalised by the goal, the crowd lifted the roof off the stadium as we urged and drove the team on. Five minutes later our reward came; a goal of breathtaking speed and one-touch passing. The move began on the edge of our own penalty area as the defence stifled a Barcelona attack and ended with Andrey Arshavin sweeping the ball into the net at the other end of the field just 17 seconds later. I flew from my seat and remember screaming a lot before becoming aware of probably the largest outbreak of 'stranger-hugging' since the VE Day celebrations in London in 1945! By the time I landed on the ground again I felt light-headed, even confused, but there is nowhere in the world I would rather have been right then. There were no more goals; we'd just beaten Barcelona at the Emirates. Perhaps it even felt a little bit like home at last.

The return leg three weeks later was always going to be an uphill battle, but I felt it was a battle we could compete in. Watching the game on TV it was clear Barcelona was the better team. But as half-time approached the scores remained level on the night, so we were still ahead on aggregate, even though we'd lost 'keeper Szczesny to injury less than 20 minutes into the game. Then, just as I started to relax, anticipating the imminent break, Messi did it again – scoring in the third minute of injury time after Barcelona regained possession following an unnecessary and risky back heel by Fabregas. Scores equal again.

When the second half got underway we won a rare corner from which Busquets headed into his own net. Incredible; against the odds we were back in front. But just seconds later my joy turned to dismay. We moved straight back onto the attack with Van Persie breaking forward, only for the assistant referee to raise his flag for offside. Unaware of the referee's whistle, the sound lost in the seething cauldron of the Camp Nou, Van Persie continued and fired his shot wide. As he turned around, the referee brandished a second yellow card towards him, followed by a red. In an extraordinary decision the referee sent off Van Persie for what he termed kicking the ball away. There was no place for a decision like that on such a night. I have seen numerous games since, in European, International and domestic competition, in which a similar action has passed without action or comment. But that night it left us with just 10 men to face Barcelona, just as we had done five years earlier in the Champions League Final. The injustice of it all really stung. Inevitably Barcelona's superiority on the night now converted itself into goals, and at the end of 90 minutes we had lost 3-1 (and 4–3 over the two games). But the question remains in my mind, the same question I'd asked after our previous encounter at the Camp Nou; what if...

There was little time to fester on the result as four days later we headed to Old Trafford for an FA Cup 6th Round tie against Manchester United – and lost again. It marked the end of our quest for cup glory. In the space of 14 days, in a sequence started at Wembley with that dark defeat by Birmingham in the Carling Cup Final that opened this book, we had crashed out of the FA Cup and Champions League too. The Birmingham defeat was the catalyst that first caused me to explore and try to understand my own relationship with my team, my Arsenal, for it appeared to me that the team was unable to shake itself free from the despair that game engendered.

In the cold light of day the fallout following the Carling Cup Final defeat was shocking. From my seat high in the Emirates I looked down on a team that seemed to have lost its purpose, its drive and its self-belief, which Wenger seemed unable to rectify. I couldn't help but reflect that the team running out after the half-time break each week to the strains of a piece of music by a band called House of Pain was just too close to the mark. We still had 11 League games to play before the end of the season and remained in the title race, but then three consecutive home draws – including dismal scoreless results against Sunderland and Blackburn – showed how the players were struggling with the psychological burden; the spirit of the team, the spirit that Wenger so often refers to, seemed absent. At the end of the third of those draws – against Liverpool – our lack of discipline left me dumbstruck and frustrated beyond belief. I had entered the house of pain and thrown away the key.

Despite our best efforts in that game we had been unable to make any impression on Liverpool's resolute defence, but due to a sickening accidental injury to Jamie Carragher the referee added eight minutes of injury time. And with seven of those minutes already played we received a dramatic lifeline when the referee awarded a penalty for a trip on Fabregas. The whole stadium collectively held its breath as Van Persie prepared to take the kick that would earn us three points. Unfazed, he lashed the ball home, granting a release of pent up angst and an eruption of hysterical celebration. All we needed to do now was regain possession and play out the last few moments. But we couldn't manage that. Liverpool pressed us back straight away, leading to some desperate, panic-stricken defending which resulted in a free-kick to Liverpool right on the edge of our penalty area. A desperate moment, which in turn grew into desperate minutes as the team protested and argued and only reluctantly moved back the required 10 yards. When Liverpool finally took the free-kick, to my immense relief the ball hit the wall and bounced away from danger towards the touchline. Just seconds remained; surely that was game over. Well it would have been had not Emmanuel Eboué, with an inexplicable and insane rush of blood, clattered into the back of a Liverpool player prompting the referee to agonisingly point to the spot. Liverpool scored their penalty – the goal recorded in the 12th minute of injury time – it was the last kick of the game. Yet another sickening moment in a season that tested the conviction of even the most loyal of fans.

We did manage a gloom-lifting win over Manchester United in the run in, but by dropping 21 points in those last 11 games after the Carling Cup Final we were condemned to finish in fourth place again, 12 points behind the winners Manchester United. It all felt so miserably familiar.

At the end of the season I admit I felt down and demoralised. The Carling Cup Final had been our chance to dispel those constant reminders in the media about how many trophy-less years we had experienced since the FA Cup win in 2005, but we'd failed in humiliating circumstances. The reaction of the team following that defeat, and particularly the performances in the League run-in, had been dispiriting. And it seemed clear to everyone that Barcelona's relentless pursuit of Cesc Fabregas would finally reach its inevitable conclusion. Unless we started adding new players to the squad it was hard to see the coming season offering any change in fortune – we were becoming the 'nearly' club. At this time, when many questioned the club's future, it misguidedly announced increased ticket prices. I was left to consider whether I could justify paying out £1310 to renew my season ticket when I was getting less enjoyment from attending games and at a time when the club appeared to have lost its direction. It was a question I discussed *ad nauseam* with many people and most just dismissed me, presuming I would automatically renew, but Steph and Dickie knew I was serious. In the end, after mentally wrestling with the dilemma and with some reservations, I renewed my ticket again for the 43rd year.

29

Seven Seasons Without a Trophy
Part 3

Within weeks of handing over my money I found myself wondering what I'd done. Gael Clichy departed, lured by the riches of Manchester City, while rumours that Samir Nasri now sat at the top of their shopping list grew stronger and stronger. After their constant plundering of all things associated with our club, not just current players but former ones too (Vieira, Platt and Marwood), I wondered if they should just go the whole way and rename themselves Arsenal North. Then, after dragging on tediously all summer, Fabregas finally went home to Barcelona just as the season began and, although Nasri still remained our player as the first game kicked off, it seemed increasingly likely that Manchester City's limitless budget would eventually lure him away too. Two games into the season it finally did. It ripped a vast gaping hole in our midfield as, just prior to the departures of Fabregas and Nasri, Jack Wilshire had suffered a serious injury at the end of July that consigned him to the treatment table for over a year; the creative heartbeat of the team silenced in three angst-inducing summer weeks.

With some relief, Wenger had started spending, bringing in Gervinho, an experienced international, and continued to invest in youth, adding Carl Jenkinson and Alex Oxlade-Chamberlain, but as the final day of the transfer window drew near he had done nothing to plug the hole in midfield. By then we had already played three games in the League, making a disastrous start to the season: a creditable draw at Newcastle followed by a 2–0 loss at home to Liverpool, and then the crushing, humiliating debacle at Old Trafford when we conceded eight – yes, eight - goals in our worst defeat for 115 years. It was hardly the way to mark our 125th anniversary season. Departures and injuries exposed the lack of experience in the squad and screamed for action in the transfer market, which was about to slam shut in just three days. These were the darkest of dark days.

Only on the final day itself did news emerge that we had signed two defenders, Andre Santos and Per Mertesacker, but the yawning midfield void remained. The idiom 'at the eleventh hour' probably doesn't emphasis just how late the club left it to plug the gap, perhaps 'at the eleventh hour and fifty five minutes' would be closer to the truth. Just minutes before midnight on 31 August the media announced the signing of Mikel Arteta from Everton and the arrival of Yossi Benayoun on loan from Chelsea. I couldn't help thinking that this late development smacked of desperation – why had we left everything so late? And I wondered if all these players would have arrived if the humiliation at Old Trafford had not been so complete. Why were we strengthening our squad amidst the turmoil of the last days of the transfer window rather than in the calm of the close season? And inevitably there was no world class signing to lift the team, the supporters or the club. From my viewpoint as a long-term fan – and I have no personal insight into what goes on behind the scenes – it just seems the management lost its way that summer.

An international break after Old Trafford meant there was no immediate way to bury the demons of that day for either players or fans. So it was some relief when the League returned to business two weeks later and we edged a 1–0 home win over newly-promoted Swansea for our first league win of the season. Yet any benefit we gained from that was blown out of the water the following week when we travelled to Blackburn - who were to suffer a traumatic season of their own - and contrived to surrender a 2–1 half-time lead against the League's bottom-placed team and lose 4–3, recording two own goals in the process. We'd played really well in the first half but seemed fragile and nervous after the break; it was horribly reminiscent of Newcastle the previous season. We ended the weekend 17th in the League, one place above the relegation zone. I had expected a tough season but not in my worst nightmares had I anticipated a start like this; we had taken just four points from our opening five games. The frustration, the anger and the despair gnawed away at me constantly.

Fortunately, we got back to winning ways in the next game, a convincing 3–0 win over Bolton at the Emirates in which Robin van Persie scored twice, netting his 99th and 100th goals for Arsenal. He provided a much needed tonic and helped lift the gloom but defeat followed, at White Hart Lane, where although we brought the game back to 1–1 early in the second half, Tottenham eventually claimed the three points with a 2–1 win. It was our fourth loss in seven League games, leaving us adrift in 15th place and fearing what might come our way over the rest of the season. However, one beacon shone brightly in the darkness: Robin van Persie, and he was up for the fight.

After the disappointment of the Tottenham game, we earned a narrow victory at home against Sunderland and then, unexpectedly, embarked on an unbeaten eight match run. We won seven and drew the other of those League games, including a stunning 5–3 win at Stamford Bridge against Chelsea. Van Persie claimed a brilliant hat-trick in that game and scored 12 times in the unbeaten run. Against all the odds we had clawed ourselves up to fifth in the table. Bizarrely this came at a time when an extraordinary series of injuries ruled out all four recognised first team full-backs to long-term lay-offs. The injuries focused my attention even more on the importance of Van Persie to the team. His goals were driving us forward, but if he were to succumb to serious injury, as he had done in previous seasons, surely the game was up.

As the year drew to a close, an incredibly disappointing draw at home to Wolverhampton Wanderers, part of the Christmas programme, reminded everyone that the team still had problems to overcome. But a narrow win at home to QPR on New Year's Eve meant we ended a roller-coaster first half of the season in fourth place, which was far better than I could possibly have imagined after the demoralising start we had experienced. In that final game of the year Robin van Persie – who else – scored the only goal of the game and with it claimed a club record of 35 League goals in a calendar year, beating by one the previous record held by Thierry Henry. Quite some achievement, which just confirmed how vital he was to any success we enjoyed on the pitch. I desperately hoped the club would wrap him in cotton wool between games for the rest of the season.

In Europe things had progressed without the angst present in the League. We won home and away in our tough Champions League play-off against Italy's Udinese to qualify for group stages for the 14th consecutive year. Then, unbeaten in our opening five games, we qualified for the knock-out phase as group winners with a game to spare, ahead of Marseille, Olympiacos and Borussia Dortmund. And this time, as group winners, at least we couldn't face Barcelona again in the last-16 round. Even so, when the draw took place it still managed to present us with tough opponents – AC Milan.

The New Year started with a tremendous and unexpected boost. Early in January the club announced that Thierry Henry, who had been training with us during the break in the U.S. Major League Soccer season, where he now plied his trade for New York Red Bulls, was about to commence a short term loan-spell back at his spiritual home. The legend returned. We all knew this was no longer the Henry who had terrorised defences half a decade before, but he's a hero, idolised by all Arsenal supporters and with back-up for Van Persie in short supply it seemed a great move. And the legend lived on when Henry returned to action as a substitute in the 3rd Round FA Cup tie at the Emirates against Leeds United. With 22 minutes left to play and the score balanced at 0–0 he came on to a rapturous welcome, and ten minutes later rolled back the years in spectacular style as he controlled a superb pass from Alex Song to stroke the ball home for the winning goal. It was a 'Roy of the Rovers' moment, it was a late Christmas present, it was perfect and for a moment I felt a little of the faded magic of the Cup seep back into my disillusioned bones.

And to be honest it was only the FA Cup that lifted the mood through January. A grating defeat at Swansea in the League left me exasperated. We scored an early goal but by the time an hour was up we were trailing 2–1. We fought our way back and ten minutes later it was all square again and – or so it seemed to me – we were ready to push on and take all three points. But no; straight from the kick-off an appalling lack of concentration allowed Swansea to immediately retake the lead while I was still celebrating our equaliser. It proved to be the final nail in the coffin of our 3–2 defeat.

At a time like that, on the back of two Premier League defeats, I guess as a fan you would not choose the next game to be against Manchester United. But they came to the Emirates a week after the Swansea game and completed a miserable month for us in the League. It was a game that seemed to mark a serious crack in the hitherto generally unshakeable relationship between Arsène Wenger and the home crowd. Although we'd gone a goal behind by half-time, we were creating chances and Alex 'The Ox' Oxlade-Chamberlain on his first Premier League start was carrying a real threat. We seemed to be generating a head of steam when 'The Ox' set up Van Persie to strike a great shot across the goalkeeper and into the net. With the score now 1-1 the mood all around the stadium lifted; I felt we had a chance. And then Wenger changed the mood. Instead of capitalising on Oxlade-Chamberlain's increasing influence out on the left, immediately after the equaliser he replaced him with Andrey Arshavin. Now while I accept that at various times over the years Arshavin has produced match-winning performances, those now seemed a long time ago, and his on-field performances during the season had lacked desire, energy and passion – the sort of qualities that Oxlade-Chamberlain displayed in abundance. The crowd was incredulous; boos reverberated around the stadium and chants of "You don't know what you're doing" followed. It seemed a shockingly misplaced decision at the time and so it proved to be. With about ten minutes left Arshavin failed to halt Valencia's run before he set up the winner for Manchester United. Wenger can be a stubborn man at times and if the rising voice of public opinion urges him to do something, then he tends to do the opposite. But I wonder if that crowd reaction hit home. Wenger substituted Oxlade-Chamberlain in each of his next four starts, but each time he replaced him with

Thierry Henry. Wenger knows no one will boo a decision to introduce Henry no matter who he replaces.

Journalists, sensing a disastrous season in comparison with our own high standards, closed in. A few days before the Manchester United game, in response to a question about whether he considered it a problem if Arsenal were not to qualify for the Champions League, chairman Peter Hill-Wood replied, "From a financial point of view, not qualifying for the Champions League is quite a blow. We have been planning for not qualifying every year so it is not a disaster, but it would be nice if we could." Nice if we could! On the day before the United game Arsène Wenger was asked a similar question, if he would consider it a disaster if we failed to qualify and he replied, "For me it would be because I want to play with the best. We want to be in there, in the top four and to play in the Champions League, and anything else would not be good enough." The responses clearly demonstrated the differing ambitions of a money man and a football man.

Three league defeats out of three was the depressing tally for January with just an FA Cup 4th Round tie to play at the Emirates to complete the month. That we were 2–0 down to Aston Villa at half-time did not lighten the dark mood that hung over the stadium that day. During the break I looked at the supporters around me and it was the same everywhere – a look of resignation, a realisation that this was no longer the team that used to terrify their opponents. The mood darkened further when Gerry revealed he had been unable to purchase the usual 'lucky' Murray Mints on the way to the game – a half-time essential! Could things get worse? With reluctance I accepted the substitute on offer – Trebor Extra Strong. Wow, what a mint. As the second half started the play seemed far more positive and, by the time I'd finished my second mint, we'd scored three times in a seven minute period to secure the game. It was a remarkable turnaround and happily brought the shutters down on what had been a less than encouraging month. Unfortunately February had much more pain lying in wait.

Actually the first half of the month offered real hope again. After a frustrating away draw at Bolton someone must have been rummaging around in an old locker because we suddenly rediscovered our swashbuckling style of old, destroying Blackburn Rovers 7–1 at the Emirates. That day it was pure pleasure to watch the team play the ball around and score goals for fun again. I had begun to think those days were long gone. A hat-trick from Van Persie as he continued his unstoppable goal-scoring run, two from Oxlade-Chamberlain, one from Arteta and of course, lastly, one from Thierry Henry. This final goal on the day set up unselfishly by Van Persie, who made it his mission that Henry would score in his last game at the Emirates as his loan deal neared its end. Three months later though, a heartless decision by the 'Dubious Goals Committee' took that goal away, crediting it instead as an own goal. Henry, though, still had one more gift up his sleeve for us. A week later he played his final League game, at Sunderland, and scored the winning goal in the last minute in a 2–1 victory. It was some return. Henry played in six League and FA Cup games, appearing for a total of two hours, scoring what we originally thought was three goals, two of which proved to be match winners. He also played 45 minutes at Milan – but there seems little point soiling his record by including that aberration. Thanks Thierry, we've missed your class and your passion.

The AC Milan game on 15 February 2012 followed exactly a year after we defeated Barcelona in that magnificent match at the Emirates, the play back then prompted and conducted by the majestic triumvirate of Fabregas, Nasri and Wilshire in midfield. A year on and we were humiliated, losing 4–0 in the San Siro, their places occupied that day – I won't say filled - by Arteta, Rosicky and Ramsey. It reflected a team, and a club, that appeared to me to have lost its way. Although there are excellent players within the first-choice eleven, the squad lacked depth because of the decision not to strengthen effectively when it was at the top. And with the long-term injuries that constantly dog us we find ourselves regularly exposed by that weakness.

With the media melt-down after Milan, our worst ever European defeat, following on from our worst League defeat since 1896 earlier in the season, I viewed with some trepidation our FA Cup 5th Round tie three days later away at Sunderland. The ensuing performance was poor, unthreatening and ineffective. We offered little and lost 2–0. My only emotion at the final whistle as I blankly watched the game on TV was dismay. But at least I was at home and could switch off and try to pretend that week had not happened; my sympathies went out to the Gooners who had travelled to those two games. Reports suggest that 5,000 witnessed the debacle in Milan and over 4,000 were at Sunderland on a cold and windy February night when the team surrendered again. I hope the club appreciates the loyalty displayed by those fans.

Our exit from the FA Cup condemned us to ending the year trophy-less again, for the seventh consecutive season. After the game, questioned on this continuing lack of silverware, Wenger responded with something new. He explained, "The first trophy is to finish in the top four. And that's still possible. I believe finishing fourth is vital for us, so let's focus on that." The club now considers that fourth place in the League is a trophy! The financial implications of failing to qualify for the Champions League are immense and should not be underestimated, but please, don't call securing that qualification a trophy.

I now feared the worst, a meltdown on par with that which followed the Carling Cup Final the previous year. And if things could get any worse, next up was Tottenham, enjoying their best season in the League for fifty years. In the build up to the game the facts were stark and clear: if we lost we would find ourselves trailing them by an impossible, unthinkable 13 points. With some trepidation I took my seat. Thirty-four painful, burning minutes later, with our defence appearing to consist of confused strangers, my greatest fears were realised – Tottenham led 2–0. My head was a whirl, a thought even crossed my mind that if they scored again before half-time I'd leave, something I have never even contemplated before – another goal and the hurt would have been just too much to bear. But that was just a fleeting moment. Strangely, despite the score, I thought we looked quite positive going forward; it was the defence that was struggling. Then, five minutes before the break, Sagna found space in the Tottenham penalty area

217

and powered a header home to lift the crowd. But it was the way Sagna grabbed the ball from the net and sprinted back to the centre circle that suggested the team believed the game was still very much alive. Three minutes later Robin van Persie did what Robin van Persie does and the score was 2–2. It was a superb goal, a goal that sent spirits soaring and one that sparked a wave of joyous celebration around the stadium. But it was about to get even better. We came out in the second half eager, hungry, positive and determined. Twenty three minutes later, following an avalanche of glorious goals, I had to keep glancing at the giant scoreboards to reassure myself I wasn't dreaming: Arsenal 5 Tottenham 2. The stadium became a living, breathing, vibrant entity that Sunday, except in the away section; it was now their turn to think about going home early, and they did in great numbers.

A week later, somewhat against the run of play, we won at Liverpool and Tottenham lost again. The feared 13-point gap was now incredibly down to just four. We had something to fight for again. And we demonstrated this new confidence in the return leg of our Champions League tie against AC Milan. Although trailing 4–0 after that dreadful night in Milan, a barnstorming first-half performance saw us take a 3–0 half-time lead. The team gave everything they had that night – showing real spirit - but couldn't get a fourth goal that would take the tie into extra time. I left the stadium that night defeated but proud.

Yet it seemed like the defeat of Tottenham had awakened something in the team and in the fans. In our next home League game we beat Newcastle 2-1 with the winning goal coming in stoppage time at the end of the game. The team never gave up, pushing for the decisive goal and deserved the win. After that we went to Everton, scored an early goal and hung on in the face of increasing pressure, giving a resolute and determined performance. The dramatic change was inexplicable; the team suddenly appeared to believe again.

There was belief around the stadium too before our next game against Aston Villa. Early spring sunshine lightened the mood further and we fully deserved the 3-0 win and, unusually, not a single goal from Robin van Persie. Instead, for the first time since 1997, two English players - Gibbs and Walcott - scored, followed by a rocket from Arteta whose experience was now beginning to have an impact and influence on the team. It was a great day. But the most remarkable statistic shone brightly from the columns of the League table. On the day of the Tottenham game – 26 February - I feared dropping 13 points behind them. After the victory over Villa – on 24 March – we were three points ahead. It was a remarkable turnaround. The grey clouds were lifting, I was loving football again and I'm sure I walked a little taller as I left the stadium that afternoon. Those clouds appeared to build up again over the Emirates towards the end of the season but ultimately they blew away on the breeze.

An unexpected defeat at Queen's Park Rangers followed the Villa game, but it just felt like a temporary blip to me. In a remarkable sequence we'd just won seven consecutive league games. As long as we could put the defeat behind us everything would be fine because Tottenham had imploded after our game in February, taking just two points from their next four games. And a blip it was. In the next game, after a towering performance, we beat Manchester City, the Premier League leaders by 1-0. As it happened I missed that game as I was on holiday in Crete. I'd identified a bar early in the holiday that showed Premier League games and settled down in a prime position with Nicola, my partner, ten minutes before kick off as the teams were announced and pundits mouthed their opinions – there was no sound. I could cope with that, but not with what followed next. As the game kicked off the picture fizzed, flickered and the Premiership's finest players disappeared only to be replaced by those of Panathinaikos and Panionios! A moment of panic, a word with the barman and thankfully service was restored to the TV that we were watching. The rest of the customers seemed generally uninterested in both options and only when I gave a yelp of delight after Arteta smashed home the only goal of the game in the dying minutes did my personal commitment receive any recognition. A local man at the next table turned to the screen, took in the player's celebrations, said "Arsenal", nodded approvingly and returned to his conversation.

A straightforward victory away at Wolverhampton Wanderers a few days later ensured I didn't notice the gathering clouds which appeared dark and threatening over the Emirates when Wigan arrived as visitors with just five games left to play. Likely candidates to join Wolves in relegation for most of the season, Wigan had recently found a new belief and were playing extraordinarily well. And that day they rushed into a two goal lead before the game was ten minutes old. They played better than us and consigned us to a 2-1 defeat. I hadn't seen that coming. We then drew our next three games, against Chelsea, Stoke and Norwich. The Norwich game, our last at the Emirates, was another which I approached convinced of a win. Having grabbed the lead after just two minutes I saw nothing to make me change my mind, but Norwich were unfazed and defensively we had a nightmare. By half time they had stormed back and were leading 2-1. It was an uncomfortable half time break. In the second half however a determined performance saw Robin van Persie turn the game around again and put us into the lead with ten minutes left to play. But it had been an unconvincing display by our defence all game and five minutes later we were exposed again as Norwich equalised – final score 3-3. Our game had kicked off at 12.45 on the Saturday, while those who were still in a position to overtake us were not playing until Sunday. Although we were occupying third place, both Tottenham and Newcastle could still overhaul us and consign us to fifth; our fate was no longer in our own hands. It was a long 24 hours to wait, but whoever or whatever the football Gods are, they were with us that day: Tottenham drew and Newcastle lost. Our fate was back in our own hands.

And so the final day of the season dawned. We were playing away at West Bromwich Albion in what was now Roy Hodgson's last match before taking over as manager of England. Win and we would secure third place and with it automatic qualification for the next season's Champions League – even better than Wenger had hoped for back in February. But if we lost and both Tottenham and Newcastle won then fifth in the League and an unwanted place in the Europa League beckoned.

That final day, I cleared the decks, got everything out of the way to listen intently as fate dealt its hand. I tuned in to Radio Five Live on headphones and watched BBC Final Score on the Red Button. Whatever happened at those three games, I needed to know I'd hear it first. I sat hunched on the sofa, unspeaking, tense and nervous - a mood or position not improved with news that Tottenham were leading Fulham 1-0 after just two minutes. But another two minutes and my mood lifted a little, we were leading 1-0 too. Then it dived headlong again; with only 15 minutes on the clock we were trailing 2-1. If the score remained like that, the unthinkable would happen and Tottenham would leapfrog us and push us down to fourth. And this year there was a question mark over fourth. Normally it would qualify you for the play-off round of the Champions League – as we know only too well – but this year, because Chelsea had reached the Champions League Final, UEFA announced that if they were to go on and win the trophy they would gain the fourth Champions League place and the team finishing fourth in the League would drop down to the Europa League. The tension was becoming unbearable.

After 30 minutes there were signs of recovery. Andre Santos scored to level the match at West Brom and Newcastle were dropping out of the picture as they trailed 2-0 at Everton. At half-time things remained the same and I was able to relax for 15 minutes. Although Tottenham still had the upper hand, if we could take the lead back at West Brom we'd be in pole position again. As the second half began I automatically shrunk back into the same huddled position on the sofa – ears and eyes straining for news. It was clear from the reports coming in that West Brom's stand-in 'keeper Marton Fulop was having a nightmare. His day got worse after 54 minutes when he contrived to punch the ball goalwards where Laurent Koscielny was able to gratefully flick it into the net. We had the lead again – 3-2 – all we had to do now was make sure we didn't make any silly mistakes. News that Tottenham had scored a second a few minutes later didn't matter as long as we held on to win. Those last 36 minutes of the season were about the longest of my life. When the referee finally blew for full-time, we'd won, secured 3rd place and gained access to the

221

riches of the Champions League for the fifteenth consecutive year – a record only bettered by Manchester United and Real Madrid. That final whistle released me; I felt the tension flow away in an instant. The worries of the last few weeks, the constant analysis of the league table, the consideration of every permutation of results, it all ended at that moment - I felt free again. But no Arsène, it didn't feel like we'd won a trophy!

It was a remarkable turnaround. There had been many dark days, days when it seemed we could lose our status as a recognised part of the 'top-four' in English football: the humiliation at Old Trafford in August, the defeat at Blackburn in September consigning us to the brink of the relegation zone, and the run of three consecutive League defeats in January which anchored us in 7th place staring upwards at teams who appeared unassailable. Yet the team stuck to its task. We scored five against Chelsea and Tottenham, seven against Blackburn and gained a stirring victory over the new champions, Manchester City, in the final run-in. And the importance of the lift the short-term loan of Thierry Henry brought to everyone should not be underestimated. With an end of season script that read like one from the movies, what had at one point appeared to be *Mission Impossible* became on that last day *Escape to Victory*. And although season 2011/12 concluded without a trophy and extended that disappointing sequence - for the third time in my 46 years supporting the team - to a seventh season, it most definitely ended on a high.

30

All About the Money

Wembley 2011 and the calamitous display in the Carling Cup Final, that's what started me thinking, really thinking. That day I witnessed the team suffer yet another gut-wrenching defeat in the final of a major competition. That was the unlucky 13th since I started supporting Arsenal. At the time I just kept asking myself over and over again "Why does this keep happening?" But now, having delved deep into all those memories and analysed my journey as a fan, I realise the process has been cathartic. I have started thinking more and more that actually I've been lucky. Not, of course, in the fact that I've witnessed so many losses in big games, but in that I have also seen my team win trophies, lots of them; it is something supporters of most teams never experience. In my formative years I remember watching TV back in the black and white days of 1969 as a deliriously happy Newcastle United won the old European Fairs Cup. I felt a misplaced jealousy of them and their supporters and wondered if I would ever see Arsenal win anything – because at that time we had been a trophy-free zone since 1953. Since that victory in 1969, Geordies have never seen their team claim another major prize and have endured relegation from the top-flight three times. The year after Newcastle won the Fairs Cup we finally got our reward when we claimed the same trophy before going on to win the Double the next season. From that time on I never envied Newcastle again and have always anticipated more success for Arsenal.

Sometimes the gap between trophies has been longer than others, but I have always felt it was only a matter of time before we won again. In fact when I look back over the years since I first found football in 1966, of the 92 professional football clubs in England just 11 have shared those 46 League titles, and three of those were one-hit wonders (Nottingham Forest 1977/78, Aston Villa 1980/81 and Blackburn Rovers in 1994/95). In the FA Cup the glory has been restricted to 16 clubs – half of those winning only once - in the same period, and only seven clubs have claimed both the League and FA Cup. The League Cup has been a little more generous, allowing 21 different clubs to celebrate victory, but the supporters of only six clubs have seen their teams win all three trophies during those years. Arsenal is one of this elite group, along with Manchester United, Liverpool, Chelsea, Manchester City and Leeds United, although elite is probably not how most would view Leeds these days. And as for relegation, well in my lifetime only two teams have been ever-present in the top division: Everton (since 1954) and of course Arsenal, with an unbroken run since 1919. I have also never seen my team in financial meltdown or suffer from gross mismanagement. So I therefore have to conclude that I have been lucky – but it still doesn't remove the hurt of those defeats in major finals. That blacklist of 13 made up of four FA Cup Finals, four losses in European finals and five League Cup Final defeats. When memories of those games manage to infiltrate the defences of my mind I don't feel so lucky.

After all these years you would think that accepting the ups and downs of a football season would get easier. But it doesn't. I think I worry and fret far more about defeats now than I ever did in the beginning, and get really down sometimes. I didn't realise that when I started writing, but as this book has grown I see it reflected more and more in the later chapters. That obsessing about individual results and the impact they have on me is clear to see. And it seems these days that the bad results bring me down far more than the good results lift me. A good result now often just brings relief, while a bad result festers and eats away at me. It doesn't sound healthy – it's 'only' football after all. It didn't used to be like that.

During the years I have followed Arsenal I've lived my life in nine-month cycles, punctuated by 90 minute footballing interludes. Wherever I am, whatever I'm doing, if Arsenal is playing I'll make sure I know what is happening in the game. I have caught up with the score while on board a Russian ship in Antarctica, I have listened nervously to live radio commentary perched on a history-soaked hillside overlooking the battlefield of Rorke's Drift in South Africa and made the ultimate sacrifice (for me anyway), crawling bleary-eyed from my bed in Queensland, Australia at 5.30 in the morning to watch live Champions League coverage. Everything else becomes of secondary importance during those 90 minutes.

Your football team, along with your family, is the only constant in life. You can change your home, your job, your relationships – but your football team is with you till death do you part. And within at a football club the fans are the only constant. The owners, directors, management and players come and go, earning their living, doing their job – to a lesser or greater degree – but for a fan it is an enduring passion and a way of life. Most fans think or talk about their club every single day of their lives. And unlike the players, fans don't have a contract that allows them to move on to another club after a few years' service. No matter how much you think this player or that player is one of us, generally he is not. If he thinks he can do better for himself elsewhere – either winning trophies or earning more – he'll go. We see it every summer at Arsenal. But for the fans it is different. The first time you push your way through the stadium's turnstile you unknowingly 'sign' a lifetime contract with that club; it is a marriage, for better or worse, but one without the escape clause of divorce.

Once you commit yourself to your team and start attending games you are trapped, but what do you get in return for your investment of love, loyalty, passion and hard cash? Generally I feel clubs are edging further and further away from their local fans – those that actually attend the games - as they look to increase their global 'brand' image and revenue. It is hard to believe now but up to 1988 the club used to appeal for fans to come to Highbury each summer and help with stadium repairs and decorating, for which they received a free season ticket in return! Those local fans deliver a fairly predictable level of revenue and so to increase that income you need to

225

open up new markets. To this end the club now organises exhausting summer tours of the Far East, and in summer 2012 added West Africa to the list, although circumstances later caused cancellation of that leg of the tour. Over six days in July they played matches in Malaysia, Beijing and Hong Kong. The marketing men then originally had the team down for the match in Nigeria just eleven days before the start of the 2012/13 season. It may be good for the club's revenue but I can't believe it is the ideal pre-season preparation for the squad.

When I first became an Arsenal fan my main worries revolved around whether I'd ever find the missing Bobby Gould card I needed to complete my collection or when I'd get to see another game. Now my worries concern the club's marketing contracts and revenue! When I started attending Highbury the stadium was an advertising-free zone. Unlike many clubs, Arsenal turned their back on the revenue available from perimeter advertising and indeed advertising in general. The matchday programme was free of adverts too; the club believed it all a little too…well, commercial, and a little tacky for a club of our stature. Sponsorships were unheard of. Today revenue gleaned from advertising and sponsorship is of vital importance. Kit sponsorship deals and stadium naming rights have a massive impact on a club's revenue. The more you read, however, about the deal with Emirates for our current sponsorships, the more it suggests that the club seriously undervalued both. But the attraction of large sums of money up front when they needed it to secure financing for the new stadium and the redevelopment of Highbury proved irresistible. It means we are now trailing a long way behind rival clubs in this area of funding. The deals with Emirates signed in 2006 run for eight years for the shirts and 15 years for the stadium, which means the club will presumably negotiate a significantly stronger shirt deal to begin in two years, while the Emirates name will remain on the stadium until 2021. And there we hit a problem. When the club sold the stadium naming rights it surrendered any historical link with our Highbury heritage. Highbury, a name known and respected around the football world, did not appear incorporated in the new stadium name, nor even was the name Arsenal, denying the stadium anything other than a corporate identity. In 2021, after 15 years in which the fans will come to accept the name, it will most likely change to something completely different. On the last day of one season we will be watching our football at the Emirates then, a couple of months later, fans will return to the stadium and be expected instantly to refer to it by its new name, the WhoKnowsWhat Stadium, making it difficult to build a new enduring affection to reflect that which we held for Highbury. And then, when that deal has run its course, the corporate logos will come down again and it will be renamed once more, and on and on. But while they wait impatiently for this next financial windfall, the club must look elsewhere to boost revenue.

In February 2012 the Deloitte 'Football Money League', more familiarly known as the 'Football Rich List', showed Arsenal maintaining their position as the fifth highest revenue earning club in world football – an improvement of five places since the last season at Highbury – but clearly demonstrated how far we remain behind the teams above in the generation of commercial income; the List divides revenue into Match day, Broadcasting and Commercial. It gives Arsenal a total annual revenue of £226.8m of which commercial revenue represents 20%. The clubs above us, Real Madrid, Barcelona, Manchester United and Bayern Munich, all have a total income significantly greater than ours, but also earn a far greater percentage of that through commercial sources. Those four clubs respectively recorded a commercial income of 36%, 34%, 31% and a blistering 56% for Bayern Munich. The restless quest by football to generate international commercial revenue is no doubt why the 2011 Italian Super Cup – the equivalent of our FA Community Shield – between Inter Milan and AC Milan took place, not in Rome, but in Beijing, China. How long before the FA follow suit?

As a season ticket holder I find the regular movement of kick off times to meet the demands of live TV coverage extremely irritating. Yet when, according to the 'Rich List', 39% of our revenue comes through broadcasting income, you can see its importance to the club, but for the supporter who attends games it is disruptive and frustrating. On the weekend of 22/23 October 2011, for example, due to the knock on effects of Thursday night Europa League matches and the normal TV disruption of the sporting programme, only three Premier League games kicked off at 3.00pm on Saturday. And throughout the whole of the 2011/12 season, of our 19 home League games just six kicked off at the traditional time. Where once 3.00pm on a Saturday was the norm, now, when you commit yourself to a large financial outlay pre-season to support your team, you have no idea when the games you have paid to watch will actually be played – neither date nor time!

But if I want my team to compete at the highest level, then I have to accept that the club can only afford to look at the bigger picture, and what I want as an individual supporter and season ticket holder is no longer that important in the world of multi-million pound businesses. Perhaps I am just losing touch with modern football, expecting my team to play at set times that I can plan around. Since 1992 and the advent of the Premier League, and with it the omnipresence of live football on TV that funded it, a whole new generation has grown up taking it as the norm that there will be Premier League football on TV on Saturday lunchtimes and teatimes, Sunday afternoon and Monday evenings. They may never actually go to a game themselves but take it for granted that the best games from each weekend will be available to them at the press of a button. This access to the top club games means the traditional start for many football fans is eroding. No longer does a child need to be introduced to football by going to a game with his Dad, brother or uncle, instead he watches the pick of games on TV and begins supporting teams that may be based hundreds of miles from where he lives, and grows up never even considering actually going to watch them play. But he'll want a replica shirt and all the rest of the paraphernalia marketed by the clubs and so revenue grows. But I think the loss of the tradition where families support the same club through the generations, which now must be under threat, is rather sad.

Arsenal is recognised throughout football as a financially well-run club, regularly held up as a shining example of how it should be done, but elsewhere other clubs continue to spend impossible sums of money. Yet this expenditure is not funded by the club's themselves, instead it is bankrolled by the new breed of billionaire club owners who appear to look at football as either an incredibly expensive plaything or a vehicle to promote their own interests. Through tight financial control, Arsenal prudently keeps its head above water, while at the same time paying back massive loans on the building of the new stadium and the redevelopment of Highbury. Meanwhile other clubs record financially crippling losses each year only for super-rich owners to tidy them away without fuss. In an attempt to control this, UEFA is shortly to introduce Financial Fair Play which aims to control and reduce losses by football clubs, with sanctions threatened for those clubs that fail to comply. Only time will tell if this move will have the required effect and even out the playing field, or whether rich men will simply employ others to discover and exploit the inevitable loopholes.

But while Arsenal under Arsène Wenger has become synonymous with a careful and considered approach to player purchase, others have not been so restricted. This limit on investment has made it ever more challenging to secure the vitally important Champions League qualification each season. Without qualification the club's income from broadcast fees and matchday earnings will plummet, leading to a reduction in overall revenue. Yet Wenger must weep sometimes when he sees how football has changed around him and how his model is struggling to survive. The impact of the stadium costs on the club forced Wenger to cut his cloth accordingly. Obliged to turn away from competing in the market for big name, big money stars, he chose instead to identify young developing talents, his commendable plan being to nurture them into the players he needs to play the style of expansive entertaining football that has become his trademark. And this system had great merit until the super-rich clubs appeared. Now, when these young stars begin to reach footballing maturity, they become targets for the money-no-object clubs. Unsettled by the media and encouraged by their agents, who stand to make a fortune for themselves if their clients move on, they soon get their heads turned. The saga drags on, destabilising the team and leaves a gaping hole in the squad when they invariably move on for the greater financial rewards offered elsewhere.

While Chelsea and Manchester City have spearheaded this change in England, clubs in other countries are adding to this growing list. In France, Paris St. Germain became 100% owned by Qatar Sports Investments in 2012 and have instantly become one of the richest clubs in the world. Also in France, in 2011, Russian billionaire Dmitry Rybolovlev acquired two thirds of Monaco. In China too it is all change as one of the nation's richest men, Xu Jiayin, brought Guangzhou Evergrande in 2010 and has now appointed World Cup-winning coach Marcello Lippi to steer the ship. And not to be outdone, their rivals Shanghai Shenhua put down a marker by buying Nicolas Anelka from Chelsea in January 2012 and later in the year added Didier Drogba to the team at a reported salary of £200,000 a week. Yet perhaps the most startling development has been in the troubled Russian region of Dagestan where billionaire owner Suleyman Kerimov bought local club Anzhi Makhachkala in early 2011 and is now investing untold millions in it. In summer 2011 Anzhi signed triple Champions League winner Samuel Eto'o from Inter Milan on a three-year deal, reportedly paying him a weekly salary of £350,000. If you can hear distant sobbing it will be Arsène Wenger crying himself to sleep, his model for the future seriously damaged by rich men with untold wealth playing their own version of fantasy football. And for Chelsea and Manchester City it has worked. In 2005 it brought – or rather bought – Chelsea their first League title for 50 years and has now delivered them the ultimate prize, the Champions League. Manchester City, meanwhile, appear set on a similar course, having, in 2012, secured their first League title for 44 years on the back of the Abu Dhabi millions.

Yet Arsenal too now has a super-rich majority shareholder. Unfortunately, of the millions the American sports magnate Stan Kroenke spent in acquiring his shares, not a penny came to the club. Yet Kroenke's arrival in that position is interesting. From the outside it seems the fall from grace of former Arsenal vice-chairman David Dein, the man responsible for bringing Wenger to Highbury and therefore instigating the footballing revolution that changed the face of the club forever, lay with his early championing of Stan Kroenke. Dein believed the club needed outside investment and without the backing of the board set out to get it. It drew the now famous response from chairman Peter Hill-Wood in regard to Kroenke that "We don't want his sort and we don't want his money." Undeterred, Kroenke began acquiring shares in the club. The Board, angered by Dein's move, unceremoniously removed him as vice-chairman in April 2007, leading him to ally himself with Alisher Usmanov and sell his shares to the Uzbekistan-born billionaire's Red and White Holdings, with Dein appointed chairman. Now two mega-rich businessmen were intent on acquiring a majority shareholding in the club. Reluctant to allow Dein back into the fold the Board suddenly found Kroenke a far more attractive proposition and, after a ruthless struggle behind the scenes, Kroenke was welcomed aboard. In September 2008 he joined the Board and in April 2011 became the majority shareholder, having grown his shares from 9.9% in April 2007 to almost 63% four years later and he continues to edge upwards. The frustrating aspect of this boardroom battle from a fan's point of view is that it must have cost him somewhere – with a quick tap on my calculator - in the region of £450m, all of which has gone to the individual shareholders, mainly former directors, who sold up. We all still wait to see what Mr Kroenke - or 'Silent Stan' - intends to do with his acquisition. And there is a little nagging question at the back of my mind. In recent years Arsenal fans have squirmed uncomfortably each summer as our best players have left: Henry, Adebayor, Clichy, Fabregas, Song and Van Persie. Is it just coincidence that Dein's son, Darren, represented or worked as an agent for all of them?

So football has changed. The question all Arsenal fans are asking now is: Can we keep up with these changes; can we continue building teams that challenge at the highest level while maintaining financial prudence? Does Arsène Wenger have a Plan B?

Success in football is relative. If a team that regularly finishes mid-table climbs to third, fourth or fifth, that is progress to celebrate, progress rewarded with European football. But if a team that consistently finishes third or fourth place then drops down to fifth, that becomes a failure by their own high standards. It seems clear, if more overseas billionaires are drawn towards the Premier League then maintaining a place in the top four will become increasingly difficult, maybe, in time, even unobtainable for those clubs outside a very *nouveau riche* minority.

Clearly football has changed much since I first visited Highbury way back in 1967 and will continue to change. Money, above everything else, now dominates the game. A successful future for the club depends as much on our ability to post successful financial results as it does results on the pitch. And after all this where does my future lie? I have to question how much longer I can continue to pay out large, ever-increasing sums of money each summer to renew my season ticket. Realistically, I know that my season ticket isn't for life; when the time comes to retire from the workplace I doubt whether I will be in a financial position to continue as a season ticket holder. The question that rattles around in my head now is, if it is going to end anyway do I just accept the end, stop renewing now and invest that money for my future. Clearly the price is never going to reduce, it will, like all things, continue to rise. Let's face it, it has grown from £19.50 for my first one in 1969 to £1,310 for my latest – yet rough figures from the Bank of England suggest that if the price had tracked inflation I'd now be paying just £265 a year for my season ticket! So yes, it will continue to increase in price. To continue purchasing a season-ticket for the next ten years would require expenditure, I'm guessing, of around £15,000. When you see it written down like that it is quite sobering. Of course you don't need to be a season ticket holder to be a supporter, I'll always be that. I'll always feel the agony and the ecstasy.

What to do now then? It is becoming increasingly difficult each year to justify the financial outlay on my season ticket. At the end of 2010/11 I came really close to calling it a day, but I was unable to take the decision to bring down the curtain on four and a half decades of regular attendance. I justified the decision to myself by saying that if the team failed to rediscover the resolve, passion and belief that I felt was seriously missing as that season limped to a close, then 2011/12 would be my last. I must admit, as the season began and we lost our opening home game to Liverpool before being destroyed at Old Trafford, I started mentally preparing myself for the end. But despite this inauspicious start the team went on to display a determination to prove their critics wrong and achieved a remarkable third place finish which I found inspiring.

So, decision time is here again. Do I save the money I would normally throw at my season ticket and invest it wisely where it can work for my future. Do I accept that the time has come to finally wave goodbye to all those disrupted weekends and inconvenient kick off times. I probably should, but perhaps there's a sign here – a pointer to what lies just around the corner. In all my years as a season ticket holder we've twice gone seven years without a trophy, but in the eighth year that sequence ended gloriously (FA Cup 1979 and League Cup 1987). In 2012 we have again racked up seven fruitless years without a trophy, so is that a sign, is there a one waiting just over the horizon? Maybe I should give it one more year…yes, that's it, just one more year…